Silva H. Ladewig
Integrating Gestures

Applications of Cognitive Linguistics

Editors
Gitte Kristiansen
Francisco J. Ruiz de Mendoza Ibáñez

Honorary editor
René Dirven

Volume 44

Silva H. Ladewig
Integrating Gestures

The Dimension of Multimodality in Cognitive Grammar

ISBN 978-3-11-099241-0
e-ISBN (PDF) 978-3-11-066856-8
e-ISBN (EPUB) 978-3-11-066865-0
ISSN 1861-4078

Library of Congress Control Number: 2020934494

Bibliographic information published by the Deutsche Nationalbibliothek
The Deutsche Nationalbibliothek lists this publication in the Deutsche Nationalbibliografie; detailed bibliographic data are available on the Internet at http://dnb.dnb.de.

© 2022 Walter de Gruyter GmbH, Berlin/Boston
This volume is text- and page-identical with the hardback published in 2020.
Typesetting: Integra Software Services Pvt. Ltd.
Printing and binding: CPI books GmbH, Leck

www.degruyter.com

For my father

Contents

List of Figures —— XI

List of Tables —— XV

1	**Introduction: cognitive grammar and gesture studies? —— 1**	
1.1	The cognitive grammar enterprise —— 3	
1.1.1	Grammar is symbolic in nature, profiling conceptual content —— 4	
1.1.2	The construal of conceptual content —— 7	
1.1.3	Discourse and the flow of cognition —— 8	
1.1.4	Gestures as part of grammar and cognitive-linguistic description —— 10	
1.2	The field of modern gesture studies —— 11	
1.2.1	Gestures and spoken language: an integrated view —— 11	
1.2.2	Gesture and language as part of linguistic theory —— 15	
1.2.3	Gestures and cognition —— 17	
1.3	A cognitive grammar and gesture studies interface? —— 22	
2	**Multimodality of grammar and its cognitive foundations —— 25**	
2.1	Grammar of gesture and its cognitive foundations —— 25	
2.1.1	Simultaneous structures —— 27	
2.1.1.1	Emic level of description —— 28	
2.1.2	Linear structures of gestures —— 30	
2.2	Multimodal grammar and its cognitive foundations —— 33	
2.2.1	Grammaticalization in gestures —— 34	
2.2.2	Multimodal constructions —— 38	
2.2.3	Multimodal syntax —— 46	
2.2.3.1	Levels of linguistic description: semantic and pragmatic relationships —— 47	
2.2.3.2	Syntactic relationships of gestures and speech —— 49	
3	**How are gestures integrated into linguistic structures? —— 55**	
3.1	Do they integrate? Four perception experiments —— 55	
3.2	Where do they integrate? Gestures realizing nouns and verbs —— 60	
3.2.1	Two examples —— 60	
3.2.2	Experiment I: Speech only —— 68	
3.2.3	Experiment II: Gesture only —— 70	

3.2.4	Experiment III: Multimodal utterances —— 75	
3.2.5	Distribution of gesture types over syntactic slots —— 80	
3.3	Why can gestures integrate? Conceptual archetypes in gestures —— 83	
3.3.1	Nouns and verbs in spoken language from a cognitive grammar approach —— 84	
3.3.2	Objects and actions in gestures —— 86	
3.3.3	Conceptual archetypes in gestures —— 89	
3.4	How can gestures integrate? Gesture and speech interacting —— 94	
3.4.1	Simultaneous use of speech and gesture —— 94	
3.4.2	Gestures replacing speech —— 97	
3.5	Summary —— 101	
4	**Semantic integration of gestures: constructing multimodal reference objects —— 103**	
4.1	Do gestures integrate? Two perception experiments —— 104	
4.2	Why can gestures integrate? —— 109	
4.2.1	Context-independent meaning of gestures —— 110	
4.2.2	Context-independent meaning exemplified —— 111	
4.2.3	The relationship between form and meaning in gestures —— 116	
4.2.3.1	Iconicity in gestures —— 119	
4.2.3.2	From iconicity to cognitive iconicity —— 122	
4.2.4	Gestural meaning as conceptual meaning – Gestures as symbolic units —— 124	
4.2.4.1	Cognitive-semiotic processes of gestural meaning construal —— 130	
4.3	How can gestures integrate? Construing multimodal reference objects —— 134	
4.3.1	Specifying gestural meaning with speech —— 135	
4.3.1.1	Representation of a vertically oriented object that may create space —— 135	
4.3.1.2	Reenacting a pushing action —— 138	
4.3.2	Merging verbal and gestural meaning —— 142	
4.3.2.1	Process of construing a multimodal reference object in the example "Ich wollte dieses ✋ ('I wanted this' ✋)" —— 142	
4.3.2.2	Process of construing a multimodal reference object in the example "und wir hinten ✋ ('and we from the back' ✋)" —— 143	
4.4	Summary —— 145	

5	**Multimodal sentences and discourse contexts: salience, attention and foregrounding —— 147**	
5.1	How are multimodal sentences integrated in the discourse? Two perception experiments —— 148	
5.2	Dynamic multimodal communication —— 152	
5.3	Salience and attention – foregrounding of meaning —— 156	
5.3.1	An emerging barrier located at a lake —— 157	
5.3.2	A scenario of pushing downward and upward —— 160	
5.4	Multimodal semantic strategies: intension and extension —— 163	
5.4.1	The extensional meaning of a surface —— 167	
5.4.2	The intensional meaning of pushing —— 169	
5.5	Summary —— 174	
6	**Conclusion —— 177**	
6.1	Cognitive grammar multimodal? —— 179	
6.2	Beyond the approach advocated here —— 183	

Appendices —— 187

References —— 203

Index —— 223

List of Figures

Figure 1 Example of a gesture realizing a syntactic slot —— 2
Figure 2 Conception of an event in terms of progressivity (adopted from Langacker 2008a: 65) —— 6
Figure 3 Discourse in Cognitive Grammar (adopted from Langacker 2001: 145) —— 9
Figure 4 Multiple channels of viewing frames (adopted from Langacker 2001: 146) —— 10
Figure 5 The stabilization and pragmaticalization of simultaneous structures in the variants of the Cyclic gesture —— 29
Figure 6 Linear structures according to Kendon (2004: ch. 7) —— 31
Figure 7 Cross-cultural comparison of the Cyclic gesture (Ruth-Hirrel and Ladewig in preparation) —— 36
Figure 8 Lexemes showing a circular motion in German Sign Language (DGS) —— 38
Figure 9 (a) Uni- and multimodal constructions (Lanwer 2017: (2); (b) uni- and multimodal constructions including gestural schematicity constructions, modified version of Lanwer's model —— 40
Figure 10 Semantic relationships between speech and gestures (based on Bressem, Ladewig and Müller 2013: 1111–1112) —— 48
Figure 11 Pragmatic relationships of speech and gesture (based on Bressem, Ladewig and Müller 2013: 1113) —— 49
Figure 12 Syntax relationships of speech and gesture (based on Bressem, Ladewig and Müller 2013: 1109–1110) —— 53
Figure 13 Sequential integration of gestures into speech —— 56
Figure 14 Grounding process exemplified in a nominal consisting of a determiner and a noun (taken from Taylor 2003: 346) —— 59
Figure 15 Transcript of the example "*Ich wollte dieses* 🖐 ('I wanted this' 🖐)" —— 62
Figure 16 Grounding of nouns according to Langacker (2008a: 276) —— 63
Figure 17 Syntactic analysis of the example "*Ich wollte dieses* 🖐 ('I wanted this' 🖐)" —— 64
Figure 18 Transcript of the example "*und wir hinten* 🖐 ('and we from the back' 🖐)" —— 66
Figure 19 Syntactic analysis of the example "*und wir hinten* 🖐 ('and we from the back' 🖐)" —— 67
Figure 20 Distribution of gestures over syntactic slots according to the findings of the speech-only condition —— 69
Figure 21 Lexical items elicited in the speech-only condition for the examples "*ich wollte dieses* ('I wanted this')" and "*und wir hinten* ('and we from the back')" —— 71
Figure 22 Lexical items elicited in the gesture-only condition for all 66 samples —— 73
Figure 23 Lexical items elicited in the gesture-only condition for the examples "*ich wollte dieses* ('I wanted this')" and "*und wir hinten* ('and we from the back')" —— 74
Figure 24 Syntactic categories used by the participants to describe a gesture realizing nominal and verbal slots (multimodal utterance condition) —— 78

https://doi.org/10.1515/9783110668568-202

Figure 25	Gesture conceived in terms of archetypical roles, grammatical notions and schemas —— 91
Figure 26	Foregrounding of verbal meaning through the use of gesture —— 95
Figure 27	Foregrounding of gestural meaning through the use of speech —— 96
Figure 28	Summary scanning in the multimodal utterances "*Ich wollte dieses* 🖐 ('I wanted this' 🖐)" —— 99
Figure 29	Sequential scanning in the multimodal utterance "*und wir hinten* 🖐 ('and we from the back' 🖐)" —— 100
Figure 30	Schematic illustration of the comparative analysis of the lexical items and gestures —— 104
Figure 31	Comparative analysis of the speech-only and multimodal utterance condition for the example "*Ich wollte dieses* 🖐 ('I wanted this' 🖐)" —— 106
Figure 32	Comparative analysis of the gesture-only and multimodal utterance condition for the example "*und wir hinten* 🖐 ('and we from the back' 🖐)" —— 107
Figure 33	Comparative analysis of the speech-only and multimodal utterance condition conducted for the whole corpus —— 108
Figure 34	Gesture in the example "*Ich wollte dieses* 🖐 ('I wanted this' 🖐)" —— 112
Figure 35	Gesture in the example "*und wir hinten* 🖐 ('and we from the back' 🖐)" —— 114
Figure 36	Peirce's (1931) triadic sign relationship —— 120
Figure 37	Example of gestures as semiotic signs —— 122
Figure 38	Distance relationships conceived for the oral-auditory mode (spoken word, onomatopoetic word), adapted from Langacker (1987a) and Wilcox (2002: 264) —— 125
Figure 39	Distance relationships conceived for the visual-spatial mode (American Sign Language sign TREE), adapted from Langacker (1987a) and Wilcox (2002: 264) —— 126
Figure 40	Cognitive iconicity in representing and acting gestures —— 128
Figure 41	Processes of semiosis for the gesture of the example "*Ich wollte dieses* 🖐 ('I wanted this' 🖐)" —— 131
Figure 42	Processes of semiosis for the gesture of the example "*und wir hinten* 🖐 ('and we from the back' 🖐)" —— 133
Figure 43	Comparison of lexical items elicited in the gesture-only and multimodal utterance condition for the example "*Ich wollte dieses* 🖐 ('I wanted this' 🖐)" —— 137
Figure 44	Comparison of lexical items elicited in the gesture-only and multimodal utterance condition for the example "*und wir hinten* 🖐 ('and we from the back' 🖐)" —— 141
Figure 45	The construal of a multimodal reference object in the example "*Ich wollte dieses* 🖐 ('I wanted this' 🖐)" —— 143
Figure 46	The construal of a multimodal reference object in "*und wir hinten* 🖐 ('and we from the back' 🖐)" —— 144
Figure 47	Comparative analyses of the lexical items elicited in the discourse condition and in the multimodal utterance condition for the example "*Ich wollte dieses* 🖐 ('I wanted this' 🖐)" —— 149

Figure 48	Comparative analysis of the lexical items elicited in the discourse condition and in the multimodal utterance condition for the example "*und wir hinten* 🖐 ('and we from the back' 🖐)" —— **150**
Figure 49	Timeline annotation in Keynote (Müller and Ladewig 2013: 305) —— **156**
Figure 50	A multimodal salience structure evolving for the example "*Ich wollte dieses* 🖐 ('I wanted this' 🖐)" —— **158**
Figure 51	A multimodal salience structure evolving for the example "*und wir hinten* 🖐 ('and we from the back' 🖐)" —— **161**
Figure 52	Process of specifying the extensional meaning in the example "*Ich wollte dieses* 🖐 ('I wanted this' 🖐)" —— **168**
Figure 53	Process of specifying the intensional meaning for the example "*und wir hinten* 🖐 ('and we from the back' 🖐)" —— **169**

List of Tables

Table 1 Distribution of syntactic slots over the corpus (elicited in the speech-only condition) —— 70
Table 2 Lexical items elicited in the multimodal utterance condition for the example "*Ich wollte dieses* 🖐 ('I wanted this' 🖐)" —— 75
Table 3 Lexical items elicited in the multimodal utterance condition for the example "*und wir hinten* 🖐 ('and we from the back' 🖐)" —— 77
Table 4 Distribution of syntactic slots over the corpus (elicited in the speech-only and the multimodal utterance condition) —— 79
Table 5 Distribution of gesture types over all syntactic positions —— 81
Table 6 Distribution of modes of representation over preferred syntactic positions —— 89
Table 7 Lexical items elicited in the gesture-only condition for the example "*Ich wollte dieses* ('I wanted this')" —— 113
Table 8 Lexical items elicited in the gesture-only condition (example "*und wir hinten* 🖐/ 'and we from the back' 🖐") —— 115
Table 9 Lexical items elicited in the multimodal utterance condition for the example "*Ich wollte dieses* 🖐 ('I wanted this' 🖐)" —— 136
Table 10 Lexical items elicited in the multimodal utterance condition for the example "*und wir hinten* 🖐 ('and we from the back' 🖐)" —— 139
Table 11 Enrichment of meaning determined in the discourse condition for all syntactic positions realized by gestures —— 164
Table 12 Processes of specification determined in the discourse condition for the syntactic positions of nouns or verbs realized by gestures —— 171

https://doi.org/10.1515/9783110668568-203

1 Introduction: cognitive grammar and gesture studies?

This book takes a usage-based approach to the integration of gestures into speech. Based on linguistic and cognitive-semiotic analyses of multimodal utterances and on naturalistic perception studies, it argues that gestures integrate on a syntactic and semantic level with speech merging into multimodal syntactic constructions. Looking specifically at discontinued utterances and their perception, it becomes evident that gestures participate vitally in the dynamics of meaning construal and may take over the function of verbs and nouns in their respective syntactic slots contributing to the semantics of the sentence under construction. With this phenomenon under scrutiny, the book takes a unified perspective on the integration of gestures with speech, following the plea formulated recently by sign language linguists to elaborate an overarching framework for studying and understanding spoken and signed language and gestures. The integration of different modes of expression to form multimodal or "composite utterances" (Enfield 2009) serves as a sample domain, showing that language and gesture "are manifestations of the same underlying conceptual system that is the basis for the human expressive ability. Thus, we propose that the general principles of Cognitive Grammar can be applied to the study of gesture" (Wilcox and Xavier 2013: 95).

> Integration of component structures into composite structures can take place at either the phonological or semantic pole of symbolic structures, or the integration can be of componential symbolic units themselves into more complex symbolic units. [. . .] Integration of component structures into composite structures with greater complexity is a central aspect of grammar, and a topic well-studied by linguists describing spoken and signed languages. One question that could be posed is whether integration can take place across linguistic and gestural systems. We propose that such integration does indeed take place, and should be studied as such. (Wilcox and Xavier 2013: 92)

This book aims to answer the question posed by both authors: "One question that could be posed is whether integration can take place across linguistic and gestural systems" (Wilcox and Xavier 2013: 92). For this purpose, cognitive-linguistic research on sign language (e.g., Wilcox 2004a) and gesture (e.g., Cienki 1998b, 2005; Müller 2008b, 2017b) will be united to investigate multimodal integration from a linguistic and usage-based perspective. By bringing together Cognitive Grammar and cognitive-semiotic/linguistic analyses of gestures (e.g., Ladewig and Bressem 2013a; Mittelberg 2006; Müller, Bressem and Ladewig 2013; Müller, Ladewig and Bressem 2013a), the book offers a framework to study multimodal utterance construction and, thus, contributes to a more general understanding of the syntactic and semantic roles of gestures in multimodal utterances. It will conclude with reflections upon the symbolic nature of grammatical classes of verbs and nouns as indicated by gestures, based on manual actions.

In order to study the syntactic and semantic integration systematically from a usage-based naturalistic point of view, the study focuses on instances of the integration of gestures into discontinued spoken utterances in which gestures replace linguistic units in utterance-final position (Figure 1).

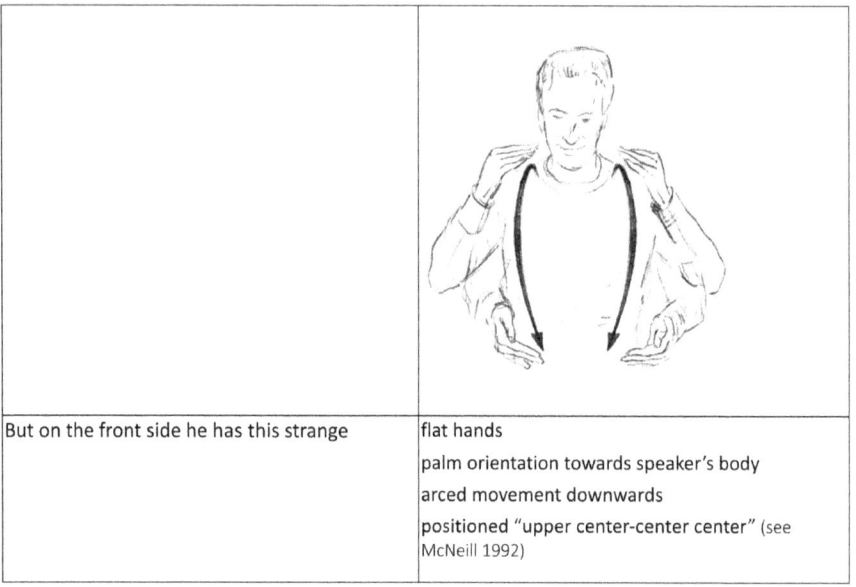

But on the front side he has this strange	flat hands
	palm orientation towards speaker's body
	arced movement downwards
	positioned "upper center-center center" (see McNeill 1992)

Figure 1: Example of a gesture realizing a syntactic slot.

In the utterances under investigation, gestures realize syntactic slots in utterance-final position, replace the spoken constituents of nouns and verbs, and complete the utterance. According to perception analyses, these multimodal utterances do not cause problems in the understanding, but recipients treat them as meaningful for the proceeding discourse.

Although this phenomenon offers revealing insights into the integration processes of speech and gestures and many researchers are sensitive to this phenomenon (e.g., Clark 1996, 2016; Engle 1998; McNeill 2005, 2007; Slama-Cazacu 1976; Wilcox 2004a), it has not been studied in depth before (Keevallik's [2013] study is an exception). This book fills this research gap, aiming to reveal the potential of gestures to realize the grammatical categories of nouns and verbs by embodying their conceptual schemas. By tracing the interactive processes between speech, particularly the grammar of spoken language, and gesture, a bridge from grammar to multimodal Cognitive Grammar is built.

The approach advocated in this book is considered as *one* possible framework to address the relation of spoken language and gesture. It allows the elucidation of the interrelation between speech and gesture on the level of grammar, taking into account the cognitive processes of meaning construal. Moreover, it aims at addressing symbolization processes in the gestural modality and, thus, gestures' potential of becoming linguistic signs. However, sure enough, by zooming in on one particular relation of both modalities, others are moved out of the attentional space, which is why the approach developed here should be treated as *one* puzzle piece for illuminating the multimodality of language.

1.1 The cognitive grammar enterprise

> Since 1976, I have been developing a linguistic theory that departs quite radically from the assumptions of the currently predominant paradigm. Called 'cognitive grammar' (alias 'space grammar'), this model assumes that language is neither self-contained nor describable without essential reference to cognitive processing (regardless of whether one posits a special faculté de langage). Grammatical structures do not constitute an autonomous formal system or level of representation: They are claimed instead to be inherently symbolic, providing for the structuring and conventional symbolization of conceptual content. Lexicon, morphology, and syntax form a continuum of symbolic units, divided only arbitrarily into separate 'components' – it is ultimately as pointless to analyze grammatical units without reference to their semantic value as to write a dictionary which omits the meanings of its lexical items. Moreover, a formal semantics based on truth conditions is deemed inadequate for describing the meaning of linguistic expressions. One reason is that semantic structures are characterized relative to knowledge systems whose scope is essentially open-ended. A second is that their value reflects not only the content of a conceived situation, but also how this content is structured and construed. (Langacker 1986: 1–2)

Cognitive Grammar was developed out of the disagreement with generative grammar which refuses to comprise meaning into the description of grammatical structures but argues instead for cognitively separated modules of syntax and semantics. Its central ideas were first spelled out in the seminal two-volume work *Foundations of a cognitive grammar* (Langacker 1987a, 1991b), establishing one research strand within the field of Cognitive Linguistics. Arguing that meaning is central to linguistic analysis, the cognitive linguists Wallace Chafe, Charles Fillmore, George Lakoff, Ronald Langacker, and Leonard Talmy started to examine language structure and language use regarding general cognitive principles and mechanisms such as perception, human categorization, iconicity attention, or memory. Each of them developed his own theory, such as conceptual metaphor theory (see Lakoff and Johnson 1980), frame semantics (see Fillmore 1985) or force dynamics (see Talmy 1988).

The theory of Cognitive Grammar "advances the controversial [. . .] proposal that essential grammatical notions can be characterized semantically" (Langacker 2008a: 103). Moreover, by claiming that "grammar [. . .] is inherently symbolic" (Langacker 1987a: 12) and that "all valid grammatical constructs have some kind of conceptual import" (Langacker 1987a: 282) meaning is equated with conceptualization. Hence, semantic and grammatical structures are conceived as having conceptual content. It is noteworthy that the term "grammar" is not used in a narrow sense, referring only to (morpho-)syntactic structures, but it is employed in a broad sense, referring to the language system as a whole, including sounds, meaning and (morpho-)syntax. Langacker further assumes that grammar is motivated by general cognitive capacities and processes, which is why he applies principles of gestalt psychology comprehensively to the analysis of language and, in doing so, draws analogies between linguistic structure and visual perception. As such, grammar is claimed to be grounded in conceptualization, which, on the other hand, is claimed to be grounded in the human's interaction with the physical reality (embodiment theory). Analyzing language from this perspective allows conclusions to be drawn about not only the relation of human language and cognition but also, as will be argued in this book, gesture and cognition.

The major premises of Cognitive Grammar will be outlined in the following pages. However, given that encompassing and enlightening résumés of its main tenets have been provided by other scholars (see e.g., Kok 2016), the basic principles that are pivotal for the enterprise followed in this book are outlined in the following sections.

1.1.1 Grammar is symbolic in nature, profiling conceptual content

The first "[o]utrageous [p]roposal," as Langacker (2008a: 5) puts it in his book *Cognitive grammar: A basic introduction,* is the well-known and fundamental claim that "grammar is symbolic in nature" (Langacker 2008a: 5) and that grammar and lexicon form a continuum, while both are claimed to be fully describable as assemblies of symbolic structures. This means that linguistic structures observable in use (usage events) are understood as merging phonological material with semantic content. This notion was inspired by de Saussure's (1916) notion of a two-dyadic sign combining the sense of a sound (*Lautbild*) and an idea (*Vorstellung*).

The view that morphemes are inherently symbolic, associating phonological representations with semantic content, is not controversial. Consider the following example to illustrate his argument. If we take the morpheme *gesture* into account, we can describe the mapping of form and meaning as follows: The phonological structure (the word's phonological pole) that comprises the smaller units of [dʒ], [e], [s], [t], [ʃ], and [ə], can be represented as [[dʒ]-[e]-[s]-[t]-[ʃ]-[ə]], where the hyphens indicate the syntagmatic combination of the components into higher-order phonological units represented by the outermost square brackets. The semantic structure (the word's semantic pole) is also complex, consisting of multiple specifications including body part, form, movement, etc., which are represented as [GESTURE]. The symbolic association forming a higher-order symbolic unit is represented by "/" in the symbolic association [[[GESTURE]/[[dʒ]-[e]-[s]-[t]-[ʃ]-[ə]]].

In contrast to lexical morphemes such as *gesture*, the symbolic status of grammatical morphemes is called into question by a number of linguistic theories. Yet, these are also considered meaningful in Cognitive Grammar. Consider the morpheme *-ing* that yields a progressive verb when combined with the morpheme *gesture*. The symbolic relationship defining each of the morphemes are [[GESTURE]/[dʒestʃə]] and [[PROG]/[ɪŋ]], where the aspectual morpheme designates the progress of the process specified by the verb *gesture*. Note that the grammatical morpheme is also responsible for the derivation of the noun into a verb. When combined, both form the complex morphological structure of [[[GESTURE]/[dʒestʃə]]-[[PROG]/[ɪŋ]]].

Now Langacker goes a step further by arguing that a basic constructional schema sanctions the formation of progressive verb forms which can be expressed by means of the following notation: [[PROCESS]/[. . .]]-[[PROG]/[ɪŋ]].

> By **schematization**, I mean the process of extracting the commonality inherent in multiple experiences to arrive at a conception representing a higher level of abstraction. Schematization plays a role in the acquisition of lexical units, if only because their conventional forms and meanings are less specific than the **usage events** (i.e. the actual pronunciations and contextual understandings) on the basis of which they are learned.
> (Langacker 2008a: 17, original emphasis)

The sequence [[PROCESS]/[. . .]] represents a schematic verb comprising a symbolic relation between [PROCESS], which is a maximally schematic semantic verb-like concept, and [. . .], a schematic characterization of its phonological pole. [PROG] stands for a semantic structure specifying progressivity and profiling specific facets of an event described. "The verb designates an entire bounded event, while the progressive, without altering the overall content, singles out just an arbitrary internal portion of that event for profiling" (Langacker 2008a: 68).

This constructional schema involves a symbolic relation between a phonological pole comprising the elements [. . .] and [ɪŋ], which are integrated syntagmatically to render [. . .]-[ɪŋ] and a semantic pole consisting of [PROCESS] and [PROG] integrated to form [PROCESS]-[PROG]. It defines the syntagmatic integration between a verb and the grammatical morpheme -*ing*, standing for the conception of an event in terms of progressivity. The diagram sketched in Figure 2 illustrates this process.

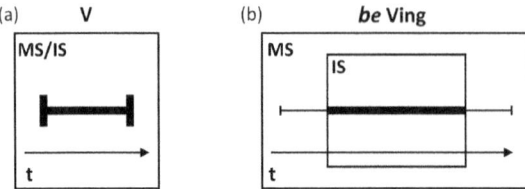

Figure 2: Conception of an event in terms of progressivity (adopted from Langacker 2008a: 65).

For the verb itself (V), there is no reason to distinguish maximal and immediate scope, so the box delimiting the temporal scope in diagram (a) is labeled MS/IS. The heavy line represents the event designated by the verb, viewed in its evolution through time. The entire bounded event, including its endpoints, appears 'onstage' within the temporal scope. Diagram (b) shows the effect of adding the progressive *be. . .-ing*. Its meaning resides in the construal it imposes on the content supplied by the verb. Specifically, it "zooms in" and imposes a limited immediate scope that excludes the endpoints of the bounded event. The composite expression *be Ving* therefore has both a maximal and an immediate scope in the temporal domain: its maximal scope encompasses the entire bounded event, of which only some internal portion falls within the immediate scope. Because the immediate scope is foregrounded, only this onstage portion of the overall event stands out as the composite expression's referent.   (Langacker 2008a: 65)

Thus, in contrast to the utterance *She gestures a lot* which designates a habitual act, *She was gesturing* implies that "such an act was under way" (Langacker 2008a: 65). Similarly, nouns are conceived schematically, involving a symbolic relaetween a phonological and a semantic pole. The sequence [[THING]/[. . .]] represents this structure in which [THING] is a maximally schematic characterization of its phonological pole. This structure can be combined with grammatical morphemes, such as the marker of plurality, which are conceived in symbolic terms like lexical items making up the sequence of [[PL]/[z]]. Thus, both structures can be integrated to form the constructional schema [[THING]/[. . .]]-[[PL]/[z]] defining a(n) (infinite) number of the THING designated by a noun.

1.1.2 The construal of conceptual content

The previous section sketched out the cognitive-linguistic view that grammar and meaning are indissociable. This argument is linked to the idea that meaning is identified with conceptualization and, thus, with the claim that meaning cannot be reduced to truth-conditional correspondence with entities of the world.

> The word conceptualization is understood in the broadest sense possible, essentially including any kind of mental experience. It thus subsumes: (i) both established and novel conceptions; (ii) not only abstract or intellectual "concepts" but also immediate sensory, motor, and emotive experiences; (iii) conceptions that are not instantaneous but change and unfold through processing in time; and (iv) full apprehension of physical, social, and linguistic context. (Langacker 2000: 26)

However, this does not mean that each and every phonological structure goes along with exactly the same conceptual meaning. Quite the opposite is the case, meaning that all aspects of conceptual structures are subject to construal, i.e., "our ability to conceive and portray the same situation in alternate ways" (Langacker 2000: 26–27). The lexical and grammatical constructions chosen to depict an event play a major role in the process of meaning construal. Consider the example of *gesture* again. If it is used as a noun, then the act of gesturing is conceived as an atemporal thing in which the successive states of the act of gesturing are coactivated, but they are conceived as accumulated and not individual. This is different when *gesture* is used as a verb. In this case, the act of gesturing is conceived more serially with its successive states. Langacker further argues that the differences in the construal of meaning are grounded in different cognitive operations framed as "sequential scanning," "summary scanning," and "conceptual reification" (Langacker 1987a, 2008a). Accordingly, the mode of sequential scanning is taken as accountable for conceiving the successive states of an event depicted. Both producer and receiver "follow along from one state to the next as the event unfolds," which is precisely why the event depicted is conceived more serially as a PROCESS (Langacker 2006: 51). A THING, on the other hand, is the product of the processes of summary scanning and conceptual reification. The single components of the event are activated holistically and the event itself is understood as a bounded space. If higher-level cognitive purposes are to be achieved, the process of conceptual reification operates. Here, groups of things are treated as single entities for the purpose of counting, for instance. These processes run automatically without any awareness of the conceptualizer.[1]

---

[1] In response to the criticism formulated by Broccias and Hollmann (2007), Langacker (2008c) has recently modified his account of the two modes of scanning based on the observation that

The conceptual content evoked by a linguistic unit can also be construed differently regarding the degrees of granularity or precision. Thus, a situation may be characterized as specific or schematic. Accordingly, the same gesture, for instance, can be described in many different ways, as shown in example (1).

(1) movement > body movement > gesture > manual gesture > recurrent gesture > cyclic gesture > cyclic gesture used in word searches

Thus, "a highly specific expression describes a situation in fine-grained detail, with high resolution" (Langacker 2008a: 55). Coarse-grained descriptions are given with the use of a less specific expression. Schematic expressions may, of course, also be deployed by speakers, such as *body movement* in example (1), which may be instantiated by more specific ones, such as *cyclic gesture*. Specificity and schematicity are essential to human language, with schemas arising from more elaborate and specific structures (see Section 1.1.1). Schemas can be found on all linguistic levels, including phonology, semantics, and grammar (see Langacker 2008a: 56).

Another aspect of meaning construal, termed "focusing," "includes the selection of conceptual content for linguistic presentation, as well as its arrangement into what can broadly be described (metaphorically) as foreground vs. background" (Langacker 2008a: 57). Accordingly, only a limited number of domains evoked by a linguistic item can be activated and if they are activated, then they are to varying degrees. Anything that is selected linguistically is rendered more prominent relative to what is not selected and, as such, is treated as more salient by speakers and addressees. Hence, a "high level of activation is a kind of foregrounding" (Langacker 2008a: 57).

1.1.3 Discourse and the flow of cognition

It goes without saying that speech events are situated in an ongoing discourse and "thus essential for understanding grammar" (Langacker 2008a: 457). A discourse comprises usage events, i.e., instances of language such as words, clauses, or intonation groups.

"certain structures override the construal imposed by others" (Langacker 2008c: 576) as in the expression "*a row of stacks of plates*" (Langacker 2008c: 576), or when a verb does not head a finite clause but is subordinated. In the latter case, "the sequential aspect may indeed be effectively or even wholly suppressed, given that the very purpose of these constructions is to impose a summary view" (Langacker 2008c: 576).

> The conceptualization inherent in a usage event includes the interlocutors' apprehension of their interactive circumstances and the very discourse they are engaged in. It thus incorporates their apprehension of the *ground* (G) and the *current discourse space* (CDS). The ground consists of the speech event, the speaker (S) and hearer (H), their interaction, and the immediate circumstances (notably the time and place of speech).
>
> (Langacker 2001: 144, original emphasis)

The current discourse space is defined as a mental space encompassing elements that are shared between participants of a conversation and grounding the communication at a given moment in time (see Langacker 2001: 144).

Langacker conceives these moments in the flow of discourse as viewing frames (Figure 3), involving the interlocutors' actions of directing and focusing of attention (illustrated by – > in Figure 3). Verbal interaction is considered successful if the different foci of attention are coordinated on the same conceptual entity, while all interlocutors have only a limited scope of attention and conception. "[W]e have a limited 'conceptual field', delimiting how much we can conceptualize or hold in mind at any given instant. Metaphorically, it is as if we are 'looking at' the world through a window, or viewing frame" (Langacker 2001: 144–145). This "window" is considered part of the immediate context of speech, including not only mental circumstances but also physical and cultural environments (see Langacker 2001: 145). A linguistic item or usage event serves the function of updating the current discourse space, including the frame currently acted upon, which Langacker calls the focus frame (Figure 3). In this sense, "a linguistic element can be *retrospective*, in the sense of making a specification concerning the prior discourse, and/or *prospective*, by virtue of evoking the subsequent discourse" (Langacker 2001: 151, original emphasis). Thus, a sequence of viewing frames advances the flow of discourse and, hence, the flow of cognition.

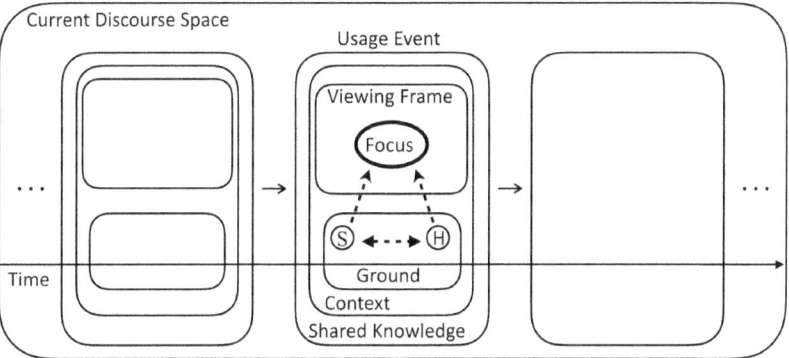

Figure 3: Discourse in Cognitive Grammar (adopted from Langacker 2001: 145).

1.1.4 Gestures as part of grammar and cognitive-linguistic description

It is indisputable that discourse does not only unfold verbally but also gesturally. Langacker (2001, 2008b) includes these observations in his theory by capturing the multidimensionality of usage events with the notions of "conceptualization channels" and "vocalization channels" (Langacker 2001: 145–146; see Figure 4).

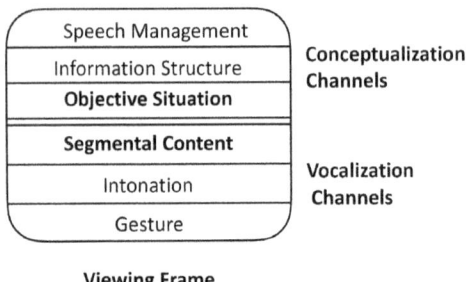

Figure 4: Multiple channels of viewing frames (adopted from Langacker 2001: 146).

Accordingly, conceptualization channels comprise speech management, including, for instance, turn management, or information structure, such as discourse topic or status, both forming the objective situation. The vocalization channels encompass segmental content, such as intonation or gesture. Consequently, Langacker includes gestures as part of linguistic analysis as they "offer independent evidence supporting the semantic analysis of particular elements and expressions" (Langacker 2008b: 249). Moreover, he points out that gestures can "indicate which facets of an overall conception are active at a given moment, thus providing clues to the shifting of attention in online processing" (see "focusing" in Section 1.1.2) and be an important resource for "developing an integrated account of grammar, processing, and discourse" (Langacker 2008b: 249). Based on these observations, Langacker underscores that gestures should be part of linguistic theory. "Granted their linguistic nature, it is important to investigate how gestures relate to other facets of language structure. One dimension of this problem is to ascertain how gestural content is integrated with co-occurring elements, both conceptually and formally. Another dimension is to investigate how the functions served by gestures relate to those served by elements of other kinds" (Langacker 2008b: 251).

This is what the book aims to do in the following chapters by combining a Cognitive Grammar and gesture studies perspective. The first theoretical frame has been introduced in this section focusing on notions crucial for the book's undertaking. We will proceed similarly in the next chapter when introducing the field of modern gesture studies. The main arguments developed in this field and a cognitive take on gesture studies will be presented.

1.2 The field of modern gesture studies

In the pages that follow, a theoretical and methodological frame of reference is introduced – that of gesture studies. This research area has developed into an autonomous field during the past 50 years, yet, it should not be considered a separate discipline as it is informed by various research strands such as psychology, linguistics, anthropology, neurology, primatology, ethnomethodology, or computer science. However, the hypothesis linking these various disciplines is that speech and gestures are tightly connected, highly coordinated and, therefore, integrated.

1.2.1 Gestures and spoken language: an integrated view

Viewing gestures as a part of spoken languages goes back to the rhetoric teachings of Quintilian, who saw gestures as companions of spoken language. He described gestures as an expression of speech acts, attitudes and emotions, and discussed their function regarding individual sections of discourse or the structure of linguistic utterances (see Müller 1998: 33). Quintilian was convinced that gestures were the natural language of humans and exhibited linguistic traits. The idea of gestures as a universal language was discussed and refined in the Renaissance (Bacon, Bulwer), the Enlightenment (Condillac, Diderot) and the Romantic Period (Vico, Herder) (see Müller, Bressem and Ladewig 2013). Gestures lost their relevance in the description of human communication when linguistics was established as an independent discipline. Spoken language was supposed to be the sole object of study for linguistics. This resulted in gestures being considered as part of "*parole*" at best, i.e., language use. Gestures were also viewed merely as an expression of emotion or having a decorative function in their relation to spoken language. This perspective was reinforced by the reasoning of the research field of nonverbal communication (see Ruesch and Kees 1969), which conceptualized gestures as a separate channel alongside speech. The interrelation of gestures and languages was generally ignored afterwards. Researchers viewed gestures as an expression of power, social status, emotion, and gender and as a means of "supporting" the meaning of speech although this supporting function of gestures has never been spelled out thoroughly.

The first microanalyses of the correlation between language and body movements (see Condon and Ogston 1966, 1967; Kendon 1972) marked the advent of the research field of modern gesture research. Pike (1967) and Birdwhistell (1970) integrated concepts of structural linguistics into the description of bodily-gestural communication and formulated the broad lines of a theory that unified language and gesture. Adam Kendon was inspired by their work and based his own studies on empirical studies of the structural argumentation of gesticulation (see Kendon 1980b) and its close coordination with language. Kendon formulated the influential idea: "[S]peech and movement appear together, as manifestations of the same process of utterance" (Kendon 1980: 208). According to him, language and gesture should be regarded as manifestations of a single process of utterance and, with this view, he created theoretical and methodical prerequisites for an integrative perspective on language use and gesture in which both modalities are equal partners. In addition to viewing speech and gestures as two forms and expressions that pursue the same rhetorical aim, Kendon also described similarities in their patterns. More precisely, he argues "that the pattern of movement that co-occurs with the speech has a hierarchic organization which appears to match that of the speech units" (Kendon 1972: 190). Hence, bodily movements and speech are hierarchically organized and highly coordinated. He detailed the gestures' structural organization in 1980, presenting an analysis of how the "flow of movement" (Kendon 1980b: 209) can be partitioned into successive units, more precisely, into "gesture phases," i.e., preparation, stroke, retraction, and hold, which can form higher-order units of a gesture phrase, comprising a preparation, a stroke, and a gesture unit, i.e., one or several gesture phrases completed by a retraction. It is interesting that a basic structure of gestures had already been observed at the beginning of the 20th century, when Ott (1902: 21), for instance, noticed that "[e]very gesture is divided into three parts – the preparation, the gesture proper, and the return". Mosher (1916: 10) also remarked that "[t]he great majority of gestures with the hands consist of three parts, which may be termed the preparation, the stroke, and the recovery." Furthermore, although argued from a prescriptive perspective, both remark that gestures can be combined linearly into sequences or series of gestures. However, similarities between spoken language and gesture on the level of these organizational patterns were first discerned by Kendon and described later by linguistic approaches to gestures (see Section 1.2.2).

Providing a vocabulary for the determination of movement phases in terms of gesture phases, serving different functions within the "movement excursion" (Kendon 1980) but also with respect to speech, set a milestone in the study of gesture and speech. Several studies aiming at detailing the picture of the gesture-speech interplay built upon Kendon's work and described various relations of linguistic units and the stroke phase.[2]

As pointed out in the beginning of this section, Kendon has always considered gestures and speech as equal partners that follow the same communicative aim (see Kendon 1983: 31). Gestures provide important information to fully understand an utterance and complement verbal information. Yet, gestures are not considered to depend upon the employment of speech or be a by-product of it. "Gesture is separate, in principle equal, joined with speech only because it is used simultaneously for the same overall purpose. The development of gesture, like the development of language, waits upon the development of a general capacity for symbolic representation" (Kendon 1983: 38). As such, gestures are capable of substituting linguistic units to fulfil the "communicative task" (Kendon 1983: 38) – a phenomenon investigated in this book.

The dichotomy between verbal and nonverbal communication was finally overcome completely with McNeill's (1985) groundbreaking essay "So you think gestures are nonverbal" in which he refers to gestures as being "verbal. They are the overt products of the same internal processes that produce the other overt product, speech" (McNeill 1985: 350). Language and gesture are, consequently, products of a mental process that controls the production of both modalities. McNeill consolidated his hypothesis with the empirically proven finding that gestures are produced mainly in conjunction with speech, are synchronized with linguistic units, develop parallel to infant language acquisition, perform semantic and pragmatic functions which are parallel to speech, and, in cases of aphasia, the production of gestures is impaired similarly to language (but see Rose 2013 for an overview of the positive effects of gestures in aphasia therapy).

McNeill's revolutionary essay incited an impassioned controversial debate on the driving force behind gestures: Either gestures and language were viewed as two semiotically different but equal parts of the process of utterance (see McNeill 1985, 1989, 1992) or gestures were thought to have a supportive function for lexical access and cognitive planning processes (see Butterworth and Hadar 1989; Feyereisen 1987; Feyereisen and de Lannoy 1991; Hadar and Butterworth 1997). This debate led to an increase in studies on the phenomena of multimodal communication.

Coming back to McNeill's approach, it should be emphasized that, although the formulations of his perspective that "gestures are an integral part of language much as are words, phrases, and sentences – gesture and language are one

---

[2] See e.g., Bressem (to appear); Chui (2005); Harrison (2010); Kendon (2004); Ladewig (2014a, 2014b); Loehr (2004); McNeill (1992); Nobe (2000); Seyfeddinipur (2006).

system" (McNeill 1992: 2) seem very similar to Kendon's proposal (see above), both scholars put forward different frameworks. Whereas Kendon argues from an interactive point of view, conceiving gestures and speech as following one rhetorical aim, McNeill opens up a conceptual take on gestures, suggesting that "gesture and speech are two sides of a single integrated process" (McNeill 1992: 274), exposing a "window onto thinking" (McNeill and Duncan 2000: 143). His work covers only a small range of gesture types, including iconic and metaphoric gestures, because he is interested in gaining insights into the processes of on-line conceptualization. Processes of stabilization and conventionalization in gestures, which are investigated by Kendon, for instance, are not in his focus of attention. He studies the speakers' idiosyncratic ways of gesturing which reveal their cognitive processes neglecting gestures that are shared by a speech community (for a discussion of the theoretical implications, see Harrison 2018; Müller 2018; Müller, Bressem and Ladewig to appear).

As pointed out earlier, McNeill is of the opinion that speech and gesture are subject to one and the same mental process: "[G]estures share with speech a computational stage; they are, accordingly, parts of the same psychological structure" (McNeill 1985: 350). This mental formation process has its starting point in a mental unit referred to as the "growth point" (McNeill 1992). Gestalt-like elements of both sides are joined together at this point in the production process. Furthermore, McNeill assumes that the different forms of thinking interact with each other during the formation process of multimodal utterances. This is expressed in the different modalities: Gestures are viewed as the visual part of thought where iconic representational processes are generated in a gestalt-like way. They unite several aspects of meaning. Speech reflects linguistic, analytical thinking. Individual, meaning-bearing elements which are joined linearly in time contribute to the overall meaning of a larger linguistic unit, such as a sentence. Language can also form different complex units that exhibit hierarchical characteristics which gestures cannot, according to McNeill.

David McNeill, like Adam Kendon, has dedicated his research to the co-expressivity of speech and gestures ever since and described multimodal utterances as forms of expression in which speech and gestures act together in conveying meaning. For this reason, both researchers are viewed as the founding fathers of modern gesture research. We must note, however, that David McNeill and Adam Kendon postulated very different theories of speech–gesture integration which sparked different schools within the research field. While David McNeill worked on a psychological theory of *language and gesture*, Adam Kendon developed an interactional approach to multimodal communication in which *gestures and speech* are described as "forms of action" (Kendon 2004: 161, 174).

1.2.2 Gesture and language as part of linguistic theory

The interest of linguists in studying gestures and speech has increased in the recent years with the possibility of analyzing larger multimodal corpora. However, a first groundwork for a linguistic approach had already been sketched out in the 1990s. Cornelia Müller's linguistic perspective on gesture (Müller 1998, 2013) combines Kendon's interest in formal and structural features of gesture with an interest in the description of the cognitive grounding of verbo-gestural meaning constitution. Moreover, she considers gestural movement as motivated (see also Calbris 1987, 1990, 2011; Mittelberg 2006; 2013) and derived from mundane actions of the hands and arms (see Streeck 1994, 2009, 2013). She is an advocate of the thesis that gestures have linguistic potential (see Müller 2013, see also Armstrong & Wilcox 2007) because both modalities accomplish a similar spectrum of function and expression. To be more precise, she shows convincingly that gestures fulfil Bühler's (1934) functions of language including expression ("*Ausdruck*"), appeal ("*Appell*") and representation ("*Darstellung*"). Still, they differ in their semiotic features, which is why a linguistic approach focuses on the medial peculiarities of gestures, i.e., their specific semiotic characteristics. This is of crucial importance in this approach because, based on Kendon's idea of "features of manifest deliberate expressiveness" (Kendon 2004: 13–14), the form of a gesture is the baseline for the construal of meaning and, thus, for a linguistic approach to gestures. Hence, gestural form features, which have been described as gestural parameters (see Ladewig and Bressem 2013a) based on sign language phonology (see Battison 1974), are viewed as potentially meaningful kinesic units. The articulatory effort behind the formation of gestures is conceived as a "communicative effort" (Müller 2014b: 130) in reference to Kendon.

> We maintain, however, a close consideration of the form specifics of a bodily performance with its single articulators. In doing so, we treat each of its form aspects as a potential meaning aspect in a multimodal depiction. This is the core idea of a form-based approach: any body movement is "work", is "effort" and we assume that when speakers move their bodies to "tell" parts of a narration, then every aspect of this "effortful movement" (to allude to Kendon's (2004) notion of "gesture as deliberate expressive movement", cf., Müller 2014b) is part of the story. (Bressem, Ladewig and Müller 2018: 228)

With the focus on the medium gesture itself, gestural patterns and structures became one of the main subjects of analysis in a linguistic approach. To be more precise, researchers shifted their attention increasingly to the description of the gestural form, which is a prerequisite for the study of gestures as motivated signs and their relation to signs of sign language. The gestural form features observable in a particular moment of gesturing, for instance, have been discussed under the notion of "simultaneous structures" (Müller, Bressem and Ladewig 2013;

see Section 2.1.1), introducing the notion of compositionality of gestural forms and proposing that gestural meanings may be composed of isolated features (see e.g., Calbris 2003, 2011; Kendon 2004; Ladewig and Bressem 2013a; Müller 2018; Ruth-Hirrel 2018; Webb 1996, 1998; for a discussion, see Kendon 2008). The idea of decomposing gestures into their meaningful segments was particularly advanced by studies on recurrent gestures (see Ladewig 2014c; Müller 2017a) and gesture families (see Bressem and Müller 2014a; Fricke, Bressem and Müller 2014; Kendon 2004; Ladewig 2011; Müller 2004), demonstrating that contrasting gestural forms discernable in varying form features are relevant for the formation of functional variants and the distribution of such variants over different contexts of use. In addition to the simultaneous orchestration of gestural form features, the temporal sequencing of gestures dubbed "linear structures" (Müller, Bressem and Ladewig 2013; see Section 2.1.2) aroused the interest of gesture scholars. Based on Kendon's (1980b, 2004) pioneering work documenting that gestures are structured linearly by gesture phases which may form units of varying sizes, the temporal arrangement of gestures has been described on various levels: Firstly, research zoomed in on the internal structure of gestures describing (a) articulatory features of gesture phases to identify Kendon's features of manifest deliberate expressiveness on the level of physical characteristics (see Bressem and Ladewig 2011), and b) the process of self-embedding to build units of higher order, such as complex strokes, gesture phrases and gesture units, by applying models from syntactic theories (see Andrén 2010; Bressem 2012; Fricke 2012). Secondly, the sequential combination of conventionalized gestures has been noticed several times. The combination of the Cyclic gesture with the Palm up open hand (see Ladewig 2014c), the Brushing aside gesture with a Palm up open hand (see Teßendorf 2014) or the Ring gesture with the pistol hand (see Seyfeddinipur 2004) are examples. It shows that the meaning and interactive function of gestures is linearly combined in a linguistic, phrase-like fashion. However, these observations only find their way into selective mentions. In other words, they have not yet been sketched out as a distinct research topic. Finally, it has been shown that several depicting gestures may combine to describe entire scenarios where a mimetic link between successive gestures is established creating a larger unit, such as an "idea unit" (Kendon 1980b). These successive gestures are related by depicting facets of a situation, event or story ("scenario", Müller, Bressem and Ladewig 2013: 723–724).

The thorough description of gestural forms is one but not the only research subject on the agenda of a linguistic approach. Obviously, the relation of gesture and speech and their integration is another. This relation has been described on the various levels of linguistic description, including prosody, semantics, pragmatics and grammar (see Bressem, Ladewig and Müller 2013; Müller, Bressem and Ladewig to appear). This aspect is spelled out more thoroughly in Chapter 2.

Finally, one concern should be addressed. A linguistic approach to gestures does not necessarily imply the assumption that gestural units resemble or are akin to units of speech. Nor does the application of linguistic terminology go along with treating both modalities as similar expressive modes. Although the borrowing of linguistic terms and notions has helped researchers to discern and describe structural similarities of both modalities, the peculiarities of the medium gesture have always been center stage in the analysis and theoretical description of gestures. This is the reason why the gestural form and, thus, the coding without sound creates the point of departure for all descriptive analyses. A linguistic approach starts from the premise that gestures can be comprehended best when analyzing them first without speech and later in relation to speech (see Chapter 2).

We have now presented three theoretical access points to the medium of gesture and its relation to language. It should be noted that this is only a brief introduction to the subject and cannot possibly be considered comprehensive. The field of modern gesture studies is an interdisciplinary research field in which the different disciplines formulate different theoretical and methodical approaches to language and gestures (see Müller, Bressem and Ladewig to appear for further information). The (cognitive-)linguistic approach to gestures in their relation to grammar will be sketched out in more detail in the subsequent chapter.

1.2.3 Gestures and cognition

The cognitive foundation of gestures has become a major research subject in the field of modern gesture studies ever since McNeill's formulation of a psychological take on gestures. Moreover, drawing upon cognitive-linguistic studies suggesting that notions such as metaphor or metonymy are general processes of human cognition, cognitive-linguistic approaches have advanced the studies on gesture. Indeed, to include other modalities than speech turned out to be a major issue in this field, because researchers have criticized the validity of linguistic data to research the processing of language. Hence, to include gestural data in the research of human cognition is regarded as a way out of "linguistic circularity" (Murphy 1996: 184), suggesting "that linguistic data are used to identify metaphors [for instance] but the main concrete predictions the theory makes are about similar linguistic and psycholinguistic data" (see Murphy 1996: 200; see also e.g., Cienki 1998b; Gibbs 1994; for a critical examination of this argument see Kertész and Rákosi 2009). Thus, gestures can offer independent evidence supporting analyses on general processes of human cognition.

Gesture research done within the framework of cognitive linguistics has evidenced ways in which gestures seem to be motivated by embodied conceptual structures. They have been shown to provide valuable insights into the bodily grounding of cognition. Manifestations of image-schematic structures were, for instance, observed in speakers' manual movements when depicting actions or manipulating virtual objects. Emerging "as meaningful structures for us chiefly at the level of our bodily movements through space, our manipulations of objects, and our perceptual interactions" (Johnson 1987: 29), they are tied to perception and motor activity and, thus, serve as a bridge to higher-level cognition. Image schemas[3] were argued to operate on many levels of meaning construal, including grammatical and semantic structures (see Brugman 1984; Langacker 1987a; Sweetser 1990), the conceptualization of emotions (see Peña Cerval 2003), metaphors (see Johnson 1987) or gestures (see e.g., Cienki 2005; Harrison 2018; Ladewig 2011; Mittelberg 2006, 2010a; Williams 2004, 2008). Based on the observation that gestural forms recur in different subjects, speakers and discourse contexts, researchers have argued that image schemas provide "skeletal structures" (Cienki 2005: 438), underlying idiosyncratic and recurrent gestures. Some exemplary cases are presented in what follows.

Cienki (1998b) not only brought in a cognitive-linguistic perspective with his identification of the image schema STRAIGHT in gestures, but he also showed that image schemas serve as a source domain for metaphors, in this case, of honesty, that may appear only in gestures. He identified further image schemas in gestures in a follow-up experimental study, including CONTAINER, CYCLE, FORCE, OBJECT, and PATH, by applying them as descriptors for gestural forms without sound. Based on his observations, he untangled the different ways in which the gesture and speech interplay in the construction of metaphoric meaning (see below). Tying in with his findings, Mittelberg expanded the list of gestural manifestations of image schemas by studying the multimodal depiction of grammatical concepts and theories in spontaneous academic discourse. Based on her identification of more "basic" image schemas that belong to the spatial motion group, she argues that "the bodily logic of force schemata, especially regarding the multimodal expression, i.e. exbodiment, of less tangible, yet crucial dimensions of meaning such as social forces and attitudes, but also affective and intersubjective dimensions of human communicative behavior" (Mittelberg 2013: 779).

Image schemas appear to play out on some level of understanding and conceptualizing gestural meaning, yet, looking at the research on the motivation of

---

[3] For a critical reflection of the notion "image schema," see Horst (2018) and (Müller and Kappelhoff 2018).

more conventionalized or "recurrent gestures" (Ladewig 2014c), Zlatev's notion of "mimetic schema" (Zlatev 2014) has proven to offer a more suitable explanation because it addresses a more concrete level of embodied meaning structure (see Müller 2017a). "The foremost theoretical role of mimetic schemas is similar to that of image schemas: to provide a basis for explaining the evolution and development of language. With the intention of avoiding the ambiguities surrounding image schemas pointed out above, [. . .] the following (hypothetical) properties of mimetic schemas are central: *preverbal, body-based, representational, intermediately specific* and *culturally shared*" (Zlatev 2014: 4–5, original emphasis)

Mimetic schemas are apprehended as more dynamic than image schemas because they are based on actions. Thus, they are semantically richer as they are more closely linked to concrete bodily experiences (see Cienki 2013b; Hampe 2005; Müller 2016; Müller 2017a; Zlatev 2014). They link instrumental actions and motor experiences with communicative actions, which can become entrenched in the case of recurrent gestures where "contexts-of-use merge with the grounding of mimetic schemas in intersubjective experiences. The result of these cognitive-semiotic and intersubjective processes is the dynamic anchoring of recurrent gestures in embodied frames of experience (understood as schematic structures of canonical experiences)" (Müller 2017a: 299).

Another process which is pivotal for understanding the motivation of gestural meaning is conceptual metonymy (see e.g., Panther and Radden 1999; Panther and Thornburg 2003; Radden 2000). Understood as operating on the level of sign formation, metonymy is described as illuminating "links between habitual bodily acts, the abstractive power of the mind, and interpretative/inferential processes" (Mittelberg 2006: 292). In contrast to metaphor (see below), the source domain is not blurred but conceptually present and salient in metonymical relations, because the process of transferring meaning takes place inside a single domain. Even though the source domain consists of a component of the target domain, the latter constitutes an elaboration of the source domain (see Panther 2005: 358). The expression "x stands for y" is typical for a metonymical relation, meaning that one entity stands for another.

Metonymical processes have repeatedly attracted the attention of gesture scholars (see e.g., Calbris 2011; Ishino 2007; Müller 1998, 2004), however, a comprehensive and systematic description of metonymical processes in gestures was supplied in Mittelberg's work on gestural meaning creation in academic discourse (see Mittelberg 2006, 2008, 2010b; Mittelberg and Waugh 2009a, 2009b, 2014). She argues that, from the perspective of the recipient, a speaker follows a gesture on a metonymical path, opening up a connection between its form and the reference object inferred. Accordingly, the gestural form is the starting point of the recipient's process of meaning construal, in which gestures are interpreted as imitations of an action, mostly with an object, or as a representation of an object (see Chapter 3).

In essence, metonymy can be considered the foundation of the construal of meaning in all gestures, because, just like verbal usage events, gestures foreground only fragments of meaning. To be more precise, with a gestural form, a speaker selects a range of semantic properties of an action, object, or event depicted, yet additional meaning aspects need to be inferred in order to understand a gesture. In reference to Jakobson (1956), Mittelberg (2006) distinguishes two metonymical processes observable in gestural sign creation, "internal and external metonymy." In the former case, the movement of the hand reflects the movement sequence of the original action, but the gestural representation is reduced to salient features of the action depicted. Hence, the whole motion sequence is not shown, but individual parts of an action schema are singled out and embodied by the hand. In the latter case, the objects, figures or shapes depicted by a speaker are contingent and, thus, external to the hand. They have to be inferred from the hand's configuration or from the ephemeral traces a speaker leaves in the air while gesturing. It is noteworthy that internal metonymy operates in all cases of gestural sign formation. External metonymy comes into play if the objects and figures depicted can be manipulated by the hands.

As has already been pointed out, metonymy is a fundamental process providing access to concrete objects and actions depicted gesturally. Yet, just like in speech, these objects and actions can be metaphorically construed. In fact, Mittelberg and Waugh (2009a: 329) describe metonymy as the first of a "dynamic two-step interpretative model suggesting that metonymy leads the way into metaphor." Hence, metaphor should not only be understood as a central process of meaning construal in verbal and signed language, but it is also a vital means for the meaning creation of gestures.

Metaphors and gestures had already attracted Wundt's attention at the beginning of the 20th century when he referred to this phenomenon as *"symbolic gestures"* (Wundt [1901] 1921: 174) and remarked that these kinds of gestures are involved in a mapping processes between different conceptual fields. According to him, a "symbolic gesture consists of a transfer of the ideas to be expressed from one conceptual field to another, thus, indicating concepts of time in terms of space, for instance, or representing abstract ideas as perceptual ones" (Wundt 1921 [1901]: 154, translation S.L.).[4]

---

4 *"Der allgemeine Charakter der symbolischen Gebärde besteht aber darin, daß sie die auszudrückenden Vorstellungen aus einem Anschauungsgebiet in ein anderes überträgt, also*

Metaphoric relations in speech and gesture have gained mounting interest in the field of modern gesture studies since McNeill and Levy (1982: 6–7) defined metaphoric gestures as a distinct gesture type in which the "form depicts the vehicle of a metaphor. The gesture is iconically related to this vehicle, not to the meaning or tenor of the metaphor. Like a verbal metaphor, a gestural metaphor conveys meaning indirectly" (Richards 1936). Subsequent research has identified different types of metaphors in speech and gestures.[5] Moreover, studies have analyzed how metaphoricity plays out in both modalities. Cienki and Müller (2008, 2014), for instance, suggest a flexible relationship between the modalities in the construal of metaphoricity by showing that different metaphors can be expressed verbally and gesturally. More precisely, they identified the following manners of orchestrating metaphoricity monomodally and multimodally, i.e., speech and gesture can simultaneously express (a) the same source and target, (b) a different source but the same target,[6] and (c) the same source and a different target. This distinction of monomodal and multimodal metaphoric meaning underscores the "modality-independent nature of metaphoricity" (Müller and Cienki 2009: 321) and reveals different forms of "thinking for speaking and gesturing" (Müller and Cienki 2009: 320). "Both the nature of the available linguistic forms as well as the expressive potential of hand-gestures which one can use in the expression of one's thoughts while speaking are significant for what thoughts ultimately get expressed" (Müller and Cienki 2009: 321). Moreover, it has implications on how metaphor is understood, i.e., either as a static property of words or gestures or "as materialized products of the process of establishing metaphoricity" (Müller 2008a: 23). Because metaphoricity may play out flexibly in the different modalities, it is also understood in more flexible terms as dynamic, gradable and having potential for being activated to different degrees in the flow of discourse (see Cameron 2002; Kappelhoff and Müller 2011; Müller 2008a, 2008b; Müller and Ladewig 2013). According to this notion, metaphoricity can span longer stretches of discourse and is not attached to single words or phrases. Moreover, it may change over the course of a conversation: It may be highlighted or backgrounded, it may emerge, be elaborated or disappear. All this is done by deploying both speech and gestures which establish a "multimodal salience structure" (Müller

---

z. B. zeitliche Vorstellungen räumlich andeutet, oder daß sie abstrakte Begriffe sinnlich veranschaulicht" (Wundt 1901 [1921]: 154).
5 See e.g., Calbris (1990, 2011); Cienki (1998a, 1998b, 2008); Ladewig (2011); Mittelberg (2006, 2008); Müller (2008b, 2017b); Nunez and Sweetser (2006); Parrill (2008); Sweetser (1998, 2007); Webb (1996, 1998).
6 See also, e.g., Calbris (1990); Casasanto and Jasmin (2012); Nunez and Sweetser (2006).

and Tag 2010: 5) as the discourse proceeds, revealing what is in a speaker's focus of attention.

This section will close with this short glimpse of a dynamic view of monomodal and multimodal meaning, which is spelled out in more detail in Chapter 5. The subsequent section outlines this book's endeavor to sketch the research field of a multimodal Cognitive Grammar.

1.3 A cognitive grammar and gesture studies interface?

The theoretical strands spelled out in the previous sections serve as anchor points for the enterprise carried out in this book. Major premises of Cognitive Grammar, such as the symbolic nature of linguistic items or the construal of meaning, will be merged with theoretical pillars of the field of gesture studies, including the multimodality of meaning and the linguistic potential of gestures, with the aim of investigating the link between grammar and gesture. In doing so, Chapter 2 ties in with the claims presented in the previous sections and presents empirical findings suggesting a close link between gesture and grammar and supporting the Cognitive Grammar and gesture studies interface proposed previously. It starts by explaining how the notion of grammar is conceived and applied in the field of gestures studies, i.e., the notion of a "grammar of gesture" (Müller, Bressem and Ladewig 2013) and of a "multimodal grammar" (Fricke 2012, 2013). The former offers a theoretical framework for the description of the structural properties of gestures, allowing them to substitute linguistic units. The latter perspective offers a methodological and theoretical framework for the description of the functional properties of gestures, allowing them to replace linguistic units and to integrate into verbal utterances. The chapter closes by summarizing recently proposed ideas on cognitive foundations of multimodal grammatical structures. The following chapters investigate the integration of gestures into the syntactic structure of spoken utterances. The starting point for these lines of thought is an empirical approach combining qualitative analyses of the interaction of speech and gesture combined with perception experiments. Each chapter begins with an introduction of the approach which is adapted to the different research questions addressed in each chapter. Moreover, two samples of the corpus serve as examples for each methodological step.

Chapter 3 investigates the integration of gestures in the syntactic structure of spoken utterances. The syntactic analyses of the 66 multimodal utterances identified in the corpus and the lexical items elicited in different perception experiments reveal that gestures preferably realize the syntactic slots of nouns and verbs that form, together with speech, multimodal constructions, such as clausemumod or nominalmumod. These findings are buttressed by three perception experiments testing the understanding of the spoken utterances and gestures with and without speech. The experiments further demonstrate that participants follow the syntactic structure of the utterance when interpreting the gestures: In noun positions, the gestures are conceived to depict objects and, in some cases, reified events. In verb positions, they are understood as depicting actions. Thereafter, cognitive foundations of the results presented previously are offered by focusing on the interaction of speech and gestures from a cognitive-linguistic perspective. More precisely, the notion of "conceptual archetypes" (Langacker 1991b, 2008a) is applied to discuss the gestures' capability of substituting nouns and verbs. Moreover, the cognitive processes of "summary scanning" and "sequential scanning" (Langacker 1991, 2008a) are introduced to account for the cognitive foundation of gestural meaning construal.

The integration of gestures into the semantic structure of spoken utterances is addressed in Chapter 4. The empirical findings of the lexical items elicited in naturalistic perception experiments allow the conclusion to be made that recipients of the multimodal utterances under scrutiny consider the gestures as integrated and adding semantic information missing in speech. The inherent meaning of gestures, i.e., the meaning of gesture conceived without speech, is examined to explore why gestures can integrate semantically into spoken utterances. It is argued that gestures can be conceived in terms of "symbolic units" (Langacker 1987a, 2008a; see also Kok and Cienki 2016; Ladewig 2012; Wilcox 2002), in which the form of the gesture occupies a phonological space and its meaning, a semantic space. These findings suggest conceiving gestural meaning as conceptual meaning. The interaction between speech and gesture on a semantic level is thereafter scrutinized by comparing the understanding of gestures with and without speech and by bringing together Peirce's (1931) concept of a triadic sign relation, Langacker's (1987a) notion of "symbolic units", and Wilcox' idea of "cognitive iconicity" (Wilcox 2004a). It is argued that recipients create a conceptual reference object ("interpretant," Peirce 1931), informed by verbal and gestural meaning, which allows them to understand the whole multimodal utterance and treat it as a meaningful contribution for the proceeding discourse.

As grammar cannot be understood without discourse, the integration of gestures in an unfolding process of meaning constitution is addressed in Chapter 5. The chapter begins by introducing the concept of a dynamic multimodal communication and methods for researching the emergence of multimodal meaning (see Müller 2008b; Müller and Ladewig 2013). By applying this approach, it is shown how speech and gesture highlight information in the flow of discourse. It is proposed, furthermore, that the realization of syntactic slots by gestures is a meaning foregrounding the strategy of speakers (see Müller and Tag 2010: 97), which can only be applied if sufficient information has been established in the flow of discourse. Moreover, it is shown that gestural meaning becomes increasingly specified the broader the discourse context becomes. The processes responsible for this meaning specification are intension and extension.

In the final chapter (Chapter 6) the results of the research presented in the book converge and are discussed regarding a multimodal conception of Cognitive Grammar. Moreover, the term "multimodality," as applied in the approach advocated here, is discussed regarding a narrower understanding in terms of "linguistic multimodality."

2 Multimodality of grammar and its cognitive foundations

As emphasized earlier, the relationship between language and gestures is elucidated from many different disciplinary perspectives, i.e., the field of modern gesture studies has been informed by many different disciplines and all of them contribute to the understanding of gesture and language. Needless to say, when studying multimodal language use, a linguistic approach should not be omitted. Yet, considering gestures as part of linguistics proper is a much-debated issue due to the primacy of spoken and written language in linguistic theory. Linguists studying gestures often find themselves in the position of justifying their research topic. However, regarding gestures as part of linguistic theory should not be omitted, considering the fact that (a) language use is as bodily as other forms of bodily expression, and (b) the functional range of gesture is related to the functions of language and is not restricted to managing social behavior or to expressing emotions (see Ruesch and Bateson 1951; Watzlawick, Beavin and Jackson 1967), as studies over the past 60 years have shown. Moreover, (c) gestures themselves have the potential to become linguistic, by either developing linguistic properties or becoming signs of fully-fledged linguistic systems.

Although the exploration of the language–gesture relationship from a linguistic perspective is still in its infancy, a fair progress in understanding their many facets has been made during recent years. Consequently, theoretical and empirical milestones will be presented in the following pages, sketching out the theoretical prerequisites for the phenomenon elucidated in the subsequent chapters.

2.1 Grammar of gesture and its cognitive foundations

The term "grammar of gesture" has been introduced to the field of gesture studies with the aim of shifting the focus to the medial properties of gestures, their motivation and their potential to become linguistic. It was developed by two projects: "The Berlin Gesture Project" leading to the interdisciplinary project "Towards a Grammar of Gesture: Evolution, Brain and Linguistic Structures," (ToGoG), which documented "those properties of form that characterize the hand(s) as a medium of expression" (Müller, Bressem and Ladewig 2013: 710),[7]

---

[7] For further information, see www.togog.org and http://www.berlingesturecenter.de/berlin gestureproject/fugestureproject. html.

as well as points of integration into grammatical structures of spoken language (see Section 2.2). Undoubtedly, the term "grammar" should be elucidated to understand the theoretical and methodological implications of this notion (see also Section 1.2.2).

The first approach of reading it is, of course, nourished by linguistic theory, describing grammars of different spoken and signed languages. As a matter of fact, this language-based grammar approach can only operate from the rule system of language itself and, thus, imposes linguistic notions and terms from language theory on gestures. In doing so, the approach (1) risks focusing only on the grammatical structures that gestures do *not* show instead of explaining in positive terms what a grammar of gestures is, and (2) forces gestures into the skeleton of language and, thus, risks missing phenomena that are gesture-specific. In the first case, gestures are always in competition with spoken and signed languages and will never be treated as a proper research phenomenon within linguistic theory. The reason is simple: Gestures do not exhibit the structures that fully developed grammars show. In the second case, gestures will be pressed into a system they have not developed themselves, which leads to a complete disregard of the medium's own properties. Birdwhistell's approach (1970) was certainly such a case. He aimed at discovering patterns and structures in gestures inspired by a linguistic theory, and, in doing so, he was indeed ahead of his time. Yet, his concepts and notions proved unpractical and inapplicable to the study of bodily movements, because the deployment of linguistic terms and notions put constraints on the study of body movements. Gestural properties could simply no longer be perceived.

The second reading is inspired by the modality itself and, thus, allows the description of the patterns and structures that we see when people use their hands to gesture. The patterns identified, however similar to or different from other modalities they may be,[8] are first described only for the modality of gesture and related to other structures found in gesture. Comparisons to other modalities, such as spoken and signed languages, are drawn only in a later step. The notion of a grammar of gesture connects with this modality-based approach. Due to this kind of reading, studies conducted within this approach did not aim to compare gesture and sign in the first place but to describe forms and uses of the hands while speaking. In other words, they were interested in describing the medium of gesture in its own right. Comparisons with linguistic

---

8 A linguist may certainly identify gestural structures that show similarities to forms of spoken or signed languages, for instance, during the phase of annotation. Yet, when describing the gestural modality as it reveals itself, these resemblances should not guide the portrayal of gestures, which is, of course, not always easy.

structures have been made in a second step to understand which properties should be considered gesture-specific, pre-linguistic or linguistic.

This research interest is accompanied by a particular methodological approach that defines gestural form as the baseline for the construal of meaning because form is meaning (see Section 1.2.2). In this sense, the notion of a grammar of gesture offers a framework for defining not only systematic gesturalness but also gestural systematicity. Gestural systematicity may show precursors of manual linguisticality. In terms of the phenomenon under scrutiny, patterns are investigated that may allow gestures to substitute elements of spoken language. These structures may explain why recipients understand utterances that are interrupted but completed gesturally. For the purpose of this investigation, two phenomena forming research strands within the framework of a grammar of gesture are presented in the following. These are the notions of simultaneous and linear structures of gestures.

2.1.1 Simultaneous structures

The notion of simultaneous structures (see Müller, Bressem and Ladewig 2013) designates different form parameters that are realized concomitantly in one gestural stroke. To be more precise, a gesture can be described in terms of a particular movement, hand shape, orientation of the palm, and position in gesture space to grasp phenomena of decomposition in the process of conventionalization, for instance. Yet, applying these notions does not entail that these different form parameters are perceived as such by a recipient. Although some form parameters may stand out and be more prominent than others (see Mittelberg 2010a; see also Chapter 3), gestures are assumed to be perceived as gestalts in which "the many individual movements can be understood only as parts of the process which embraces them, and it is indeed only thus that they attain their particularity" (Koffka 1938 [1915]: 377). Following Andrén (2010: 84), we could therefore argue that gestures are "weak Gestalten" (Köhler 2007 [1938]: 29), meaning they are holistic entities, but "we are not completely blind for the 'parts', i.e., the move(s) and hand-shape(s) and so forth that make up gestures as acts, even though we tend to see 'through' them, to the overall acts as intentional wholes, and primarily to the stroke phase of these movements." The form parameters borrowed from the description of signs (see Battison 1974; Stokoe 1960) can, thus, be deployed to address particular form aspects of such gestural gestalts systematically (see Ladewig and Bressem 2013a).

The notion of simultaneous structures comprises both gestures' articulatory (etic) and meaningful (emic) features. However, the emic level of description is in the center of attention in what follows. Approaches to elucidate gestures on the level of articulatory features have been outlined elsewhere (see Bressem and Ladewig 2011; Ladewig and Bressem 2013a).

2.1.1.1 Emic level of description
The idea that varying meanings are discernable in contrasting gestural forms was put forward early (de Jorio 1832/2000; Neville 1904; Wundt [1901] 1921) but pursued only selectively (see Efron[1941] 1972; Sparhawk 1978) until the rise of gesture studies in the 1990s. Calbris (1990) was among the first to conduct extensive and compelling research of the semantic structure of gestures. Aiming to "elucidate the signifying structure of the gestures" (Calbris 1990: xv), she developed a "physico-semantic classification" (Calbris 1990: xvi) based on the physical characteristics of gestures which are linked to signification. One group of gestures studied extensively is that of Wiping Away gestures (see Bressem and Müller 2014a, 2014b; Harrison 2018), which she subsumed under the notion of gestures of "separation" (Calbris 2003: 31–37). This type of gesture is motivated by the schema of cutting, yet, it "no longer evoke[s] just the act, but its result or the intention of its result, i.e. negation, total refusal" (Calbris 2003: 35; see also Fricke, Bressem and Müller 2014). With analyses of this kind, her research aimed to fathom the meaning of recurring physical components, their motivation and conceptualization (see Calbris 2003, 2008, 2011). Over and above, they paved the way for further research on the meaningful segments of gestures which was particularly advanced by studies on recurrent gestures (see Harrison 2018; Ladewig 2014c; Müller 2017a) and gesture families (see Bressem and Müller 2014a; Fricke, Bressem and Müller 2014; Kendon 2004; Ladewig 2011; Müller 2004; Ruth-Hirrel 2018). This research demonstrated that some parameters out of the clusters of form features may stabilize in form and meaning (semanticization) and, thus, become the core of a gesture (family). With one or two parameters taking over a particular meaning, the other form parameters become free to adopt other meanings and functions sensitive to the local exigencies of meaning creation and interaction. Similarly, the form parameters additional to the core of a gesture may stabilize in the continuing process of conventionalization and, thus, define a meaning variant of a recurrent gesture or a gesture family.

Consider the example of the Cyclic gesture – a gesture grounded in the movement pattern of a continuous rotational movement, performed *in situ* and away from the speaker's body (see Ladewig 2010, 2011, 2014b; see Figure 5). This movement pattern was identified in a corpus study of German as expressing the meaning of cyclic continuity in all contexts in which the gesture was

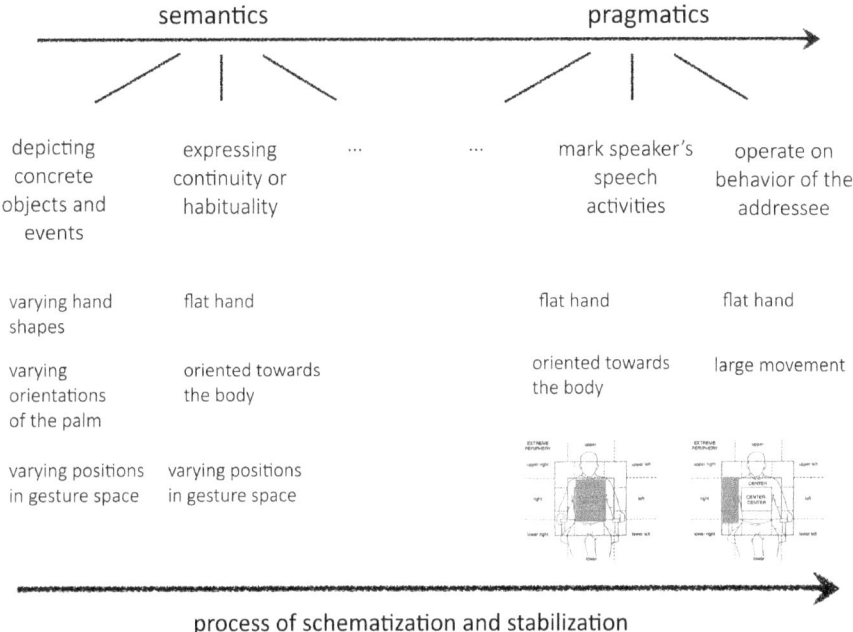

Figure 5: The stabilization and pragmaticalization of simultaneous structures in the variants of the Cyclic gesture.

deployed, i.e., descriptions, word and concept searches, and requests.[9] Local meanings are embodied by the additional parameters, i.e., hand shape, orientation of the palm, and position in gesture space, which may be randomly deployed depending on the idiosyncrasies of gesturing but which may also be deployed more systematically and, thus, define the variants of the Cyclic gesture. More specifically, the Cyclic gesture used in word or concept searches, for instance, is positioned in the center of and close to the speaker's body. When used in requests, it is located in the peripheral gesture space and with a large movement size. In both cases, the form parameters embody a deictic function of either referring to oneself or addressing an interlocutor.

Structures of this kind have been observed for other recurrent gestures as well. Their observation allowed researchers to argue for a "rudimentary morphology" (Müller 2004: 254; see also Harrison 2018) or "emerging 'morphosemantics'" (Kendon 2004: 224). Moreover, it was shown that these stabilized

---

[9] Further analyses of this pattern can be found in, for example, Duncan (2002); Müller (2000, 2004); Parrill, Bergen and Lichtenstein (2013); Zima (2014a, 2017).

simultaneous structures reflect different stages in the process of conventionalization in which an increase of stabilized clusters of form parameters goes hand in hand with the process of lexicalization, grammaticalization or pragmaticalization (see Ladewig 2010, 2011, 2014b, 2014c; see Figure 5). Processes of grammaticalization clearly establish the turning point between a grammar of gesture and a multimodal grammar, i.e., the instantiation of grammatical categories in other modalities, such as gestures (see Section 2.2). Such stabilization processes have primarily been studied from the perspective of signed languages. The approach outlined here zooms in on the gestural side of the continuum to elucidate the stages between singular, idiosyncratic gestures and fully conventionalized gestures (see Harrison 2018 for the discussion of the dimensions between action and gestures). In order to study these processes of stabilization, a simultaneous structures approach and, thus, a focus on the segments a gesture is "composed of" is essential. Without examining the emic units of gestures, their development into linguistic units could not be explored.

2.1.2 Linear structures of gestures

Not only are gestures structured by articulatory features and different form parameters, but they are also organized in temporal sequences. These sequential organizations of gestures have been referred to as "linear structures" (Müller, Bressem and Ladewig 2013: 722–726), comprising both the internal organization of gestures in terms of gesture phases and their arrangement in gesture sequences. It has developed into a major research subject within gesture studies for both methodological and theoretical reasons. First of all, the determination of gesture phases is an important prerequisite for analyzing the interrelation of gesture and speech, because the interrelation of gestural and verbal units in the process of multimodal meaning creation can be studied only when the meaningful parts of the gesture are identified, i.e., the stroke and the hold. Secondly, with the definition of gestural segments, the complex and hierarchical organization of movement segments (see Birdwhistell 1970; Kendon 1972; Pike 1967) becomes describable and can be linked to structures of spoken language. Interestingly, the internal structure of gesture had already been described at a time when video recordings and, thus, the minute analysis of gestures were not feasible at all. It was at the beginning of the 20th century that Ott (1902: 21), for instance, noticed: "Every gesture is divided into three parts – the preparation, the gesture proper, and the return." Similarly, Mosher observed a three-component structure of gestures when he argues that the "great majority of gestures with the hands consist of three parts, which may be termed the preparation, the stroke, and the recovery" (Mosher 1916: 10). With these descriptions, both coined the terms that have later been subsumed under the notion of "gesture phases," which were elaborated further by numerous gesture scholars (see Bressem and Ladewig 2011; Duncan n.y.; Kendon 1972, 1980b; Kita, Gijn and van der Hulst 1998; Seyfeddinipur 2006). The hierarchy emerging in the linear combination of gesture phases, first described by Kendon (1972, 1980b, 2004: ch. 7), has been defined as "gesture phrases" and "gesture units." Accordingly, a stroke alone or a stroke plus a preparation may form a gesture phrase. The whole excursion of the hands from one rest position to the next forms a gesture unit (Figure 6).

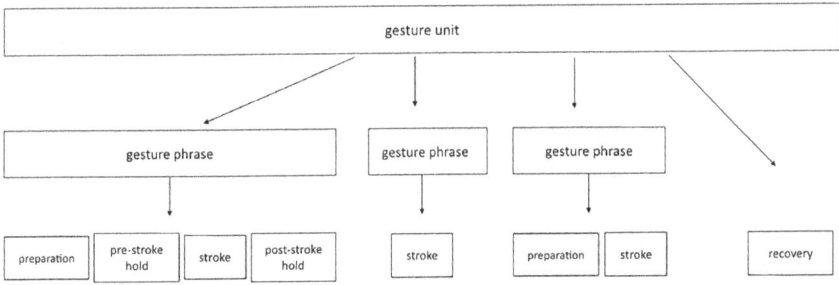

Figure 6: Linear structures according to Kendon (2004: ch. 7).

A fundamental property of language was brought up with the hierarchy illustrated in Figure 6 and related to gesture. More precisely, Fricke argues that gestural segments can be self-embedded to form higher order units and, thus, exhibit the property of recursivity. She suggests the following phrase structure rules that govern the formation of higher order units (Fricke 2013: 744):

$$GU \rightarrow \begin{cases} GP\ Retr \\ GU\ GU(GU1 ... GUn)\ Retr \\ GU\ GP\ GP(GP1 ... GPn)Retr \\ GU\ (GU1 ... GUn)\ GP(GP1 ... GPn)\ (GUn+1 ... GUz)\ Retr \\ GP(GP1 ... GPn)GU(GU1 ... GUn)\ (GPn+1 ... GPz)\ Retr \end{cases}$$

$GP \rightarrow (Prep)\ SP$

$SP \rightarrow S(\ S1...Sn)$

$S \ \rightarrow (Hold)\ s\ (Hold)$

Accordingly, the smallest element a gesture can be composed of is the stroke, which can be self-embedded to form complex structures of strokes – a "stroke phrase" (SP) – which has been referred to as complex strokes (see Bressem 2012, to appear; Fricke 2012). A stroke with or without a preparation (Prep) may form a gesture phrase (GP). One or multiple gesture phrases followed by a retraction (Retr) may form a gesture unit (GU), which can be simple (GP+Retr) or complex ($GP_1 \ldots GP_n$+Retr). If a gesture unit shows no complete relaxation at its completion ("partial retraction", see Kendon 1980b; Seyfeddinipur 2006), it is conceived of as a "secondary gesture unit." A gesture unit exhibiting full relaxation, on the other hand, forms a "primary gesture unit," which is, at the same time, the highest unit in the hierarchy comparable to the constituent category "sentence" (S) in grammars of vocal and signed languages, as Fricke (2013: 744) argues.

With this structure, Fricke differentiates recursion from iteration in gestures. Moreover, she argues that "[b]ased on the assumption that recursion is specific to the language faculty in the narrow sense (FLN), then the recursion of co-speech gestures forces them to be considered as an integral element of language" (Fricke 2013: 745). In this vein, she defines resembling structures in the gestural and verbal modality. As these structures belong to the realm of grammar, the phenomenon of gestural recursivity also constitutes a research subject within the concept of a multimodal grammar (see Section 2.2)

All in all, the concept of linear structures makes visible gestures' capability of forming temporal structures in a systematic way. Some of these temporal structures resemble linguistic structures but not all patterns necessarily have to do so in order to be subsumed under this notion. Other structures identified so far are the following:

1. Gestural repetition, resulting in the multiplication of the same gestural meaning (iteration) or in the creation of a new gestural meaning (reduplication) (see Bressem 2012, 2014, 2015, to appear);
2. gesture sequences, i.e., the sequential combination of conventionalized or recurrent gestures, such as the Brushing aside gesture combined with a Palm up open hand (see Teßendorf 2014) or the Ring gesture combined with the pistol hand (see Seyfeddinipur 2004; for more examples consult Ladewig 2014c); and
3. gesture scenarios, where a mimetic link between successive gestures is established creating a larger unit such as an "idea unit" (Kendon 1980b: 218). These successive gestures are related by depicting facets of a situation, event or story (see Müller, Bressem and Ladewig 2013: 723–725).

Concluding, the approach of a grammar of gestures offers a framework for elucidating and describing the properties of the medium "gesture" itself, as it sets the description of form center stage. With their application, comes the belief that linguistic structures are not a matter of substance but a matter of form (see de Saussure 1916; Hjelmslev 1974) and, thus, they are considered independent of a particular modality (as signed languages have already proven). Gestures, on the other hand, are, of course, not conceived of in terms of forming a linguistic system in their own right but as potential candidates to become linguistic. Hence, as pointed out earlier, the approach offers to unravel those characteristics of gestures that are gestural (see McCleary and Viotti 2009; Müller 2018), those being on their way to become linguistic and those that are linguistic and have entered a language, be it spoken or signed. Linking these research aims to the enterprise undertaken in this book, it is the interest here to identify those properties that enable gestures to substitute linguistic items and, thus, show properties that may become linguistic (see Chapter 6).

2.2 Multimodal grammar and its cognitive foundations

Recent years have seen an upsurge in the interest of linguists in gestures and, with it, a multimodal approach to grammar has started to develop. This approach advocates the view that linguistic structures can be found in modalities other than spoken language. This has clearly been shown for signed languages but here, the idea that gestures can be grammatical functions and, thus, may become linguistic is underscored.

Two major lines of thoughts are perceivable within this research area arguing (a) that gesture and grammar converge at particular points in time, i.e., when gestures recur or when speech and gesture co-occur regularly, and become entrenched to a certain extent, and (b) that gestures are capable of instantiating structural and functional properties exhibited by the language system of discrete languages. Thus, the former comprises processes of grammaticalization and, thus, the end of the continuum introduced in the previous section and also the frequent co-occurrences of speech and gesture and the emergence of multimodal constructions (see Section 2.2.2). The second addresses the gestural execution of grammatical functions, yet in these cases, the gestures do not necessarily have to be grammaticalized. In other words, gesture can take over functions of linguistic units by realizing a syntactic slot, for instance, and, thus, by being integrated into the structure of speech (see Section 2.2.3). These lines of thought will be outlined in the following.

2.2.1 Grammaticalization in gestures

The first research strand of a multimodal approach to grammar draws on the emergence of recurrent gestural patterns that may form monomodal constructions, i.e., a form-meaning pattern entrenched in our cognitive system. This idea is grounded in the "imagistic formalisms of cognitive grammar" (Cienki 2015: 210) and the symbolic status of both linguistic and gestural units. As McNeill (1992) claims in his psychological approach, gestures and speech form one cognitive system in which gestures reveal the imagistic side of thinking. Moreover, based on the notion of "thinking for speaking" (Slobin 1987), the idea that a particular kind of thought is mobilized for the purpose of gestural communication, reflecting imagistic aspects of thinking, was discussed under the notion of "thinking for gesturing" (Cienki and Müller 2008; Kellerman and Hoof 2003). Empirical findings supporting this line of thought are supplied by studies investigating the development of gestures into linguistic elements of signed languages, such as discourse markers, or lexical or grammatical morphemes. These studies adduce evidence that single form parameters can undergo processes of stabilization in form and meaning. Such form parameters often constitute the core of recurrent gestures, such as the hand configuration or the movement of the hand (e.g., Bressem 2012, to appear; Bressem and Müller 2017; Janzen 2012; Janzen and Shaffer 2002; Ladewig 2011, 2014b; Pfau and Steinbach 2006; Shaffer and Janzen 2000; Wilcox 2004b, 2005). The Palm up open hand, for instance, used in spoken discourse to express agreement or to seek agreement for the discursive objects presented on the open hand, was observed in many signed languages such as American Sign Language (see Conlin, Hagstrom and Neidle 2003), Danish Sign Language (see Engberg-Pedersen 2002) or Turkish Sign Language (Zeshan 2006) where it is used as a grammatical marker or a discourse marker (see Pfau and Steinbach 2006; Pfau, Steinbach and van Loon 2014). Since functional similarities between gestures and signs were observed in this case, it appears logical that the Palm up open hand used as a sign has developed from the recurrent Palm up open hand gesture (Pfau, Steinbach and van Loon 2014).

Other recurrent gestural patterns that were found to embody grammatical functions are gestures expressing negation (see Bressem and Müller 2014a, 2017; Harrison 2009, 2014, 2018), aspectuality (see Boutet, Morgenstern and Cienki 2016; Cienki and Iriskhanova 2018; Duncan 2002; Ladewig 2014b; Ruth-Hirrel 2018) or plural (see Bressem 2012, 2014, 2015, to appear). Based on the functional similarities observable in recurrent gestures and signs of signed languages Pfau, Steinbach and van Loon (2014: 2146) conclude that beyond lexicalization, certain manual and non-manual co-speech gestures that accompany spoken utterances may also fulfill well-defined grammatical functions when used by signers; that is, they may grammaticalize. Grammaticalization may either proceed directly from gesture to grammatical marker (route II) or may involve an intermediate step, at which the gesture undergoes lexicalization (route I). We have argued that diachronic changes that take a gestural element as input – that is, route II and the first step on route I – are modality-specific, while the change from lexical to grammatical element parallels grammaticalization phenomena that have been described for spoken languages.

The emergence of linguistic structures in gestures, similar to that in spoken or signed languages, is grounded in processes of abstraction, schematization and decontextualization. They give rise to lexical, grammatical and discursive items. As Langacker puts it,

> [a] lexical item embodies the commonality in form and meaning **observable across a substantial number of usage events** (i.e. actual utterances in their full phonetic detail and contextual understanding). Its acquisition comes about through the reinforcement of **recurrent features**, the progressive entrenchment of whatever aspects of form and **meaning are constant across events**. It thus involves a process of **decontextualization**, whereby non-recurrent features are filtered out, as well as **schematization**, for it is only by abstracting away from specific points of fine detail that commonalities become apparent.
>
> (Langacker 1999: 2, emphasis added)

In this way, abstract schemas of gestures can emerge that can be classified as modality-independent and modality-specific at the same time. First of all, schemas such as aspectuality, plural, negation, or emphasis are entrenched in spoken language systems, signed language systems and gestures, and, thus, should be conceived as modality-independent. On the other hand, their form varies in the manual and verbal modality due to the different medial properties that the voice and the hand show. The Cyclic gesture, for instance, is defined as a recurrent gesture forming part of a gesture family (see Section 2.1.1). Researchers have argued that the core meaning of this movement pattern – cyclic continuity – has emerged from experiences with cyclic motions and the recurrence and repetition of events through time (see Ladewig 2011, 2014b; Ruth-Hirrel 2018). Moreover, recent corpus studies have revealed that the expression of aspectuality is the prototypical and, thus, central function of this gesture, because a large number of tokens co-occurred with verbal aspectual meanings. In more detail, Ruth-Hirrel (2018) and Ruth-Hirrel and Ladewig (in preparation), who compared Cyclic gesture tokens co-expressed with predicates expressing aspect in English (n = 254), German (n = 97) and Farsi (n = 31), showed that the Cyclic gestures relate systematically to the expression of aspectual meanings in all three languages and that it co-occurs with categories proposed by Vendler (1957, 1967); (Figure 7;

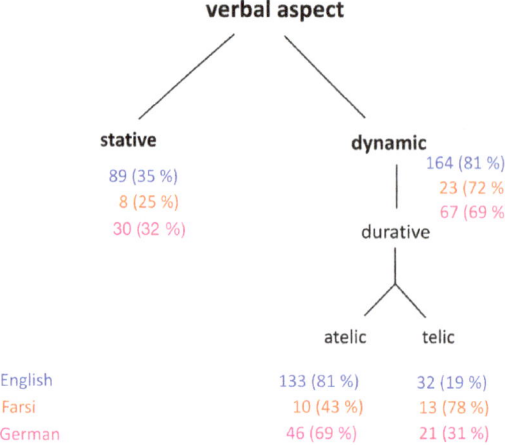

Figure 7: Cross-cultural comparison of the Cyclic gesture (Ruth-Hirrel and Ladewig in preparation).

see also Harrison's case study of "multimodal progressive utterances" [Harrison 2018: 212] composed of "be + -ing with the Cyclic gesture").

According to the numbers shown in Figure 7, most tokens in English and German are co-expressed with atelic durative aspectual expressions, followed by stative and telic construals. Most tokens in Farsi were accompanied by durative, telic expressions, followed by telic and stative construals. Ruth-Hirrel and Ladewig (in preparation) conclude that the Cyclic gesture foregrounds durativity and continuity in all contexts even if states are expressed verbally because, as a matter of fact, states also endure.

It is interesting that the distribution of the Cyclic gesture over the different types of aspectuality goes hand in hand with stabilizations in form, at least in German and English. Stative constructions in English, for instance, were used at the sides of the speaker's body. German stative constructions were co-expressed with Cyclic gestures exhibiting a relaxed flat hand, oriented towards the speaker's body. Cyclic gestures used with English progressives (always atelic expressions) were performed with asynchronous, bimanual movement at a frequency greater than expected. German does not show grammaticalized aspect such as the progressive, but the Cyclic gestures co-expressed with atelic constructions also showed a form pattern, which is the open hand oriented towards the body and the fingers touching each other, i.e., they were held together (for a comprehensive account, see Ruth-Hirrel 2018; Ruth-Hirrel and Ladewig in preparation).

The insights emerging from these observations are twofold. First of all, continuative aspectual meaning appears as the prototypical meaning of Cyclic gestures, as it is directly related to their experiential source. Secondly, the different stabilized patterns and their distribution over different dimensions of aspect make visible entrenchment processes of both types and tokens. Taking frequency of use regarding a specific meaning or function into account (see Geeraerts, Grondelaers and Bakema 1994), it appears that "token frequency gives rise to the entrenchment of instances, type frequency gives rise to the entrenchment of more abstract schemas" (Evans 2006: 118). In relation to the processes of schematization and decontextualization (see Langacker 1999: 2), we can argue that the formational and semantic core expressing aspectual meaning in the contexts examined constitutes the type of the Cyclic gesture, whereas its instances form entrenched and stabilized tokens. Speculating about the further development of the Cyclic gesture, it can be argued that this movement pattern enters the sign language system as a marker of aspectuality (see Ladewig 2014b; Ladewig and Bressem 2013a). In fact, the continuous circular movement has been observed in American Sign Language (ASL) and German Sign Language (DGS) as a marker of continuative aspect (see Klima and Beluggi 1979: 306; Meir 2012: 102; Padden 1988: 254). The processes underlying this development would be the entrenchment of an abstract schema due to type frequency, decontextualization from its situated meanings, and schematization, giving rise to the abstract schema of continuative aspect.

Grammaticalization processes of this kind have been discussed by sign linguists as well (see above) and among them, Sherman Wilcox (2004b, 2005) has suggested two routes from gesture to language to fathom the different dimensions of such processes. He stated that the first route leads from gesture to a grammatical morpheme via a lexical morpheme and the second from gesture to a grammatical morpheme via a marker of intonation/prosody. Several examples were given for modal verbs in ASL, among them the development of the modal verb CAN. Researchers argued that this marker of possibility has developed from the lexical sign STRONG, which has itself emerged from a gesture expressing upper body strength (see Janzen and Shaffer 2002; Shaffer and Janzen 2000; Wilcox 2004b; Wilcox and Shaffer 2006; Wilcox and Wilcox 1995). Interestingly, this gesture has been identified as a recurrent one, forming part of the repertoire identified for German and expressing the meaning "strength", "force" or "power" (Bressem and Müller 2014b: 1584).

The development of the Cyclic gesture into a marker of continuative aspect fits well into Wilcox's first route. Accordingly, it is conceivable that the gesture based on the bodily experiences of circular motions and cyclic events has developed into the lexical item of TIMES/HOUR, ALWAYS or PROCESS, with clearly slightly different forms, and later developed into a grammatical marker of continuative aspect (Figure 8).

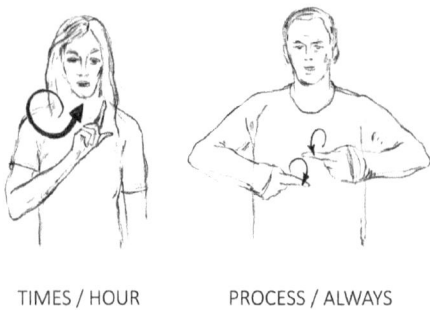

TIMES / HOUR   PROCESS / ALWAYS

Figure 8: Lexemes showing a circular motion in German Sign Language (DGS).

To sum up, gestures have the potential to become linguistic, as the compelling body of research demonstrates. Yet, with the current discussion on the emergence of signs in mind, it appears noteworthy and crucial for the understanding of the view advocated here that the ideas outlined argue for a continuous development from gesture to sign and not for a "cataclysmic break," as has been claimed elsewhere (see Singleton, Goldin-Meadow and McNeill 1995). With the latter notion, a "*categorical difference*" between gesture and sign is diagnosed which is "*a consequence of a decision to restrict the concept of gesture to spontaneously used gestures*" (Müller 2018, orginal emphasis; see also Harrison 2018), as was done by McNeill (1992), and has framed a whole research school ever since.

It is noteworthy that the grammaticalization of gestures has attracted more sign language researchers than gesture scholars so far, although fundamental claims were made when the field of gesture studies was in its infancy (see Kendon 1988a). This is most likely due to the fact that linguists started to join the scientific exchange about gestures relatively recently. However, with the increasing interest of linguists in gestures and multimodal communication, the gesture's potential to achieve a linguistic status is being explored more and more. One of the growing topics within this research strand is the formation of entrenched multimodal assemblies, so-called "multimodal constructions," with which the next section deals.

2.2.2 Multimodal constructions

Departing from the theory of Cognitive Grammar and pointing out that "there are variable DEGREES to which gesture can have linguistic status," Cienki (2015: 508, original emphasis) describes two paths gesture can take to become linguistic. The first path is based on the cognitive grammatical claim that all linguistic units are abstracted from usage events. Processes of abstraction go hand in hand with schematization, i.e., the "reinforcing [of] whatever commonalities recur across a number of usage events, being inherent in these events at any level of granularity" (Langacker 2007: 425; see Section 2.2.1). Accordingly, schematic units abstracted from usage events exhibit prototype structures that become entrenched due to their recurrent deployment. Because usage events can be verbo-gestural and because verbo-gestural usage events may recur, not only speech but both modalities speech and gestures can undergo processes of abstraction and become entrenched units when used in a sufficient number of events (for a discussion of the term "sufficiency," see Zima 2014a: 27). Hence, the frequent co-occurrences of speech and gesture may be candidates for establishing a link between gesture and grammar observable on different time scales. The phenomenon dubbed "multimodal constructions" (Bressem 2012; Zima 2014b) is one outcome of such processes (see the special issue of Linguistics Vanguard 2017 (3) for more information) and is developing into a major strand within linguistic approaches to gestures. It starts from the premise that constructions (see Bybee 2006; Goldberg 1995, 2006) regarded as basic units of language are multimodal in nature. Goldberg's (2006: 5) original idea considers "[a]ny linguistic pattern [. . .] as a construction as long as some aspect of its form or function is not strictly predictable from its component parts or from other constructions recognized to exist. In addition, patterns are stored as constructions even if they are fully predictable as long as they occur with sufficient frequency." Accordingly, construction grammar approaches (see Croft 2001; Goldberg 1995, 2006; Hoffmann and Trousdale 2013) posit that linguistic units of all levels of grammatical descriptions, i.e., morphemes, words, idioms, phrasal patterns, etc., can become constructions. With the interest in multimodality, this notion has been expanded to integrate gestures and other forms of bodily behavior. The exigency for such a multimodal constructions approach is simply the fact that language use itself is multimodal. As Hoffmann (2017: 1) points out "[s]ince authentic spoken utterances are very often accompanied by gesture, it seems logical to assume that cross-modal association and chunking could also result in multimodal constructions: constructions that on top of verbal properties also contain information on gesture, facial expressions, body posture, etc."

Because the inclusion of gestures into linguistic theory is a much-debated issue (see Section 2.1), the application of a construction grammar approach to gestures calls forth similar concerns. Hence, considering stable gesture–speech co-occurrences as single expressive units finds very critical stances, arguing, for instance, that constructions can only be considered multimodal if gestures are obligatory to speech (see Ningelgen and Auer 2017; Ziem 2017). Yet, the number of such cases is assumed to be very limited (for a discussion, see Chapter 6).

However, we find approaches advocating the view that Goldberg's notion can be applied to both speech and gesture if the notion is treated more flexibly, encompassing different degrees of entrenchment, schematization and scope. Based on the idea that "constructions are mentally stored with different degrees of schematicity," Lanwer (2017: 2), for instance, argues that "differences between multi- and unimodal constructions can always be a matter of schematicity, at least with respect to gestural features which are not part of phonetic articulation" (Lanwer 2017: 2). He proposes with this definition that one and the same construction could be stored as a verbal, monomodal pattern which can be added by conventionalized gestures at a more specific level of schematicity (Figure 9a).

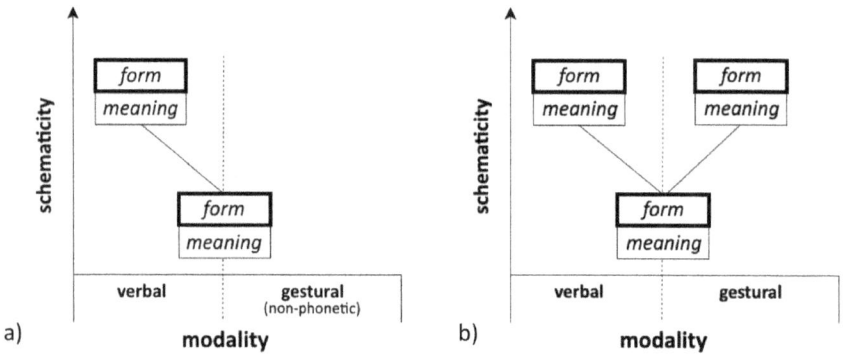

Figure 9: (a) Uni- and multimodal constructions (Lanwer 2017: 2); (b) uni- and multimodal constructions including gestural schematicity constructions, modified version of Lanwer's model.

This model is flexible enough to include language and other forms of bodily expressions. However, what should be taken notice of in the attempt to formalize multimodal representations is that gestures also show different degrees of schematicity, first and foremost, conventionalized gestures. For this reason, the emergence of more abstract and schematic patterns should be included in Lanwer's model. A first attempt is made in Figure 9b.

In order to exemplify this line of thought, we focus on the Throwing away gesture, which has recently been suggested as a potential candidate for forming a multimodal construction because researchers have observed systematic co-occurrences of its gesture tokens with particular verbal items, such as modal interjections. For this reason, Bressem and Müller (2017) refer to these gesture–speech units as the "Negative-Assessment-Construction," in which the gestural element is characterized as follows:

> It is characterized by a particular kinesic core: a lax flat hand oriented vertically with the palm facing away from the speaker's body flapping downward from the wrist. The form of the gesture is based on actions of throwing away middle-sized roundish objects sitting in the palm of the hand that one wants to get rid of: a rotten fruit, the core of an apple, a crumpled piece of paper for the trash. All these actions have a shared goal: clearing one's body space of such unpleasant or useless objects. When used in relation with speech, Throwing Away Gestures enact these actions: The hand now metaphorically throws away topics of talk and qualifies the rejected arguments, ideas and actions as uninteresting and void. In this way, the gesture acquires a particular meaning, namely that of getting rid of, removing and dismissing annoying topics of talk by throwing them away from the speaker's body. (Bressem and Müller 2017: 3)

Now, what speaks for a schematized pattern of the Throwing away gesture? In order to answer this question, we compare the use of a singular and a recurrent gesture. The gesture depicting the disposal of a piece of paper into a waste basket serves as a candidate of the first gesture type and a Throwing away gesture used with the German particle *egal* ('never mind') for the second. Both gestural performances are claimed to be grounded in the action of throwing something away, i.e., literally performing the act of throwing an object somewhere into a remote space. Yet, both performances would differ in gestural form because both showed different degrees of specificity based on the varying distance to their experiential root. To be more precise, the singular gesture in the first case is much closer to its derivational base than the recurrent form and, thus, expected to be performed in a much more elaborate way, including a specific hand shape depicting the form and size of the object thrown away and a movement pattern that is most probably directed towards the goal of the throwing action, for instance, a basket. Moreover, the quality of the movement would probably differ due to its embodiment of a certain extent of force and effort to move the virtual object held by the hand. As such, we would assume many more parameters to be semantically loaded in order to mime the underlying action (see Bressem, Ladewig and Müller 2018) than in the case of the recurrent Throwing away gesture. Tokens of this gesture do not depict the action of throwing something away in the first place, which means they do not embody the action in its very concrete sense but rather as "a schematized scene of mundane actions" (Bressem and Müller 2017: 6), which can be conceived of as a "cognitive scene" at the same time. Accordingly, the gesture, although originally motivated by a concrete action, instantiates a more abstract scheme, namely that of

> the 'Away Action Scheme' – a shared experiential frame that is grounded in mundane actions of moving or keeping away annoying objects. The elements included in this action scheme are an unpleasant situation (starting point) in which annoying objects are in the immediate surrounding (cause). These are removed through an action of the hand

(action), which then leads to removal of the objects and a neutral situation (endpoint) [. . .]. These elements make up the experiential frame and the schematic cognitive scene on which the semantics and the pragmatics of the 'Negative-Assessment-Construction' rests. (Bressem and Müller 2017: 6)

In a similar vein, the Cyclic gesture mentioned in the previous section going along with the progressive in English can be conceived of as a multimodal construction, and recent work by Ruth-Hirrel (2018) or lends support to this argument (see also Harrison's [2018: 212] case study of "multimodal progressive utterances"). By following Cienki's (2017) approach of considering central and peripheral variants of the Cyclic gesture (see below), she makes a good case for treating gestures as constructions, because "[g]estural constructions, like spoken language constructions, create higher-level meanings that cannot be strictly predicted from the component symbolic structures that comprise them. They are distinct symbolic entities. They also exhibit variable degrees of schematicity and conventionality, as is the case with spoken language constructions" (Ruth-Hirrel 2018: 224). Her argument aligns perfectly with the treatise on schematization processes in gestures given in Section 2.2.1. However, like Bressem and Müller (2017), she expands the notion of recurrent gestures or gestural constructions to include linguistic items and introduces the "'Tell me' Joint Action Construction" as a particular variant of the Cyclic gesture, which Ladewig (2011, 2014b) has described as Cyclic gestures of requests. According to Ruth-Hirrel (2018: 217), the construction "complements the question that is expressed in speech by foregrounding a process that is left implicit by the spoken expression." Interestingly enough, the Cyclic gesture of this English multimodal construction is positioned in the interactional space, in the same way as the Cyclic gestures used in requests found in German. Hence, these gestural tokens are used with interactional purposes, because they are performed with larger movements and/or in peripheral spaces of the speaker's body (see Bavelas et al. 1992; Ladewig 2011, 2014b; Ruth-Hirrel and Wilcox 2018; Sweetser and Sizemore 2008). Ruth-Hirrel (2018: 219) concludes that because Cyclic gestures used with questions were strongly associated with interactional space, the "hypothesis that the Cyclic gesture and the location in interactional space are the obligatory symbolic structures in this gestural construction" is supported. Moreover, she remarks that other bodily behaviors are associated with this construction, such as eye gaze or single-handedness. These observations should be investigated further.

Another recent study fostering the notion of multimodal constructions elaborates on Bressem's (2012, to appear) idea of conceiving beats as function rather than a distinct gesture type. Accordingly, Ruth-Hirrel and Wilcox (2018) argue that beats are superimposed on pointing gestures and, thus, form "complex beat-point constructions." In line with other authors, they demonstrate that simple beats and beat-point constructions hold specific relationships to speech by aligning with pitch accents. With such a close interrelation with speech on the level of intonation, both types were found to interact with verbal expressions of stance-taking. Complex beat-point constructions are, thereby, used to add extra emphasis to the information expressed. In other words, while "multimodal constructions that incorporate pointing can establish and direct attention to reference points (Place structures) without the help of beats, the integration of beats and points emphasizes that certain stancetakers and their stances are particularly important to the speaker's message" (Ruth-Hirrel and Wilcox 2018: 486). As such, this extra emphasis would not be conveyed without the gesture.

Bringing it all together, it becomes immediately clear that the point of departure in the studies presented is a stable gestural form-meaning pattern (monomodal construction) that regularly co-occurs with linguistic constructions.[10] Yet, the base for defining these instances as multimodal constructions is not only the regular co-occurrence of both modalities but should be seen in the interaction between both and, thus, in the creation of a meaning that does not evolve from its parts. Gestures very often make explicit or foreground aspects of verbal meaning.

However, a particular perspective on multimodal constructions comes with the studies outlined, namely a gesture-based view (see Bressem and Müller 2017). In other words, whereas the studies presented depart from the gestural side of constructions and investigate their distribution over particular linguistic structures, the growing research of multimodal constructions has started out mainly from their verbal part. Mittelberg (2017b), for instance, argues to consider the German existential construction "*es gibt*" ('there is/are') as a multimodal construction when observed in its multimodal environment. Her argument is based on the observation that this verbal construction goes along with varying forms of the open hand, such as the palm up or palm lateral, and that exactly these gestures enact the experiential root of the verbal construction which is, among others, giving and holding (see also Müller 2004). With this insight, she concludes "that linguistic constructions that recruit basic embodied manual actions and interactions with the physical and social world are particularly likely to be

---

10 See also Harrison's discussion of the "grammar–gesture nexus" defined as "a mechanism for the regularity that we observe when people spontaneously gesture. These are specific bindings of grammatical and gestural form that occur when speakers express [grammatical notions such as] negation. The genesis of a grammar–gesture nexus in spoken language is the established linguistic conventions of negation on the one hand, and the corresponding actions that gestures may reproduce on the other" (Harrison 2018: 45).

instantiated multimodally and thus also engender emergent multimodal patterns, or clusters, of experience" (Mittelberg 2017b: 5).

Zima (2014a, 2014b, 2017) also investigates the interrelation of particular linguistic expressions and gestures, i.e., linguistic motion constructions of English, including [V(motion) *in circles*], [*zigzag*], [N *spin around*], and [*all the way from* X PREP Y]. Her findings suggest that all of them show "strong associations with recurrent forms of gestures" (Zima 2014a: 27), frequently specifying the path and manner of motion expressed in the verbal construction. Moreover, she finds that the different constructions investigated recruit different gestural forms. In more detail, while the [V(motion) *in circles*] construction, for instance, is accompanied by multiple circular gestural movements, the [*all the way from* X PREP Y] goes along with a larger range of different movement patterns. Zima concludes with these observations that the constructions investigated have not only a verbal but also a gestural structure.

Lanwer (2017) does not investigate gestures but head nods co-occurring with linguistic constructions, more precisely with German appositions. He shows that head nods vary regarding the type of apposition with which they co-occur. To be more precise, whereas head nods mainly align with the first element in loose appositions such as "prime minister Carstensen" (Lanwer 2017: 4), head nods align chiefly with the stressed syllable of the second element in narrow appositions like "my guest| Peter Sloterdijk" (Lanwer 2017: 4). He concludes that the "different verbal patterns evoke different conceptual groupings firstly by way of using distinctive prosodic features. Consequently, these patterns can be described as two different verbal constructions" (Lanwer 2017: 10). Moreover, based on the highest frequencies of co-occurrence determined for narrow appositions, he concludes that these constructions are more inclined to be instantiated multimodally.

These studies like many others (e.g., Andrén 2010, 2014; Bressem 2012, to appear; Kok 2016; Kok and Cienki 2016; Schoonjans 2017, 2018; Schoonjans, Brône and Feyaerts 2015; Stickles 2016), all have in common that they start from the premise that usage events are multimodal in nature and that "chunking should also result in multimodal constructions: verbal constructions that also contain information on gesture, facial expressions, body posture, etc." (Hoffmann 2017: 4). However, it is still debated which criteria allow us to consider a gesture–speech ensemble a multimodal construction. When shifting the attention to the introduction of this section, the notion of "sufficient frequency" (Goldberg 2006: 5) appears as one of the main conditions. Another is that of entrenchment. Both are certainly crucial for defining constructions, but both are also fuzzy (for a discussion of the notion of entrenchment see e.g., Schmid 2007, 2015). As Zima (2014a: 27) rightly points out: "What frequencies rates are to be regarded as sufficient, i.e. recurrent enough, to serve as proofs of mental entrenchment, however, is unclear." She argues that, similar to verbal constructions observed in real-time interactions which are not simply instantiated but adapted to the needs of the ongoing interactions (see Auer and Pfänder 2011), gestures might also be deployed to meet the exigencies of the *in situ* meaning creation. Zima and Bergs' (2017: 2) proposal of "a continuum from constructions which are only infrequently and loosely connected to co-speech gesture use to constructions which are frequently and systematically co-instantiated with a given gesture" is certainly a practicable approach given that not every linguistic item is accompanied by a gesture. As such, her idea is in line with Kok's findings of "gesture-attracting items" (Kok 2016: 212) showing a high frequency of gesture-accompanied words such as deictic expressions and "gesture-repelling words" (Kok 2016: 213) including epistemic verbs. Interestingly enough, Bressem and Müller (2017) suggest a similar idea to Zima and Bergs' (2017), although they start from a gesture studies perspective, meaning that they investigate a particular gesture and its relationship to linguistic constructions.

Cienki (2017) picks up on this discussion and offers another solution to the problem by attributing prototype theory a central role in the emergence of multimodal constructions. He states that constructions comprise both a deep and a surface structure where "the deep structure of a construction can be seen as a set of tools that can be drawn upon to express the construction (surface structure). The surface structure is thus a metonymic representation of some (if not all) elements of the construction" (Cienki 2017: 3). Based on the assumption that the deep structure includes information about which gestures may co-occur with a construction, every construction is considered to be potentially multimodal. Hence, some elements of this potential may be instantiated and appear at the surface, while others may not. All in all, by conceiving constructions in terms of prototypes, Cienki does not aim to answer the question of what aspects belong to a multimodal construction as entrenched elements, but he rather brings up the question of how central or peripheral an element is to the deep structure of a construction.

Two conclusions can be drawn based on this short precis of the growing body of research on multimodal constructions. First of all, as argued from the first minute of the increasing field of gesture studies, gesture and speech are tightly connected and the link between them can be looser or stronger. Secondly, gestures *contribute meaning that is not made explicit in speech*. The assumption pursued in this book is that gestures do not express exactly what is conveyed verbally and, thus, emphasize verbal information only rarely. The reason for this claim lies in the different medial properties, as pointed out earlier. This is possibly one of the many reasons why humans did not give up on gesturing even when they managed to develop fully fledged linguistic systems. The different modalities humans dispose of share the load of communicating information. Due to their medial characteristics, some modalities are more suitable for conveying specific information than others. Gestures are, for instance, deployed to express spatial information, whereas gaze is very easily used for fulfilling interactive functions. In this sense, the argument that gestures can only form multimodal constructions if the evolving meaning is more than the meaning of its parts is somewhat redundant, because gestures cannot but contribute their own meaning aspects to verbal constructions. Thus, if this is held as an argument for defining constructions, it should be elaborated further. What can also be observed when looking at constructions is that some gestures are more tightly linked to verbal constructions than others and, therefore, appear to be more entrenched. This aspect has been brought up by many studies on constructions and should also be investigated further. All in all, the notion of constructions offers a way to tackle the issue of the systematic link evolving between the two modalities speech and gesture, which is why it is worth continuing research on this phenomenon.

A third and final phenomenon discussed under the concept of a multimodal grammar is multimodal syntax, referring to cases of gesture–speech interaction, in which gestures instantiate structural and functional properties of the syntax of spoken languages. Here, we leave the strand of research that investigates recurrent form-meaning patterns emerging from recurrent multimodal usage events to shift the attention to singular gestures.

2.2.3 Multimodal syntax

As has been mentioned previously, the claim that gestures and spoken language are integrated, forming two sides of the process of utterance, is pivotal for the field of gesture studies (see Section 1.2). However, as convincingly as this claim has been tested empirically, results are unclear regarding a concept of language. In fact, what theories of language are pursued in gesture studies remains mostly unreflected in the body of literature. Notably, regarding the distinction between language use and language system, it appears that the integration of gestures into speech is widely accepted, whereas the integration into the language system is a much-debated issue. The dispute concerning the notion of multimodal constructions proves the skepticism (see Section 2.2.2). Some researchers investigating multimodal syntax clearly establish a relationship between gestures and the language system, because they argue that gestures are capable of embodying syntactic functions. With this notion, another relationship of gesture–speech integration is added, namely a syntactic relationship. Before introducing this dimension of gesture–speech interplay, the focus is briefly shifted to other dimensions of gesture–speech interaction discussed from a linguistic perspective.

2.2.3.1 Levels of linguistic description: semantic and pragmatic relationships

So far, the relationship and integration of language and gestures has been studied mainly at the level of language use. As has been mentioned previously, researchers had already found in the 1960s that the flow of speech is synchronized with the flow of gesturing (e.g., Condon and Ogston 1967). Ever since, the integration of speech and gesture has attracted the attention of researchers and built the foundation of the field of gesture studies (see Section 1.2). In order to describe the reciprocal relationship in the process of multimodal meaning creation, the notion of co-expressivity is of core importance, which McNeill described thus: "Co-expressive but *not redundant:* gesture and speech express the same underlying idea unit but express it in their own ways – their own aspects of it, and when they express overlapping aspects do so in distinctive ways" (McNeill 2005: 22, original emphasis). Both modalities, the gestural and the verbal, can be viewed as co-expressive if they refer to the same object in discourse (see Engle 2000: 26). Yet, this does not entail that speech and gesture have to be expressed simultaneously. In fact, they can stand at a certain temporal distance from each other. According to this definition, gestures can be pre- or post-positioned or they can be used in parallel but need to refer to the same unit to be considered as establishing a relationship. As a matter of fact, gestures can also stand alone, i.e., without speech, but in this case, they may connect to an utterance or form an utterance in their own right (see below).

Based on this temporal relationship between speech and gesture, both modalities have been specified regarding the levels of semantics, pragmatics and syntax (see Bressem, Ladewig and Müller 2013 for an overview). These different relationships will be presented in the following, though it is important to note that gestures, like language, are multifunctional.

On the semantic level, the following relationships have been defined: complementary, contrary and substitutive (Figure 10). To be more precise, if speech and gesture stand in a complementary relationship to each other, both modalities share semantic characteristics, yet, the gesture adds information to the speech and, thereby, modifies the linguistic content. If they stand in a contrary relationship to each other, the two different modes of expression each transmit different information, in that the gesture supplements information. When gestures replace speech, they substitute linguistic information (for a discussion of

complementary/ supplementary	Speech and gesture share semantic features but the gesture contributes semantic features to speech
contrary	Speech and gesture do not match in the semantic features and do not form an overlapping set of features
replacing	gesture substitutes speech

Figure 10: Semantic relationships between speech and gestures (based on Bressem, Ladewig and Müller 2013: 1111–1112).

the term "replacement," see Chapter 6). Modification is probably the semantic function which is observed most frequently.

Though research literature often refers to a redundant relationship of speech, assuming that the modes of expression in these cases convey more or less identical information, we argue that a redundant relationship is quite rare or not observable at all. In this regard, we follow McNeill's concept of co-expressivity, which does not include redundancy (see above). Indeed, when looking more closely at the semiotic properties of both modalities, it appears highly improbable that both convey redundant information. Although both speech and gesture may resemble each other to a certain extent, as shown in Section 2.1, they still express meaning differently, because language makes use of the oral-auditive means whereas gesture deploys visual-spatial means (yet, both are grounded in and employ the body).

Gesture and speech can also be integrated on a pragmatic level, thus, accomplishing a pragmatic function. If this is the case, they can relate to the speaker him-/herself or to the addressee by operating on the level of interaction or discourse (Figure 11). If they regulate or structure the behavior of the speaker, for instance, to express that he or she wants to maintain the right to speak (see Bohle 2007; Ladewig 2014c; Streeck and Hartge 1992), or when a gesture expresses a negative attitude regarding what has been said (as seen in the so-called "Brushing aside gesture"; see Bressem and Müller 2014a; Teßendorf 2014), gestures definitely operate on the level of interaction and perform a modal function. When regulating the behavior of others and, thus, are related to an addressee, they fulfill a performative function (see Müller 1998). This is the case when a speaker wards off the arguments of a dialogue partner with gestures or interrupts him or her with gestures. When gestures operate on the level of discourse, they perform a discursive function (see Müller 1998). This can be observed frequently in repetitive, accentuated gestures, which are often mistakenly called contentless beat gestures (see Efron [1941] 1972; Ekman and

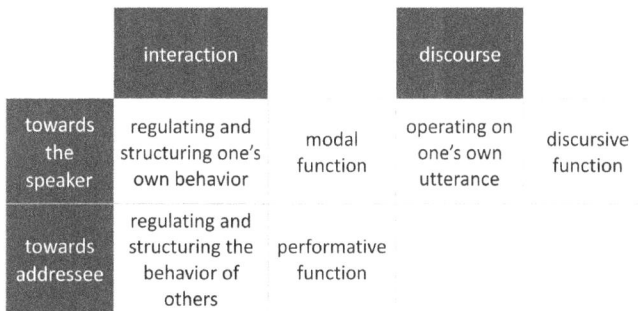

Figure 11: Pragmatic relationships of speech and gesture (based on Bressem, Ladewig and Müller 2013: 1113).

Friesen 1969; McNeill 1992; for a discussion of this notion, see Section 2.2.2 and Bressem 2012, to appear; Ruth-Hirrel and Wilcox 2018).

2.2.3.2 Syntactic relationships of gestures and speech

That gestures are linked to the syntactic structure of spoken utterances has been mentioned many times in the literature (see Bohle 2007; Clark 1996; Enfield 2009; Fricke 2012; Goodwin 1986; Harrison 2009, 2018; Harrison and Larrivée 2016; Ladewig 2012, 2014a, 2019; Slama-Cazacu 1976; Streeck 1988, 1993, 2002, 2009, 2016). However, arguing that gestures can be integrated into the syntax of speech and, thus, expanding the scope of verbal grammars to include gesture, pushes the envelope further. With this claim comes the issue of whether the language use or the language system should be conceived as multimodal. One of the authors to tackle this issue is Ellen Fricke, who combines a semiotic and functional grammar approach to gestures. Fricke (2012) spells out the major tenets for a theory of a multimodal grammar in her book *Grammatik multimodal: Wie Wörter und Gesten zusammenwirken* ('Grammar multimodal: How speech and gesture work together'), which addresses the overarching question of the extent to which the faculty of language and the grammars of single vocal languages can be considered as multimodal. To tackle this issue, she discusses different phenomena of gestures becoming linguistic or adopting linguistic functions, arguing that, first of all, co-speech gestures can be typified and semanticized independently of verbal utterances. This relates to grammaticalization processes discussed in Section 2.2.1. Secondly, based on her analysis of the linear structures of gestures, she argues that it is possible to analyze co-speech gestures independently of speech in terms of constituency. Building on that, she claims that gestural segments can be self-embedded to form higher order units and, thus, exhibit the property of recursivity (see Section 2.1.2). Thirdly, she argues that gestures can be integrated into the language system because they are capable of instantiating structural properties of discrete language systems.

According to Fricke (2012: 252), two ways of integrating gestures into language, more precisely into nominal phrases, can be distinguished: integration by position or the cataphoric integration. The former comprises cases of gestures substituting verbal constructions and the temporal overlap of gestures and speech. The latter refers to the integration of gestures by cataphoric expressions, such as *like, like this,* or *such a*. Fricke attends to the latter by examining the co-occurrence of the German cataphoric expression *son* ('such a') and singular gestures (iconic gestures in McNeill's terms). She coins this phenomenon "multimodal attribution" because the deictic expression in these cases demands a qualitative description found in a modality other than speech, namely gesture. By qualifying the nouns gestures are co-expressed with, gestures replace verbal adjectives and fulfill the function of an attribute. These observations lead Fricke to conclude that gestures are systematically integrated into the syntax of a spoken language and, thus, into the language system. Consider the following example taken from her sample:

> The German speaker [. . .] describes the façade of the Berlin State Library: She uses the noun phrase *sone gelb-goldenen Tafeln* 'such yellow golden tiles' accompanied by a gesture modeling a rectangular shape. On the verbal level, the adjective *gelb-golden* expands the nuclear noun, modifying it at the same time by reducing its extension to tiles with a specific characteristic of color. On the gestural level, the rectangular shape performed by the hands of the speaker fulfills an analogous function of modifying the nuclear noun. The resulting intersection of both extensions is a set of tiles with a specific characteristic of color (yellow golden) and a specific characteristic of shape (rectangular).
> (Fricke 2013: 747–748)

This pattern, which is observed frequently in multimodal noun phrases, allows speakers to divide labor between speech and gesture when communicating qualitative information. Accordingly, speakers tend to refer to aspects of shape in gestures, whereas information on color is transmitted verbally (see Fricke 2013: 748).

Sure enough, the observation that gestures provide qualitative information when used with cataphoric expressions is not new (see Ehlich 1987; Fricke 2007; Streeck 2002, 2009, 2016; Stukenbrock 2010). Yet, Fricke conducts the first systematic analysis of this phenomenon of gesture–speech interaction and discusses its implications for functional syntactic theories. She states that, in the cases under scrutiny, gestures may replace adjectives and fulfill the function of an attribute by expanding the nucleus of a noun phrase and reduce the extension of its reference object. Based on these observations, Fricke (2013: 746–747) concludes "that the attributive function of modifying the nuclear noun in a noun phrase can also be instantiated solely by gesture." She conceives the phenomenon of "multimodal attribution" as a point of multimodal integration and, thus, a transition point between linguistic monomodality and linguistic multimodality in its narrow sense (see Fricke 2012: 257). Accordingly,

> [m]ultimodality in the narrow sense occurs when the media involved in an expression belong to different sense modalities and are structurally or functionally integrated in the same code or, alternatively, manifest the same code, e.g., 'gesture–speech ensembles' (Kendon 2004). In the broad sense of multimediality, the media involved belong to the same sense modality, e.g., 'language–image ensembles.' It is worth pointing out that both kinds of multimodal ensembles differ with respect to their specific potential for establishing and instantiating grammatical structures and functions. (Fricke 2013: 751)

Many more works on the integration of gestures or bodily practices by way of cataphoric expressions have been supplied in recent years (see Barske and Golato 2010; Lindwall and Ekström 2012; Ningelgen and Auer 2017; Streeck 2016; Stukenbrock 2010, 2014, 2015, 2016). Stukenbrock (2014), for instance, who pursues a more interactional perspective informed by conversation analysis, gives an encompassing account of the German deictic expression *so* ('like this'), including not only the situated context of the expression but also other forms of bodily expressions. Based on her analysis of verbal instructions, she (2014: 19) argues that "[a]s a gesturally used deictic, 'so' can be conceived of as a multimodally embedded and embedding practice which provides a grammatical link between verbal and visual bodily resources within and across 'turns' and actions. In instructional sequences, it assumes participant-role specific, locally adaptable multimodal functions."

Ningelgen and Auer (2017) are in line with Fricke's and Stukenbrock's claims when they support the claim of a gesture–grammar link between the German expression *so* and singular gestures. They even attest this gesture–speech ensemble the status of a multimodal construction. Yet, only specific tokens of this cataphoric expression should be included in the verbal side of the construction. Referencing to Streeck's (2002) and Fricke's (2012) analyses of the German *so*, Ningelgen and Auer (2017) criticize that both authors equate the stressed and the unstressed form of this expression and promote the idea that only the former may acquire a constructional status. To be more precise, only those forms of *so* that are accentuated should be considered as performing a deictic function and, thus, warrant Streeck's claim that *SO* (in its stressed form)

> can serve as a "flag" that alerts the interlocutor that there is extralinguistic meaning to be found and taken into account in making sense of what is being said right now. Gaze direction combines with the flag by serving as a pointer to the location where additional

meaning is found. In their combination, *so* and the gaze shift serve to direct the interlocutor's visual attention to the hands and incorporate the work of the hands into the grammatical structure of the talk. (Streeck 2002: 582)

Hence, whereas *SO* with such a deictic function, as in "*und dann SCHLÄFT er SO*" ('and then he sleep like this'; see Ningelgen and Auer 2017: 3), is considered part of a multimodal construction, *so* as a vagueness or focus marker, as in "*irgend so ne komische RUSsin*" ('LIKE some strange Russian woman'; Ningelgen and Auer [2017: 7]), is not regarded a part of a multimodal construction even if gestures such as recurrent gestures with metapragmatic functions are co-expressed with this particle.

A second phenomenon subsumed under the notion of multimodal syntax has been investigated in detail by Bressem (2012, 2014, 2015, to appear). She shifts the attention to a particular movement pattern, namely repetitive gestural movements which can grammaticalize to mark plurality (see Section 2.2.1). Based on a data corpus consisting of 173 repetitions comprising 895 strokes, she differentiates two types of gestural repetitions: (a) repetitions in gesture creating a gestural unit without creating a complex gestural meaning (iteration), and (b) repetitions in gesture creating a complex gestural unit and a complex gestural meaning (reduplication). These two forms show differences in their kinesic structure and in their way of multimodal meaning creation. Accordingly, while iterations comprise sequences of at least two *preparation-stroke* or *stroke-stroke* units, reduplications are limited to *stroke-stroke* sequences. Briefly speaking, iterations show preparational phases, reduplications do not. Regarding their relationship with speech, Bressem notes that most repetitions investigated co-occur with their lexical affiliates, which means the gesture does not precede or succeed its verbal reference item. However, regarding their interaction with the semantics of the utterances, both types behave differently, as has already been addressed. Gestural iterations, for instance, specify and modify verbal meaning. If they are co-expressed with nouns, they act as an attribute, because they specify the co-expressed object regarding form and size information and, thus, extend the nucleus of the noun phrase. In cases of co-occurring predicates, gestural iterations specify the manner of the action, thus, taking over the function of adverbial adjectives. According to Bressem, gestural reduplications, on the other hand, convey similar semantics as speech, which is why she ascribes them only a supporting or emphasizing function. She grounds her argument in the observation that in these cases, the semantics of speech and gesture is less important, but the prosodic structure is in the focus of attention, thus, putting forward the idea of a rudimentary gesture prosody (see Bressem 2012, to appear). Interestingly, those tokens expressing lexical meaning co-occur with particular constructions, namely verbs or verb phrases. When expressing grammatical meaning, they span whole utterance constructions.

To conclude, gestural repetitions are not integrated with speech by means of a deictic expression, indicating the necessity to include information other than speech. Rather, they are linked by position and function, because they deliver important information to understand the meaning the speakers want to convey. Bressem's findings expand the range of syntactic constructions that gestures may realize. In other words, what Fricke demonstrates for the cataphoric integration of gestures into noun phrases is now shown for the temporal overlap of repetitive gestures with other linguistic constructions, more precisely, with verbs and verb phrases, at least in cases of gestural iteration. Yet, from a theoretical perspective, Bressem would not argue that gestures are integrated into the language system of discrete languages, but that they form part of utterances on the level of language use – an argument also put forward in this book.

Coming back to the different levels of linguistic description, gestures and speech may be related on a syntactic level by position or cataphoric expressions (Figure 12). Gestures can, for instance, be integrated cataphorically into speech by using verbal deictics, including *such (a), like, here, like this*, taking over the function of attributes. Moreover, they can replace verbal adverbs and adjectives when being co-expressed with verbs or nouns. The third phenomenon addressed in Figure 12, the substitution of linguistic items by gestures, is based on the study presented in the subsequent chapters (see also Ladewig 2014a, 2019). As becomes visible, in all cases discussed here (except for gestural reduplications), gestures add meaning to a multimodal utterance, thereby, replacing verbal items, such as adjectives or adverbs, that fulfill particular syntactic and semantic functions. In this view, some gestures can be regarded as realizing such syntactic slots, at least in the cases where they are tightly connected to verbal items in speech.

	replacing speech	temporal overlap	temporal succession
positional integration	fills a syntactic gap	executed simultaneously with speech	
cataphoric integration		verbal deictics (like, here, this, such)	

Figure 12: Syntax relationships of speech and gesture (based on Bressem, Ladewig and Müller 2013: 1109–1110).

In a nutshell, although a fair amount of research discussing a gesture–grammar link has been presented in this chapter, this research strand is still in its infancy. Three major lines of thought have hitherto been distinguished. Firstly, gestures can be linked to grammar by becoming grammaticalized themselves, thus, emerging as stable forms or monomodal constructions from the recurrence of multimodal usage events. Secondly, from these multimodal usage events, conventionalized speech–gesture combinations may arise in the form of multimodal constructions. Here, gestures are linked to the grammar of spoken language. Thirdly, gesture can be related to grammar by realizing particular syntactic constructions. These cases comprise the cataphoric integration of gestures and the gestural substitution of syntactic slots, such as adjectives or adverbs, and nouns and verbs, as will be discussed in the pages to come.

3 How are gestures integrated into linguistic structures?

The central topic of this chapter is the identification of anchor points for gestures to integrate into spoken utterances and the determination of the gestural properties making the substitution of linguistic units possible. As has been pointed out in the previous chapters, the recipients of the utterances under scrutiny do not treat them as problematic for the proceeding discourse. On the contrary, they even respond to these utterances, thereby, reflecting an understanding of such utterances. This is particularly interesting, as these gestures replace the semantic centers of the utterances they are integrated into.

In what follows, four questions will be addressed which aim at giving a descriptive and explanatory account of sequentially constructed multimodal utterances.
1. Do recipients of the utterances under scrutiny consider the gestures part of the spoken utterances?
2. What linguistic units are substituted by gestures?
3. Why can gestures replace linguistic units?
4. How do speech and gestures interact in creating multimodal utterances?

In order to answer these questions, a qualitative analysis of all examples found in the data was conducted using the different tools presented in the following chapters and in the appendix. This analytical step was followed by four naturalistic perception experiments in which the comprehension of the single gestures and multimodal utterances were tested.

In what follows, the results of the micro- and quantitative analysis will be presented, using two examples representative of the corpus. It will be shown that gestures preferably replace the linguistic constructions of nouns and verbs. Based on these results, the argument is put forward that gestures embody the conceptual archetypes of these constructions which are objects and actions and that the underlying syntactic structure of the verbal utterance influences the perception and conception of gestures by imposing particular cognitive modes on the gestures.

3.1 Do they integrate? Four perception experiments

So far, the integration of speech and gesture has mainly been studied regarding their temporal relationship, using examples in which gestures and speech are co-expressed. Many scholars of gestures agree upon the observation that gestures precede or end at the phonological peak of an utterance, that they add meaning to or specify the meaning transmitted by speech, covering the same "idea unit" (Kendon 1972, 1980b), and that both modes of expression perform the same pragmatic function. Moreover, studies have shown that gestures may anticipate the meaning of the utterance, as they often precede a "lexical affiliate" (Schegloff 1984). These cases of synchronization between speech and gestures were framed as the phonological, the semantic and the pragmatic synchronization rule (see McNeill 1992: 25).

Linguists studying further integration processes of speech and gesture have only recently taken the syntactic integration of gesture into speech into account. Fricke (2012, 2013), coining the term "multimodal attribution," demonstrated that gestures can be integrated syntactically into noun phrases of a spoken utterance by adopting the position of an adjective which functions as an attribute. Bressem (2012, 2014, to appear) showed that repetitive gestures can add information to the nouns and verbs they are co-expressed with, thus, taking over the functions of adjectives and adverbs. Her findings can certainly be applied to all kinds of depictive gestures (see Chapter 2 for further information).

What these studies showed is that gestures are not only integrated into spoken utterances by being performed simultaneously with speech and synchronized with the semantic and pragmatic content of an utterance. They can also be integrated into utterances by taking over syntactic (and semantic) functions of spoken linguistic units.

The gestures under scrutiny are also studied regarding their syntactic and semantic integration into spoken utterance. Yet, the phenomenon differs from the cases studied so far. In the latter, the gestures are integrated sequentially into the spoken utterances, meaning that the expression of speech and gestures shows a linear structure in time (Figure 13). Accordingly, the syntactic and semantic gap exposed by the interruption of the speaker correlates with the absence of speech.

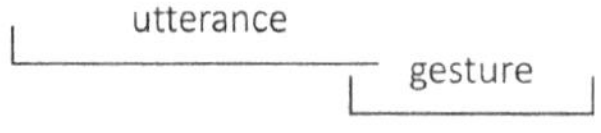

Figure 13: Sequential integration of gestures into speech.

All examples identified in the data (see Appendix A) were analyzed qualitatively regarding the prosodic features and the syntactic and semantic functions of the verbal units. Furthermore, each gesture inserted into the speech gaps was described thoroughly, applying a linguistic (form-based) approach (see Chapter 2 and Appendix B).

The qualitative analysis was complemented by four perception experiments in which the 66 utterances identified served as stimuli.

Speech-only condition. In the speech-only condition, the spoken utterances of the corpus were written down on sheets of paper and handed out to the subjects. The participants were asked to read the utterances and fill in words, phrases, or clauses they considered best suited for the speech gaps. The list of utterances encompassed only the utterances in which the gestures joined in. No further information on the context was supplied. A total of 15 subjects (ten female, five male) participated. The average age was 23 years. The group of participants was different from the other five experiments (the fifth is introduced in Chapter 5).

The speech-only condition was treated as a control condition, conducted to learn (a) whether the subjects consider the utterances to be interrupted and fill in lexical items, and (b) whether the syntactic functions determined by investigating speech only correlate with the functions determined when both speech and gesture are under examination.

Gesture-only condition. In this condition, video clips only of the gestures were shown to the participants. No further information on the preceding verbal utterance or the larger verbal context was given. The subjects were asked to write down words, phrases, or clauses they considered best suited for the meaning of the gestures. A total of 15 subjects (ten female, five male) participated. The average age was 25 years. The group of participants was different from the other five experiments (the fifth condition is introduced in Chapter 5). This experimental condition aimed to show whether syntactic units and functions can be allocated to the gestures alone. Put differently, the question of whether the gestures themselves are conceived to realize syntactic information was addressed.

Multimodal utterance condition. Clips of the sequentially constructed multimodal utterances were shown to the participants in the second video condition, and they had to write down their choices on a sheet of paper (8 out of 15). In a second version, the clips were included in a pdf file which the participants could watch privately on a computer (7 out of 15). A total of 15 subjects (ten female, five male) participated. The average age of the group of participants was 27 years. This group also participated in the discourse condition (see Chapter 5) with a time lag of six months.

The video clips only encompassed the utterance. No contextual information was given to the participants. The participants were asked to watch the videos and to write down words, phrases, or clauses they considered best suited for the syntactic gaps of the utterance written down on the paper sheets or the pdf file. People were not asked to pay particular attention to the gestures.

This condition addressed the questions of whether the recipients of the multimodal utterances consider the gestures part of the utterance and how speech and gestures interact when integrating with each other.

Manipulated multimodal utterance condition. The participants watched manipulated multimodal utterances in the final video condition. In these cases, the verbal utterances were combined with gestures taken from other examples of the corpus. To be more precise, gestures that were originally used in verb positions were combined with utterances exhibiting a nominal syntactic gap and *vice versa*. In practical terms, the audio track of one video was laid over another video. Only a random sample of 14 manipulated videos were tested. The task was the same as in the multimodal utterance condition. The video clips were shown to the participants and they had to write down their choices on a sheet of paper. A total of 15 subjects (twelve female, three male) participated. The average age was 24 years.

Although this experimental condition yielded interesting and valuable data, it is discussed only briefly in the chapter because only a small sample was tested. The basic problem laid in the difficulty to manipulate naturalistic data in a way in which the participants do not become distracted. It turned out to be challenging to match parameters, such as voice or background sounds, when laying the audio track of one video over another. Consequently, only those videos in which the subjects showed a similar voice (regarding age and gender) and interacted in a similar setting and those videos where the background noise was similar could be manipulated.

This condition was executed to corroborate or question the findings yielded by the multimodal utterance condition.

The lexical items elicited in the experiments were analyzed syntactically applying a cognitive grammarian approach (see Langacker 2008a) to ascertain whether the conceptualizations materialized by speech and gesture designate different or similar conceptual referents. In doing so, the foundation for investigating the cognitive–interpretative processes of the multimodal utterances under scrutiny was laid.

The lexical items elicited were determined based on their underlying grounding process. Grounding provides the interlocutors access to the content evoked by a nominal or finite clause. "A grounding element specifies the status vis-à-vis the ground of the thing profiled by a nominal or the process profiled by a finite clause" (Langacker 2008a: 259). Two types are differentiated: nominal grounding and clausal grounding. "Through nominal grounding (e.g. *the, this, that, some, a, each, every, no, any*), the speaker directs the hearer's attention to the intended discourse referent, which may or may not correspond to an actual individual. Clausal grounding (e.g. *-s, -ed, may, will, should*) situates the profiled relationship with respect to the speaker's current conception of reality" (Langacker 2008a: 259).

The element grounded through nominal grounding, for example, designates an instance (represented by I in Figure 14) which is conceptualized against the appropriate domain (represented by the square box in Figure 14). It is identified by both speaker (S) and hearer (H), participating in a specific speech event, i.e., the ground.

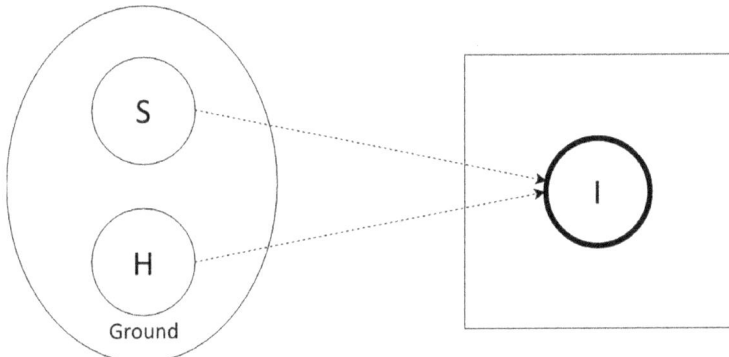

Figure 14: Grounding process exemplified in a nominal consisting of a determiner and a noun (taken from Taylor 2003: 346).

The instance is conceptualized against the appropriate dominion (represented by the oval in Figure 14). The process of singling out and identifying a discourse referent is represented by intermittent arrows in Figure 14.

The grounding element foreshadows the trajectory of a syntactic construction in the online syntactic processing of utterances. Thus, it allows recipients to "project" the unfolding of grammar (see Auer 2005).

The lexical items elicited in the different experimental conditions were coded according to these grounding processes. Hence, nominals were identified by way of particular grounding elements, such as (definite, indefinite) determiners or (absolute, universal, relative) quantifiers. Clauses were determined by means of clusters of features pertaining to the verb and its subject, including the number agreement of the verb with its subject, the nominative cases of the subject and tense inflection, and modal verbs. Of course, ungrounded structures were also identified in the data corpus, such as predicate nouns, comprising nouns that predicate a property of a nominal or non-finite clause. However, their occurrence was very limited. Elements grounding a clause were further distinguished regarding the verb's complements. Accordingly, clauses may be grounded by plain verbs profiling a temporal relationship or a PROCESS, but such processes may be also be specified regarding the participants involved in the process (tr = trajectory, lm = landmark) or its circumstances (modifier). Gestures may realize all the structures explained: nouns, verbs with and without complements, modifiers or clauses themselves. As has been pointed out previously, all lexical items elicited were coded for these different linguistic structures. This was done for a particular reason, namely the semiotic complexity of gestures. Gestures can convey complex semantic information reflected by clause structures in spoken language, as will be discussed in more detail in Section 3.3.2. Accordingly, what is transmitted sequentially in spoken language can be expressed by only one gestural form. A clause such as *He is walking over a hill* may be signified gesturally by an index finger which is moved along an ephemeral, arced line. The trajectory is, thereby, depicted by the hand shape. The process the trajectory executes is conveyed by the movement of the hand. Modifying information, such as the local circumstances, are transferred by the movement pattern. As the purpose of this study is to elucidate the cognitive processes of the recipients when interpreting gestures replacing speech, it is important to differentiate whether they consider both the hand shape and the movement to gain access to their embodied concepts or whether either one of them is more in the foreground. Consequently, clauses were specified regarding the temporal relationships and their participants and circumstances.

3.2 Where do they integrate? Gestures realizing nouns and verbs

Before presenting the quantitative analysis of the lexical items elicited in the different experimental conditions, two exemplary cases of the corpus are presented. They are addressed first from a qualitative, micro-analytic perspective and later serve to exemplify the quantitative results.

3.2.1 Two examples

The first example shows an instance of sequential gesture–speech integration in which the gesture is used in noun position. The second example shows an instance in which a gesture is inserted in the syntactic gap of a verb.

Example 1: Gesture in noun position (*Ich wollte dieses* ✋ / 'I wanted this' ✋)
The first example is taken from a parlor game adapted from the game *Tabu* ('taboo'), a guessing game. In this game, one person explains a word to his/her teammates who have to guess the word. The challenge is to avoid the semantically related items listed on a computer screen.

In the situation illustrated in Figure 15, a woman explains the word *Staumauer* ('concrete dam') to her teammates who fail to guess the word. When the playing time has expired, her teammates start discussing her explaining strategy. At one point of the discussion, one teammate starts criticizing the guessing words offered to his team, whereupon the game leader, who was responsible for describing the word, defends her explanation strategy by saying *Mann ich wusste nich wie ich's umschreiben soll* ('Man, I didn't know how to describe it'). The teammate asks whether *Leuchtturm* ('lighthouse') was the right term, whereupon the game leader negates his question by saying *Nein Stausee. Ich wollte dieses* ✋ ('No barrier lake. I wanted this' ✋; see the transcript in Figure 15).

She interrupts her utterance and, while looking at her recipients, performs a gesture which is composed of five strokes. This multi-stroke sequence is executed with both hands, showing a flat configuration, a palm oriented towards her body, and an up and down movement that is repeated four times. The first stroke begins on the definite determiner *dieses* ('this'). The following four strokes fill a pause. After the performance of the multi-stroke sequence, a second speaker responds by raising the question *Wand. Durfte man Wand sagen?* ('Wall, were you allowed to say wall?'; see Appendix C and Chapter 5).

The integration of the multi-stroke sequence into the interrupted utterance can be analyzed on different levels. The constant intonation at the end of the utterance indicates a breaking off (see Appendix C and below). The speaker's utterance has not yet been completed, but her communicative activity appears to shift from the verbal activity to a gestural performance because the speaker is engaged in a bodily communicative activity after breaking off her utterance. Both verbal and bodily activity are performed in temporal relatedness. This temporal succession of both modalities already suggests considering the gestures as part of the utterance. As has been described above, the first stroke of the multi-stroke sequence overlaps the last word of the spoken utterance, which is the definite determiner *dieses* ('this'). The following three strokes fill the subsequent pause. No time gap between the different strokes and between speech and gesture is noticeable. As such, the gesture appears to "dock" onto the utterance and, thus, becomes a part of it (see Figure 13 for a schematic representation of this process).

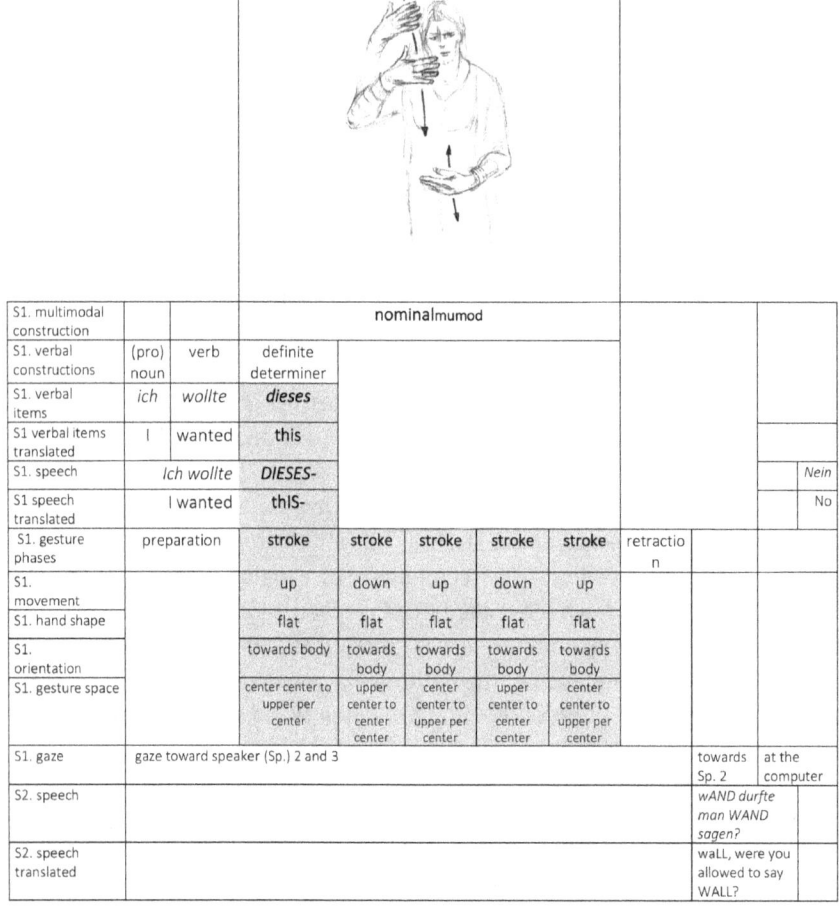

S1. multimodal construction				nominalmumod						
S1. verbal constructions	(pro) noun	verb	definite determiner							
S1. verbal items	ich	wollte	*dieses*							
S1 verbal items translated	I	wanted	this							
S1. speech		*Ich wollte*	*DIESES-*							Nein
S1 speech translated		I wanted	thIS-							No
S1. gesture phases	preparation		stroke	stroke	stroke	stroke	stroke	retraction		
S1. movement			up	down	up	down	up			
S1. hand shape			flat	flat	flat	flat	flat			
S1. orientation			towards body	towards body	towards body	towards body	towards body			
S1. gesture space			center center to upper per center	upper center to center	center center to upper per center	upper center to center	center center to upper per center			
S1. gaze		gaze toward speaker (Sp.) 2 and 3							towards Sp. 2	at the computer
S2. speech									wAND durfte man WAND sagen?	
S2. speech translated									waLL, were you allowed to say WALL?	

Figure 15: Transcript of the example "*Ich wollte dieses* 🤚 ('I wanted this' 🤚)".[11]

A similar conclusion can be drawn when analyzing the syntax of the spoken utterance. That is to say, if we take the idea of gesture and speech as equal partners in the process of utterance formation seriously (see Kendon 1980b), we

---

[11] The full transcripts of both examples can be accessed in Appendix C. The annotation of speech follows roughly GAT2 (Selting et al. 2011). Hence, capital letters mark accents in speech. Hyphens represent constant intonation.

can argue that the gesture in this example realizes the slot of a noun because the definite determiner *dieses* ('this') takes a noun and, thus, grounds a nominal (Figure 16). Hence, both modalities form a multimodal nominal.

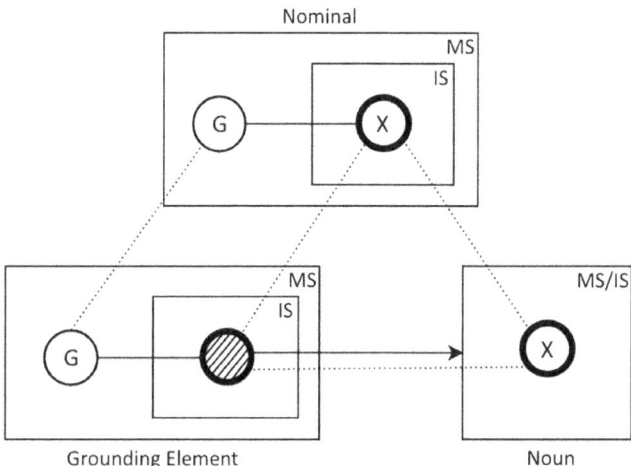

Figure 16: Grounding of nouns according to Langacker (2008a: 276).

A schematic representation of this process is shown in Figure 17, illustrating the stepwise process of forming a multimodal utterance from a cognitive grammar perspective which always includes the units with which meaning is expressed and its mental representation. Accordingly, it is argued that different schemas are instantiated and elaborated by the linguistic elements we use (represented by the solid arrow and marked by shading in Figure 17). An instance, thus, the argumentation, fleshes out a schema and, therefore, specifies it. It inherits the structure of a schema which is common to all its instances. When a schema is extended, represented by a dashed line in Figure 17, it is transformed to a certain extent. In the example under scrutiny, the schema of a flat, vertical surface, represented by the shaded rectangle, is embodied by a gesture, which is then extended to a mental reference object, a THING, showing this particular form (see Chapter 4). Hence, the definite determiner, the gesture is juxtaposed with, profiles the meaning of an object exhibiting a vertical surface as an instance of a type. This instance is not expressed verbally but gesturally. "A **definite** determiner profiles an instance that the speaker has singled out for attention; the speaker also supposes that the hearer, too, can uniquely identify the instance" (Taylor 2003: 354, original emphasis). Of course,

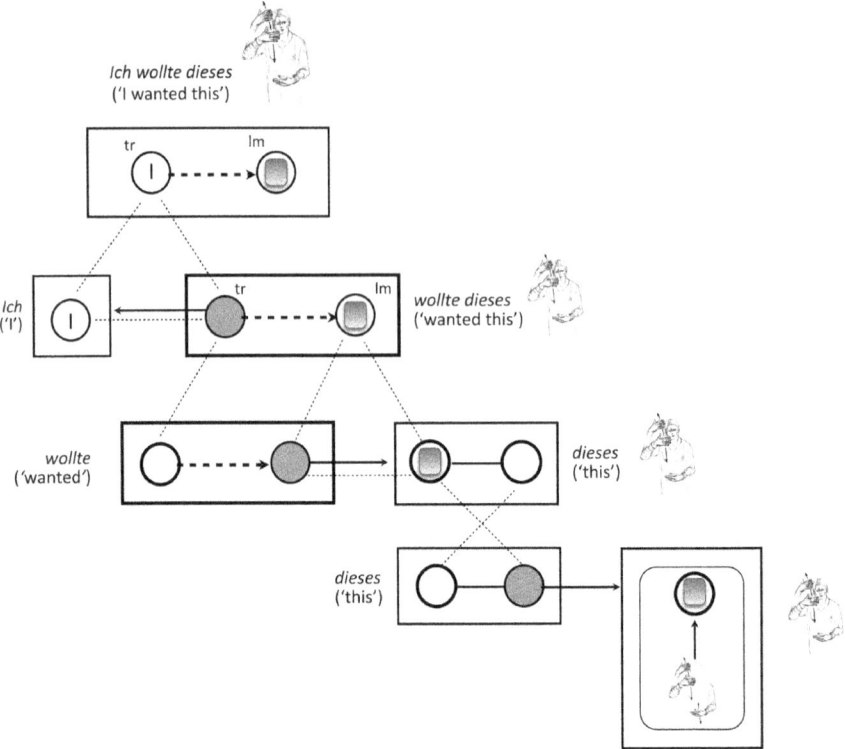

Figure 17: Syntactic analysis of the example "*Ich wollte dieses* 🤚 ('I wanted this' 🤚)".

misunderstandings may occur and, thus, the speaker may be mistaken in his/her supposition (see Taylor 2003: 354), which may lead to an interactive process of negotiating meaning. In the example under scrutiny, one of the recipients interpreted the gesture as referring to a wall, because he responded with the question *Wand, durfte man Wand sagen?* ('Wall, were you allowed to say wall?'), whereupon the speaker looks at the computer screen and says *Nein* ('No').

It appears noteworthy to point out that the definite determiner does not fulfill a deictic function here, because it is not accompanied by a focus accent, i.e., "the semantically and pragmatically most relevant of the actual phonetic prominences in the intonation phrase. It indicates, and foregrounds, the focus of the utterance" (Selting et al. 2011: 19). Adverbs or definite determiners used with such a focus accent fulfill a deictic function "instructing the recipient to perceive visually the simultaneous occurrence of bodily behavior" (Stukenbrock 2015: 421, translation S.L.).¹² In these cases, the gestures are inserted into the utterance by cataphoric integration (Fricke 2012, 2013; Streeck 2002; see Section 2.2.3), which is not observable in the example discussed here.

The outcome of the qualitative analysis presented above suggests regarding the gesture as forming part of the utterance creating a sequentially constructed multimodal utterance.

Example II: Gesture in verb position (*und wir hinten* 🖐 / 'and we from the back' 🖐)
The second example is taken from a conversation between four women sharing experiences they had had when arriving home from a party. The story told by one of the women deals with an incident in which she, her sister, and their grandmother came home from her wedding party. When arriving at the apartment house, the speaker's sister notices that she has forgotten the key to her apartment. In order to get into it, she tries to climb up to the window, but her grandmother standing at the window in the apartment tried to stop this undertaking.

Miming her grandmother, the narrator says *geh runter* ('get down') and explains what her grandmother was doing (*und die hat immer geschubst* / 'and she was pushing all the time'). While doing so, the narrator executes two pushing movements forward and away from her body using both hands. Afterwards, she describes what she was doing by saying *und wir hinten* ('and we from the back'). She then interrupts her verbal utterance and performs one pushing movement upward and away from her body (Figure 18). A second speaker (speaker Su in Figure 18) responds to this verbo-gestural performance by asking *Echt?* ('Really?') and starts to laugh out loud. The narrator looks at her and affirms by saying *Ja* ('Yes').

The relatedness and intertwining of speech and gesture, both forming a sequentially constructed multimodal utterance, can be described on various levels. The constant intonation at the end of the utterance indicates its interruption. However, the narrator's bodily movements fill a pause, which suggests that she is still engaged in a bodily, communicative activity.

Speech and gesture are tightly intertwined, similar to the previous example. On a temporal level, the gesture considered to form part of the utterance is prepared while the speaker is uttering the personal pronoun *wir* ('we') and the first syllable of the following adverbial modifier *hinten* ('from the back', literally:

---

12 "*Anweisung, das simultan stattfindende körperliche Geschehen visuell wahrzunehmen*" (Stukenbrock 2015: 421).

S1. multimodal construction			clause_multimodal				
S1. verbal constructions	C	(pro)noun	adverbial modifier				
S1. verbal items	und	wir	hin	ten		Yes	
S1 verbal items translated	and	we	from the	back			
S1. speech			und wir hin	tn-	0.5s	Ja	(laughing)
S1. gesture phases		preparation		stroke		partial retraction	hold
S1. movement				straight upward			
S1. hand shape				flat hand			
S1. orientation				away body			
S1. gesture space				upper center			
S1. gaze	forward					towards Sp.2	forward
S2. speech				Echt?		(laughing)	
S2. speech translated				Really?			

Figure 18: Transcript of the example "*und wir hinten* 👋 ('and we from the back' 👋)".

'behind'). The stroke of this gesture begins on the second syllable of the adverbial modifier and fills the subsequent pause of half a second. It is followed by a retraction and a hold[13] (Figure 18).

---

[13] Gestural strokes or holds are usually considered to be the only gesture phases having the potential to carry meaning (see e.g., Kendon 1980b; Kita, Gijn and van der Hulst 1998). However, in this case, the retraction should also be regarded as meaningful, since it is part of the underlying action mimed by the gesture. Further support is given by the articulatory feature "tension" reflected in the hand's configuration, which is maintained through the performance of the retraction (see Bressem and Ladewig 2011; Ladewig and Bressem 2013a). Additionally, the hand is not led into the rest position but is brought into a hold. See Jantunen (2015) for more research on meaningful transition phases from the perspective of sign language.

On the syntactic level, the gesture can be considered as realizing the slot of a verb grounding a clause, as Figure 19 aims to illustrate. Accordingly, after uttering the beginning of the second main clause *und wir hinten* ('and we from the back'), a gesture joins in. Following the Subject-Verb-Object structure of this main clause, the gesture occupies the position of the finite verb, which, in second position, follows the subject *wir* ('we'). Moreover, as the clause under investigation is combined with the precedent main clause *die hat immer geschubst* ('and she was pushing all the time') by the coordinating conjunction *und* ('and'), both clauses exhibit the same word order. Hence, like in the precedent main clause, the constituent following the pronoun *wir* ('we') and the

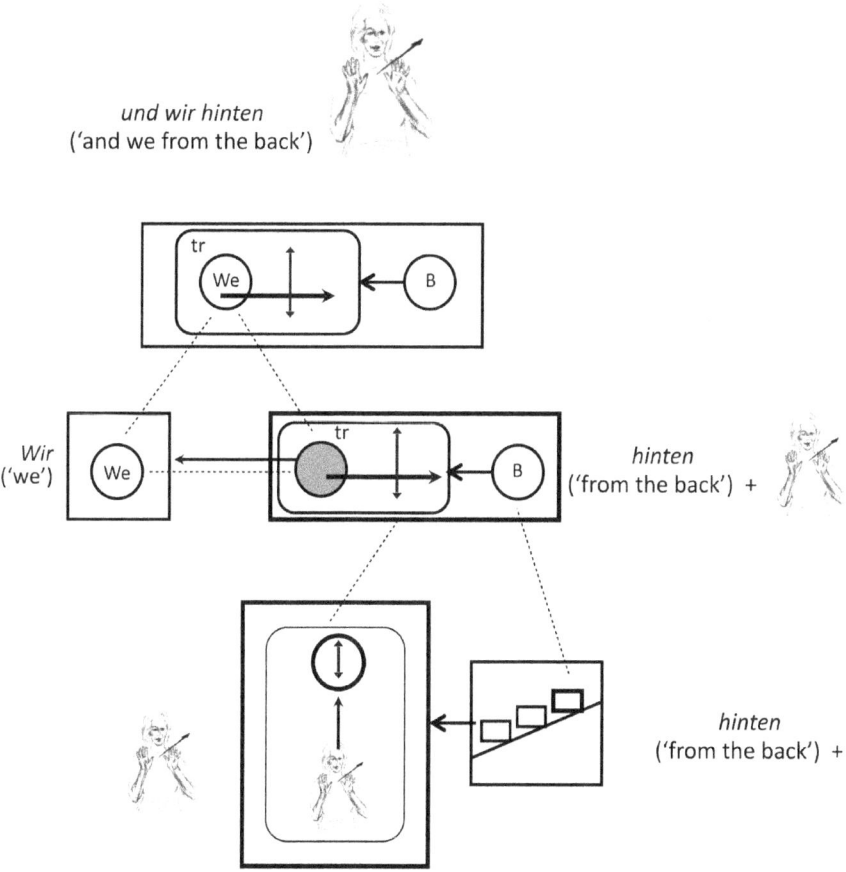

Figure 19: Syntactic analysis of the example "*und wir hinten* 👋 ('and we from the back' 👋)".

modifier *hinten* ('from the back', literally: 'behind') should be a verb profiling a PROCESS which is embodied by a gesture in this example.

Based on these observations, the gesture can be considered part of the utterance where both speech and gesture form a sequentially constructed multimodal utterance.

The findings of the qualitative analysis were tested in the naturalistic perception experiments which will be presented in the following sections. As outlined in Section 3.1, the experiments aimed to show (a) whether the recipients of these multimodal utterances consider the gestures part of the utterance by realizing particular syntactic slots, if so, (b) what verbal units are preferably replaced by gestures, and (c) how speech and gestures interact in creating multimodal meaning. The two examples introduced above serve to exemplify the outcome of the different experiments. We begin with two experiments that tested the understanding of both modalities, speech and gesture, independently (Sections 3.2.2 and 3.2.3). The understanding of the multimodal utterance was tested in the third experiment, presented in Section 3.2.4.

3.2.2 Experiment I: Speech only

The first step to take when addressing the question of how recipients interpret gestures realizing syntactic slots is to characterize these syntactic slots regarding their grounding process. Consequently, the first perception experiment was based on speech only (speech-only condition, see Section 3.1). The only stimuli the recipient had at hand were the spoken utterances written down on sheets of paper. The utterances were given to the participants, whose task it was to write down the lexical items they considered best suited for the syntactic gaps.

The aim of the experiment was to ascertain whether the recipient considers the utterances under investigation as discontinued and, if so, what syntactic slots are exposed through the interruption of the utterance.

As Figure 20 reveals, the syntactic constructions of nouns and verbs are the preferred slots realized by gestures. Accordingly, 332 nouns (36.2 %) and 290 verbs (31.6 %) were identified out of the 917 lexical items elicited.

The lexical items in noun positions form part of noun or prepositional phrases, in verb positions, they form part of analytic verb forms or verb phrases. The participants chose clausal constructions to fill in the syntactic gaps in 9.2 % of the cases (84 lexical items).

Based on the syntactic constructions determined for the lexical items elicited, the examples of the data corpus were specified according to the syntactic slots they exhibited. Table 1 lists the distribution of the syntactic slots over

3.2 Where do they integrate? Gestures realizing nouns and verbs — 69

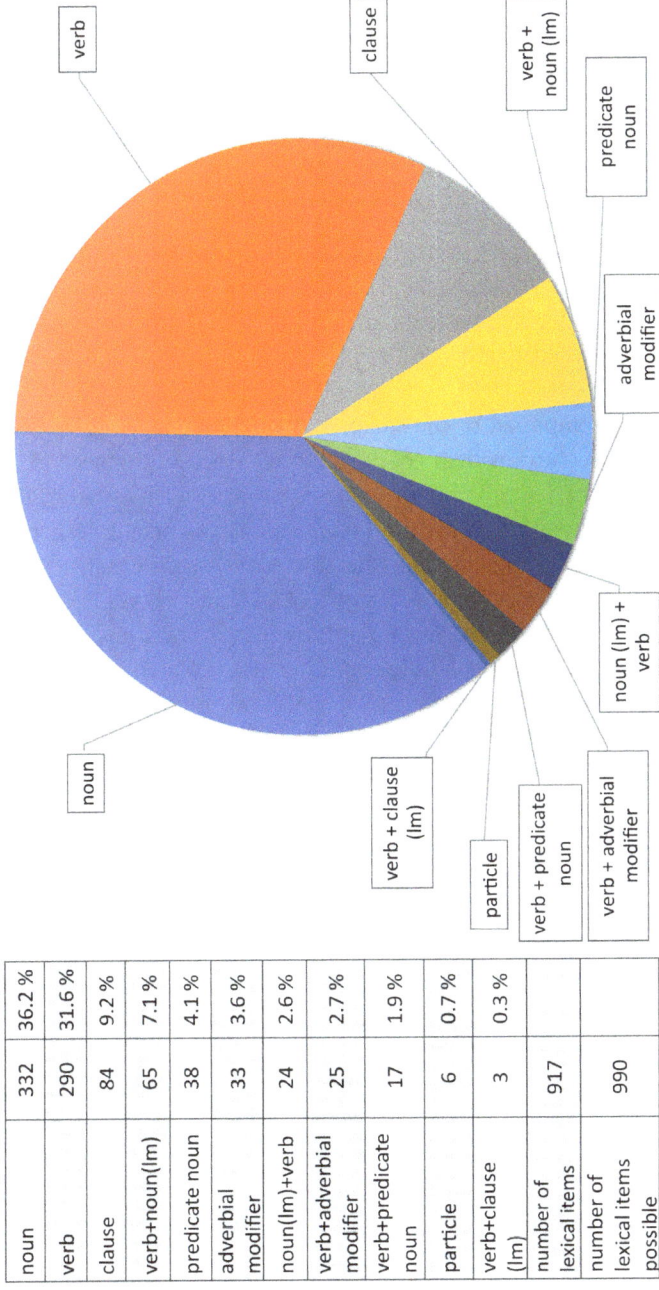

noun	332	36.2 %
verb	290	31.6 %
clause	84	9.2 %
verb+noun(lm)	65	7.1 %
predicate noun	38	4.1 %
adverbial modifier	33	3.6 %
noun(lm)+verb	24	2.6 %
verb+adverbial modifier	25	2.7 %
verb+predicate noun	17	1.9 %
particle	6	0.7 %
verb+clause (lm)	3	0.3 %
number of lexical items	917	
number of lexical items possible	990	

Figure 20: Distribution of gestures over syntactic slots according to the findings of the speech-only condition.

Table 1: Distribution of syntactic slots over the corpus (elicited in the speech-only condition).

Noun	Verb	Clause	Total
29	29	8	66

the whole corpus. Accordingly, 29 examples show the syntactic slot of a noun (forming part of a nominal), 29 show the syntactic slot of a verb (grounding a clause), and eight show autonomous clause structures. These findings reveal that noun and verb positions are preferably realized by gestures in the utterance–final position.

These results are exemplified by the samples illustrated in Section 3.2.1. In the first example, the gesture realizes the position of noun, in the second, it realizes the position verb. Yet, when both verbal utterances were tested in the speech-only condition, the participants used more complex syntactic constructions to "fill" the syntactic and semantic gaps. Moreover, these constructions participated in different processes of specifying spoken items (Figure 21). To be more precise, in the case of the first example, for which a noun position was determined (Section 3.2.1), the speech-only condition also revealed a noun, yet, it serves as a direct object or landmark of a verb construction (Figure 21). Hence, it specifies a process regarding its participants but still forms part of a nominal grounded by the definite determiner *dieses* ('this'). In the second example, for which a verb was determined (Section 3.2.1), the speech-only condition also revealed a verb grounding a clause, yet again, it is specified either by nouns serving as landmarks or by adverbial modifiers (Figure 21).

As will be seen in the course of this chapter, these findings are in line with the results yielded by the analysis of the whole corpus, which is why both examples are considered as representative cases. This means, more precisely, that if the recipients perceived the spoken utterances only, i.e., without the gestures, they used "more material" to "fill" the syntactic and semantic gap. As soon as the recipients perceived both speech and gesture, they used less material (see Section 3.2.4).

3.2.3 Experiment II: Gesture only

The first two experiments were conducted to test the understanding of both modalities, speech and gesture, individually. Speech was examined in the first experiment, revealing nouns and verbs as the majority of syntactic slots exposed

3.2 Where do they integrate? Gestures realizing nouns and verbs — 71

ich wollte dieses ('I wanted this')

Lexical items	Lexical items (translated)	Syntactic category	No.
Boot mal sehen	'boat see' ('[to] see this boat')	noun(lm)+verb	1
Teil	'part'	noun	1
Ereignis nicht missen	'event not miss' ('[to] miss this event')	noun(lm)+verb	1
Schiffshebewerk sehen	'ship canal lift see' ('[to] see this ship canal lift')	noun(lm)+verb	1
schon immer mal sehen	'always see' ('always wanted to see this')	verb+adverbial modifier	1
Jahr mal hinfahren / Mal wirklich hin / Jahr dort hin	'year go there' ('[to] go there this year') / 'time really there' ('[to] go there really this time') / 'this year there' ('[to] go there this year')	noun(modifier)+verb	3
Ding umfahren	'thing drive round' ('[to] drive round this thing')	noun(lm)+verb	1
Wunder sehen	'wonder see' ('[to] see this wonder')	noun(lm)+verb	1
Wort nicht mehr hören	'word hear any more' ('[to] hear this word any more')	noun(lm)+verb	1
Wochenende schwimmen	'weekend go swimming' ('[to] go swimming this weekend')	noun(lm)+verb	1
Dingsda	'thingummy'	noun	1
Panorama immer schon mal fotografieren	'panorama always to photograph' ('always wanted to photograph this panorama')	noun(lm)+verb	1
Bauwerk auch mal betreten	'building also enter' ('also wanted to enter this building')	noun(lm)+verb	1

und wir hinten ('and we from the back')

Lexical items	Lexical items (translated)	Syntactic category	No.
haben dann gefragt, was das soll	'asked what this is all about'	verb+clause (lm)	1
haben geschoben	'were pushing'	verb	1
wurden immer mehr zusammen gequetscht	'were squeezed together more and more'	verb+modifier	1
hatten keine Chance	'didn't stand a chance'	verb+nominal (lm)	1
dagegen	'against'	adverbial modifier	2
sind gestürzt	'are fallen' ('fell')	verb	1
dann auch	'then too'	adverbial modifier	1
haben daran gezogen	'pulled on it'	verb+adverbial modifier	2
haben es abbekommen	'got it' ('got hurt')	verb+(pro)noun(lm)	1
konnten nichts dagegen tun	'couldn't do anything against (it)'	verb+adverbial modifier	1
hatten keinen mehr	'didn't have anyone anymore'	verb+(pro)noun(lm)	1
haben geschlafen	'were sleeping'	verb	1
haben zurückgeschubst	'pushed back'	verb	1

Figure 21: Lexical items elicited in the speech-only condition for the examples "*ich wollte dieses* ('I wanted this')" and "*und wir hinten* ('and we from the back')".

by the interruption of the utterances. The understanding of gestures without speech was tested in the second experimental condition. Accordingly, the participants watched short video clips of the gestures identified in the data and wrote down a lexical item they considered best suited for all gestural meanings.

The findings are visualized in Figure 22, revealing that a range of different syntactic constructions was used by the recipients to describe the gestures. Among the constructions used most often are nouns (20.2 %), clauses (17.7 %), nominals (14.7 %), verbs+nouns (as a tr+lm construction, 14.1 %), or adverbs (10.2 %). Interestingly, verbs only were used in just 6.7 % of the cases. Hence, when recipients consider only the gestural form, they conceive of it as depicting a whole scene, such as a person engaged in an action with an object, or they focus on single aspects, such as the direction of a movement. These construals with different meanings are reflected in the diverse syntactic constructions that recipients used to designate gestural meaning, ranging from simpler units, such as nouns, to more complex constructions, such as verb+noun constructions or autonomous clauses. Briefly, although the gestural form certainly provides the basis for the construal of meaning (see below), a broader range of semantic information is considered to be transmitted by a gestural form (without its verbal context). This broad range of meaning is reflected in a range of different syntactic constructions. Moreover, it is by no means the case that one specific form prompts only one specific meaning expressed by a very limited range of lexical items.

As Figure 23 shows, the lexical items elicited for the two representative cases show a wide range of different syntactic constructions. Accordingly, in order to describe the gesture perceived in the first example, the recipients deployed verb constructions such as *wischen* ('to wipe'), nouns such as *Wand* ('wall'), *Bildschirm* ('screen'), or *Fenster* ('window'), adverbs such as *hoch und runter* ('up and down') or autonomous clauses including *Öffne das Ding mal* ('Just open this thing') or *Bist du verrückt* ('Are you crazy'). In the second example, the participants also used different syntactic constructions ranging from verbs such as *werfen* ('to throw'), nouns such as *Basketball* ('basketball') or *Tanz* ('dance') to autonomous clauses such as *Sie wirft einen Ball* ('She's throwing a ball'). Hence, although the meanings of the lexical items elicited can be "mapped" onto the gestural forms, recipients construed these forms very differently. In some cases, they referred to actions or objects, in others, they designated directions or whole scenes (see Chapter 4 for a thorough analysis of the semantics of the gestures). These different meaning construals are echoed in the diverse syntactic structures of the lexical items.

3.2 Where do they integrate? Gestures realizing nouns and verbs — 73

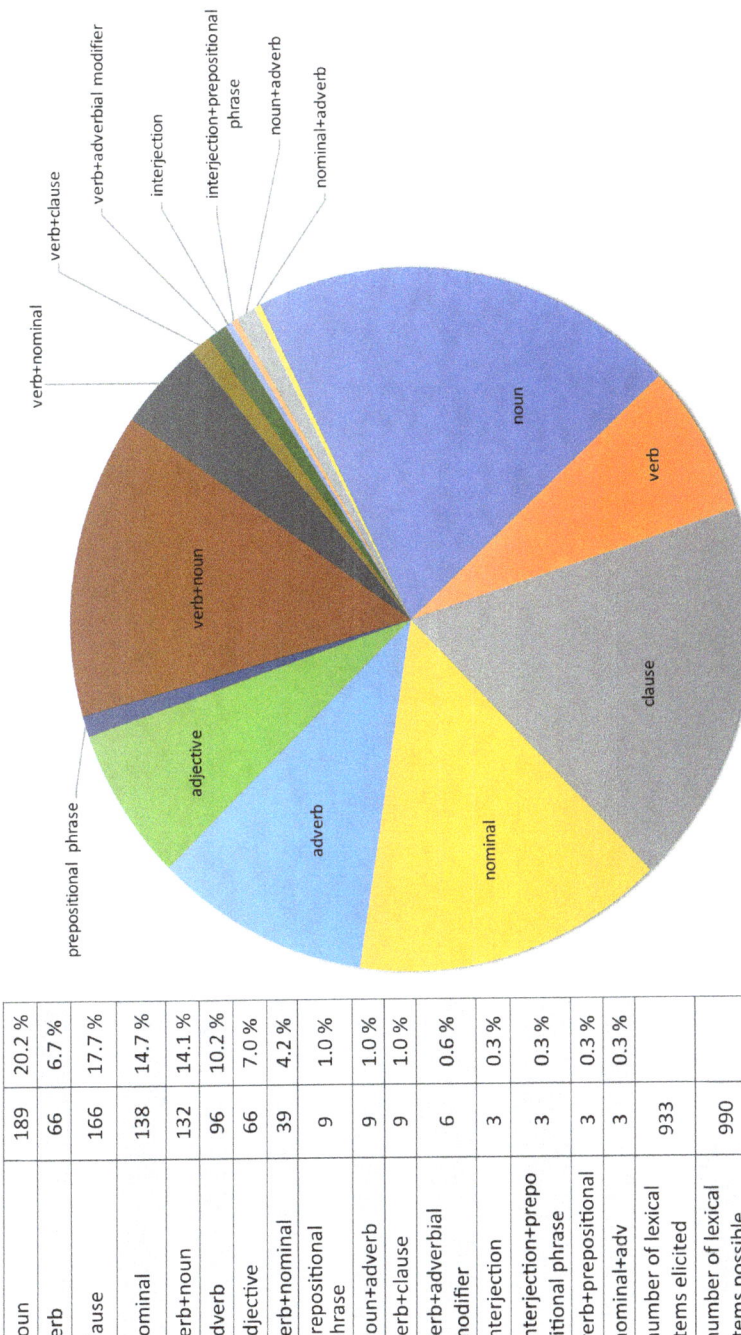

noun	189	20.2 %
verb	66	6.7 %
clause	166	17.7 %
nominal	138	14.7 %
verb+noun	132	14.1 %
adverb	96	10.2 %
adjective	66	7.0 %
verb+nominal	39	4.2 %
prepositional phrase	9	1.0 %
noun+adverb	9	1.0 %
verb+clause	9	1.0 %
verb+adverbial modifier	6	0.6 %
interjection	3	0.3 %
interjection+prepositional phrase	3	0.3 %
verb+prepositional	3	0.3 %
nominal+adv	3	0.3 %
number of lexical items elicited	933	
number of lexical items possible	990	

Figure 22: Lexical items elicited in the gesture-only condition for all 66 samples.

3 How are gestures integrated into linguistic structures?

Lexical items	Lexical items (translated)	Syntactic category	No.	Lexical items	Lexical items (translated)	Syntactic category	No.
Öffne das Ding doch mal.	'Just open this thing.'	clause	1	hopp in die Luft	'hopp into the air'	interjection+ prepositional phrase	1
Klappe	'clapper'	noun	2	Sie wirft einen Ball	'she's throwing a ball'	clause	1
senkrechte Fläche	'vertical surface'	adj. modifier+ noun	1	Volleyball, Basketball	'volleyball', 'basketball'	noun	3
Bildschirm, Wand, Fenster	'screen', 'wall', 'window'	noun	3	etwas hochdrücken, etwas hochschieben	'(to) press,' '(to) push something upward'	verb+ noun(Im)	2
wischen	'(to) wipe'	verb	1	Ball werfen (Korb werfen)	'(to) play the ball (make a basket)'	verb+ noun(Im)	1
Abgrenzung (in der Höhe)	'limits (in the height)'	noun	1	Volleyball spielen	'(to) play volleyball'	verb+ noun(Im)	2
hüpfend (dynamisch)	'jumping (dynamically)'	adj. modifier	1	Tanzstil	'dancing style'	noun	1
hoch und runter	'up and down'	adv. modifier	2	hochheben	'(to) lift upward'	verb+ adverbial modifier	1
auf und zu	'open and closed'	adv. modifier	1	etwas schieben	'push (shove) something'	verb+ noun(Im)	1
Sie ist irritiert. Sie aufgeregt.	'She is confused.' 'She' excited.'	clause	2	Bewegung (Tanz)	'movement (dance)'	noun	1
Bist du bescheuert?	'Are you crazy?'	clause	1	Sportübungen ausübend	'doing sport exercises'	verb+ noun(Im)	1

Figure 23: Lexical items elicited in the gesture-only condition for the examples "*ich wollte dieses*
('I wanted this')" and "*und wir hinten* ('and we from the back')".

These findings suggest that a gestural form alone does not prompt a particular meaning and it does not "trigger" a particular construction with which this meaning is expressed verbally. The process of attributing meaning to the gestural form, as was required in this experimental condition, is, on the one hand, highly dependent on the individual ways of perceiving gestures and, on the other hand, shaped by the subjective experiences of the recipients. Emblematic gestures form an exception, but these were found only rarely in the data (see Section 3.2.5).

3.2.4 Experiment III: Multimodal utterances

The third experiment aimed at testing (a) what syntactic slots are realized by the gestures and whether they differ from the syntactic positions determined in the first experiment (see Section 3.2.2), and (b) how speech and gestures interact in creating multimodal meaning. To put it another way, the question of whether the syntactic structure of an utterance has an impact on the understanding of the gestures under scrutiny was addressed.

The analysis of the syntactic structure of the first example reveals that the multi-stroke sequence realizes the syntactic slot of a noun because *this* grounds a nominal. This analysis is confirmed by the results of the third video experiment, in which the participants watched video clips of the multimodal utterances. Accordingly, the construction of a noun or of adjective+noun could be determined in 13 out of 15 lexical items elicited. The participants referred to entities such as *Ding* ('thing'), *Fenster* ('window'), or *Bild* ('picture') (Table 2). What also becomes visible is that the meanings differ to a great extent from both the speech-only and the gesture-only condition. Whereas the recipients referred to entities being in motion or showing a vertical dimension in the multimodal utterance condition, the lexical items elicited in the speech-only and the gesture-only condition diverge and present a rather broad range of possible meanings (this aspect is addressed in more detail in Chapter 4).

Furthermore, it is interesting to note that the syntactic structure of the utterance opens up a wider scope of interpretation. The syntactic structure is ambiguous, as is revealed by the outcome of the speech-only condition. The interrupted utterance can be completed by two different syntactic constructions, i.e., either by a noun, as explained before, or by a predicate. In fact, most subjects in the speech-only condition named a noun *and* a verb phrase as their lexical choice, in which the noun served as the direct object or the landmark of the verb. When looking closely at the syntactic structure of the utterance, this result does not

Table 2: Lexical items elicited in the multimodal utterance condition for the example "*Ich wollte dieses* 👆 ('I wanted this' 👆)".

Lexical items elicited	Lexical items (translated)	Syntactic category	No.
Ding, Gerät	'thing'	noun	3
Ding, was sich öffnet	'thing that opens'	noun+clause modifier	1
längliche Ding	'longish thing'	adjective+noun	1
große Ding	'big thing'	adjective +noun	1
Ding vertikal	'thing vertical'	adjective+noun	1
Wandteil / Glas / Fenster / Bild / Plakat	'wall' / 'glass' / 'window' / 'picture' / 'poster'	noun	5
Öffnen (Platten, die aufgehen)	'opening (panels that open)'	noun	1
Auf- und Runterklappen zeigen	'to show an up-and-down flapping'	noun(lm)+verb	1
vorne dran	'in front of (it)'	adverb	1

come as a surprise, because the German verb *wollen* acts either as a transitive verb requiring a nominal, such as in *Ich wollte dieses Bild* ('I wanted this picture'), or as a modal verb requiring a verbal complement consisting of another verb and its complements, as in the case of *Ich wollte dieses Boot sehen* ('I wanted to see this boat', Figure 21). In the speech-only condition, 13 out of 15 lexical items favored the construction of *wollen* ('[to] want') as a modal verb. One of the participants considered the verb to be transitive.

In the second example, the gesture realizes a verbal syntactic slot. After uttering the beginning of the second main clause *und wir hinten* ('and we from the back'), a gesture joins in. It is prepared while the speaker is uttering the personal pronoun *wir* ('we') and the first syllable of the following adverb *hinten* ('from the back', literally: 'behind'). The stroke begins on the second syllable of this adverb and fills the subsequent pause. It is followed by a retraction and a hold. Following the Subject-Verb-Object structure of a main clause, it can be argued that the gesture replaces a main verb, following the subject *wir* ('we') and, thus, grounding the clause. This analysis is substantiated by the results of the multimodal utterances condition, in which all the subjects named a verb to refer to the meaning of the syntactic gap (Table 3).

Table 3: Lexical items elicited in the multimodal utterance condition for the example "*und wir hinten* ✋ ('and we from the back' ✋)".

Lexical items elicited	Lexical items (translated)	Syntactic category	No.
haben gedrückt	'have pressed'	verb	3
haben geschoben	'have pushed / push'	verb	8
gegengedrückt	'have pressed against'	verb	1
angeschoben	'pushed start'	verb	1
hochgedrückt	'pushed up'	verb	2

To conclude, what the analysis of both examples suggests is that the meaning of the gesture is adapted to the syntactic information provided by speech when they realize a particular syntactic slot.

These findings are in line with the results yielded by the quantitative analysis of the corpus of lexical items elicited in the multimodal utterance condition (Figure 24). This means that the participants did not use a wide range of syntactic constructions to describe the gestures, but they followed the syntactic structure of the utterance. Accordingly, when gestures realized the syntactic slot of a noun, recipients used noun or adjective+noun constructions to "fill" the syntactic gap, forming multimodal nominals. If the syntactic structure exposed the slot of a verb, the recipients used verbs to fill the syntactic gap, thereby, forming multimodal clauses. To be more precise, 404 lexical items out of the 435 lexical items elicited for these 29 examples exhibiting a nominal syntactic slot showed a noun. Similarly, 446 out of the 480 lexical items elicited for the 32 cases exhibiting a verbal syntactic slot showed a verb. Moreover, when comparing both the speech-only with the multimodal utterance condition, it becomes clear that the lexical items elicited in the multimodal utterance condition are not triggered only by the semantics of the utterance. From a semantic perspective, the lexical items elicited in both conditions differ to a great extent. Therefore, it can be argued that a gesture brings in its own meaning that is, furthermore, adapted to the syntactic structure of the utterance.

It appears noteworthy to address the distribution of syntactic constructions over the examples of the corpus. When comparing the speech-only and the multimodal utterance condition, it becomes noticeable that the distribution of the syntactic slots differs slightly. Similar to the speech-only condition, the lexical items elicited in the multimodal utterance condition also show a dominance of nominal constructions (404 out of 913; 44 %) and verbal constructions

3 How are gestures integrated into linguistic structures?

	nominal syntactic slot determined for	verbal syntactic slot determined for 32 samples
	lexical items possible: 435	lexical items possible: 480
verb	8	446
noun	404	
clause	2	
adverb	4	
verb+adverb		23
verb+object		14
verb + predicate		15
particle	1	26
empty verb construction		25

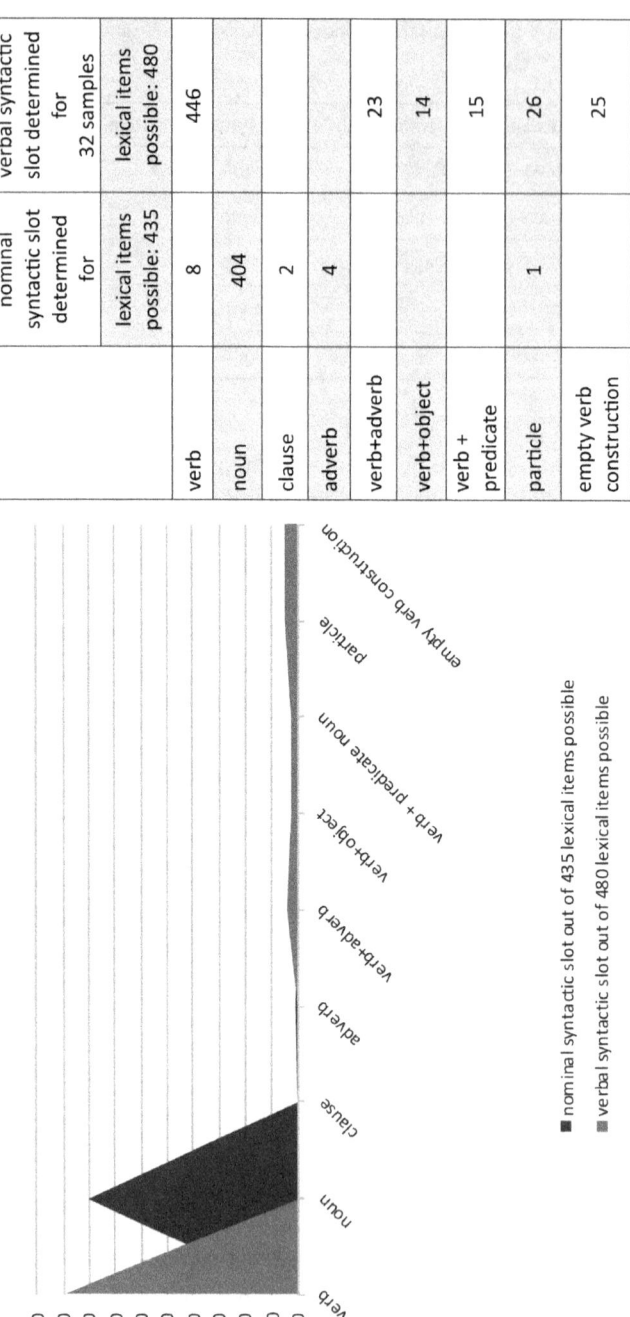

■ nominal syntactic slot out of 435 lexical items possible
■ verbal syntactic slot out of 480 lexical items possible

Figure 24: Syntactic categories used by the participants to describe a gesture realizing nominal and verbal slots (multimodal utterance condition).

(446 out of 913; 49 %). Yet, clausal constructions were 4 % less often used by the subjects. Apart from some variations due to unfilled slots in the questionnaires of the experiments, these differences arise from two samples of the corpus that are ambiguous regarding clausal and verbal constructions. Both examples were considered as clause constructions in the speech-only condition but conceived as verbal constructions in the multimodal utterance condition. Hence, 30 examples exhibiting a noun and 32 examples exhibiting a verb were identified in the multimodal utterance condition based on the lexical items (Table 4).

Table 4: Distribution of syntactic slots over the corpus (elicited in the speech-only and the multimodal utterance condition).

	Noun	Verb	Clause	Total
Speech-only condition	29	29	8	66
Multimodal utterance condition	30	32	4	66

A similar effect can be observed in cases of syntactic constructions in which a syntactic object is possible, as in the case of *Ich wollte dieses* ('I wanted this'), *Ich wollte schnell mal* ('I just wanted fast'), or *und die unten* ('and they downstairs'). In the speech-only conditions, the participants were inclined to use more complex constructions consisting of a verb and a noun that function as an object or landmark.[14] On the other hand, in the utterance condition, the participants deployed either a noun or a verb in these ambiguous cases. Based on these findings, it can be argued that the gestural modality (a) disambiguates syntactic slots and (b) narrows down the range of constructions used by the participants. Accordingly, when combining visual and auditory information, the attention clearly shifts from the construal of a complex scene framed by a verb and its complement(s) to the conception of an entity referred to by a noun or an action designated by a verb.

---

14 The noun(lm)+verb construction was coded for cases in which the spoken utterance was interrupted after a demonstrative pronoun, (in)definite article, or possessive pronoun. In these cases, the grounded element would be considered a nominal. The verb+noun(lm) construction was coded if the immediate constituent was a subject, an analytic verb form or a verb phrase.

3.2.5 Distribution of gesture types over syntactic slots

This section shifts the attention to the gesture type that preferably realizes nouns and verbs of spoken utterances. The gestures identified form the semantic centers of the units they construe together with speech, namely multimodal nominals and multimodal clauses. Hence, they can be considered as carrying the semantic weight of these multimodal utterances. Therefore, it is interesting to ascertain whether gestures that show a more or less stable meaning, such as emblems or gestures that are spontaneously created and linked indexically to the speech situation, are used to realize the syntactic slots.

The distributional analysis of the gesture types over the preferred syntactic position addresses this issue and uncovers that, against the assumption advocated in the literature (see McNeill 2005, 2007), not conventional but spontaneous gestures are most often used to replace speech (Table 5). These gestures, referred to as "singular gestures" (Müller 2010b, 2017a), "referential gestures" (Müller 1998), "iconic gestures" (McNeill 1992), or "representational gestures" (Kendon 1980b; Kita 2000), are regarded as spontaneous form-meaning mappings that unfold their meaning through the temporal overlap with speech. They were used in 63.3 % of the cases in a noun position, 68 % realized syntactic slots of verbs; and they realized clauses in 100 % of cases. When replacing nouns, 53.3 % of the gestures were performed non-pantomimically, meaning that no other body parts were involved in the gestural depiction (see Bressem, Ladewig and Müller 2018 for more information on pantomimic and non-pantomimic gestures). The gestures were performed in a pantomimic way in 10 % of the cases. When realizing verbs, 56 % of the gestures were used in a non-pantomimic and 13 % in a pantomimic way. Recurrent gestures realize nouns in 33.3 % of the cases, out of which 13 % are Palm up open hand gestures, 7 % are Throwing away gestures, 3.3 % are Sweeping away gestures, and 10 % are Pointing gestures. Verbs are realized by recurrent gestures in only 15 % of the samples. No Palm up open hand gestures are used in these positions. The gestures identified in verbal slots are Throwing away gestures (3 %), Sweeping away gestures (6 %), Cyclic gestures (3 %), and Pointing gestures (3 %). Emblematic gestures make up the smallest number of speech-replacing gestures. They realize nouns in 3.3 % of the cases and verbs in 16 % of the cases.

In a nutshell, gestures characterized by the absence of linguistic properties and obligatory presence of speech (see McNeill 2005, 2007) realize linguistic units in most cases. Singular (spontaneous) gestures together with recurrent gestures amount to about 90 % of all gestures used in the corpus. These two gesture types have both only been selectively characterized as serving the function of replacing speech.

3.2 Where do they integrate? Gestures realizing nouns and verbs

Table 5: Distribution of gesture types over all syntactic positions.

66 Syntactic slots	Singular gestures			Recurrent gestures				Pointing	Emblematic gestures
	Non-pantomimic	Pantomimic	Palm up open hand	Throwing away	Sweeping away	Bimanual asynchronous Cyclic gesture			
Noun: 30 gestures	16 (53.3 %)	3 (10 %)	4 (13 %)	2 (7 %)	1 (3.3 %)	/		3 (10 %)	1 (3.3 %)
Verb: 32 gestures	18 (56 %)	4 (13 %)	/	1 (3 %)	2 (6 %)	1 (3 %)		1 (3 %)	5 (16 %)
Clause: 4 gestures	4 (100 %)	/	/	/	/	/		/	/

To sum up, this section investigated whether and, if so, what syntactic positions are realized by gestures in the utterance-final position. Nouns and verbs turned out to be preferably replaced by gestures. Together with speech, these gestures, mostly created spontaneously, form multimodal nominals and clauses. When these gestures are perceived without speech, they are conceived of as realizing a broad range of syntactic units and meanings (for more information on the relationship between form and meaning, see Chapter 4). More precisely, they may convey a complex scene, a thing, or a temporal relationship, prompting the use of nominals, verbs, adjectives, or adverbs to describe the meaning of the gestures.

When speech and gesture merge, recipients follow the syntactic structure of the utterance to interpret the meaning of the syntactic gap and, as such, of the multimodal utterance. The gestures in noun positions are conceived to depict entities and, in some cases, reified events or, in more general terms, THINGs. In verb positions, they are considered as depicting temporal relationships or PROCESSes. Accordingly, the range of construed reference objects is reduced by the syntactic positions realized gesturally. However, gestures can also disambiguate the syntactic structure, as some cases of the corpus have shown.

These findings accumulate evidence that speech provides a frame that "coerces" a particular understanding of the gesture according to the slot realized.[15] Thus, what has been shown for words belonging to particular syntactic categories (see Goldberg 1995; Kaplan 1976) can also be applied to gestures. Although gesture do not show fixed syntactic categories, as Section 3.2.3 revealed, the syntactic structure of an utterance coerces them into particular categories. These can then coerce certain conceptualizations of the gestures, like verbs or nouns do. Accordingly, when gestures are perceived without speech, recipients are free to interpret the gestures by drawing on their preferential way of perceiving movements based on their own bodily experiences. When speech and gesture merge, spoken language provides an interpretative frame for the construal of gestural meaning. In these cases, gestural meaning is adapted to the syntactic (and semantic) information provided by the syntactic slot realized gesturally. This aspect is elaborated further in Section 3.4.

---

15 See Michaelis (2004) on constructional coercion.

3.3 Why can gestures integrate? Conceptual archetypes in gestures

The previous section revealed that (spontaneous) gestures can replace nouns and verbs of spoken utterances. Gestures and speech interact in specific ways to construe multimodal meaning, as will be discussed in the next sections and chapters. However, before tackling the issue of creating multimodal meaning, this section addresses gestures' capability to replace nouns and verbs of spoken utterances. This topic deserves an extended treatment of its own as it is pivotal for both understanding the interaction of gesture and speech on the level of grammar and contributing to an understanding of gestures as potential candidates for developing linguistic structures. Accordingly, the focus of this section is to define "nounish" or "verbish" properties of gestures that may qualify them to replace nouns and verbs of spoken language.

Regarding spoken language, such properties can be determined on a syntactic and a phonological, morphological, or a semantic level of description. Syntactic features regarding, for instance, grounding elements, and the position or the function of a linguistic unit were consulted in the analysis presented in the previous section. Yet, syntactic features alone do not answer the question regarding why gestures adopt the positions and functions of nouns and verbs of speech as they refer to the structural and functional properties of the linguistic units that gestures replace.

Phonological and morphological features can also be consulted to distinguish nouns and verbs. Prosodic stress, for instance, is a helpful means to discriminate both notions in the English language. Correspondingly, Arciuli and Slowiaczek (2006: 2) show that whereas "disyllabic nouns exhibit first syllable stress, most disyllabic verbs exhibit second syllable stress [...] Both native and non-native speakers of English are sensitive to these stress differences across nouns and verbs" (see also Kelly and Bock 1988; Sereno 1986). Moreover, words can be grouped according to inflectional characteristics, which again correlate with the syntactic categories of nouns and verbs. In German, a verb agrees with a subject in person, number, tense, and case. Nouns inflect regarding case, gender, and number. However, whether phonological or morphological criteria apply to gestures, meaning whether gestures are, for instance, accentuated differently or whether they show particular morphological features when substituting nouns and verbs, remains a matter of speculation at this point of the investigation.

Semantic criteria apply to define sub-categories of nouns and verbs, such as concrete or abstract entities. Nouns are distinguished regarding count and mass nouns, for instance. Verbs are sub-categorized regarding their reference to actions, processes, and states. Yet, whether semantic information can and should be consulted to differentiate nouns and verbs is treated controversially within the theory of grammar.

The theory of Cognitive Grammar "advances the controversial [. . .] proposal that essential grammatical notions can be characterized semantically" (Langacker 2008a: 103). Moreover, by claiming that grammar is inherently symbolic and that "all valid grammatical constructs have some kind of conceptual import" (Langacker 1987a: 282), meaning is equated with conceptualization. This means that both semantic and grammatical structures are understood in terms of a conceptual structure (see also Chapter 1). With this fundamental assertion, the theory of Cognitive Grammar is a useful framework for tackling the issue of why gestures can replace nouns and verbs and whether they can be considered to exhibit characteristics of these categories. Firstly, the gaps created by interrupting spoken utterances are not only syntactic but also semantic in nature, which means that discontinued utterances not only leave a structural gap but also interrupt the flow of meaning construction. Secondly, in view of the fact that the study examines the understanding of gestures and, as such, the sense evoked in the recipient's mind, theories of cognition and conceptualization are certainly a field of reference when exploring these processes of understanding. Moreover, as meaning is treated as a subjective phenomenon in the Cognitive Grammar framework, it proves beneficial in the current investigation, because, similar to speech, gestures reflect a speaker's perspective on a depicted situation. Thirdly, as has been pointed out in Chapter 1, the theory of Cognitive Grammar considers "gestures as an integral part of linguistic expression" (Langacker 2008b: 250) and, as such, offers points of anchorage for gesture studies.

3.3.1 Nouns and verbs in spoken language from a cognitive grammar approach

Cognitive Grammar distinguishes nouns and verbs by alluding to their conceptual referents. Accordingly, nouns are conceived as profiling[16] things and conceptualizing prototypically physical objects. Verbs are understood as profiling processes. They conceptualize "participants interacting energetically in a 'force-dynamic' event" (Langacker 2008a: 103). Using this conception, basic

---

16 Profiling frames "what the expressions designate (or refer to) within the conceived situation" (Langacker 2008a: 43). A cup with coffee in it designates a container. It is understood as the conceptual referent of an expression (see Langacker 2008a: 66).

grammatical categories are defined in symbolic terms and "can be given uniform semantic characterizations" (Langacker 2008a: 23). Of course, not all representatives of the categories "noun" and "verb" can be conceived as referring to entities or (inter)actions. A noun, for instance, can also refer to an action ("murder") or a process ("growth"). However, as Langacker points out convincingly, the use of the different grammatical categories of nouns and verbs makes visible how an event is conceptually *construed*. This means that the grammatical choice of the speaker makes visible his or her perspective on a speech event. Langacker (2008a: 95) sketches out his idea of meaning construal based on the use of different grammatical categories by using the example of the verb "explode" and the noun "explosion" (see also Langacker 1991b). "While invoking the same conceptual content, they differ in meaning because of how they construe it: unlike explode, which directly reflects the event's processual nature, explosion construes it as an abstract thing derived by conceptual reification. It is precisely by virtue of this conceptual contrast that the expressions belong to different grammatical categories" (Langacker 2008a: 95).

These differences in the construal of meaning are based on different cognitive operations framed as "sequential scanning," "summary scanning" and "conceptual reification" (Langacker 2008a). The mode of sequential scanning imposes a processual or temporal view on a situation and considers the successive states of an event. Thus, the event or activity is conceived more serially, and the producer and the receiver "follow along from one state to the next as the event unfolds" (Langacker 2006: 51). Consequently, a situation described is conceptualized as a PROCESS.

A THING is a product of the processes of summary scanning and conceptual reification. Summary scanning refers to the cognitive mode by which the event described is considered as an atemporal thing. The different states of the event are coactivated in such a way that the successive states are conceived and perceived as accumulated and not individual, which results in conceptualizing a situation as bounded. The single components of the event are activated holistically. If higher level cognitive purposes are realized, the process of conceptual reification is activated, where things are treated as single entities for the purpose of counting, for instance. These processes run automatically without any awareness of the conceptualizer.

> Indeed, what makes objects prototypical is precisely the fact that the grouping and reification are so natural and automatic (perhaps effected by low-level processing) that we are only aware of their product. While a rock does consist of substance discernible at multiple contiguous locations, our capacity for object recognition is such that we automatically pull these together to produce the conscious apprehension of spatial continuity.
>
> (Langacker 2005: 125)

Coming back to the example given by Langacker, the lexical items "explode" and "explosion" cannot be considered as semantically equivalent. Although the word "explosion" does not add anything to the conceptual content of "explode," the semantic content is construed differently, i.e., in terms of a THING not a PROCESS.[17]

Although the application of semantic criteria to nouns and verbs in spoken language may be debatable for some cases, implementing a semantic distinction between the grammatical categories of nouns and verbs provides an instrument for reasoning why gestures preferably replace these categories: In a similar way, language gestures can depict entities and actions, and they do so by reenacting instrumental actions, drawing shapes in the air, molding three-dimensional objects, or embodying characteristics of entities (see Müller 1998, 2014a). This aspect is elaborated in the subsequent paragraph. Moreover, the issue of "nounish" or "verbish" will be tackled based on the empirical findings discussed previously.

3.3.2 Objects and actions in gestures

Gestures depicting objects and action have already been distinguished by Wundt (1916) in his description of a "gesture–language." Though stating that gestural equivalents to nouns, adjectives, or verbs of spoken language cannot be defined clearly, he argues that gestures or *Gebärden*[18] ('signs of sign language') symbolize notions comprising the three logic categories: *Gegenstand* ('objects'), *Eigenschaften* ('qualities'), and *Zustand* ('states') (Wundt 1921 [1901]: 197). Accordingly, entities are either embodied by the hands that turn into a 'continuous, plastic reproductions ("*dauernde, plastische Nachbildungen*", Wundt 1921 [1901]: 178) or they are co-denoted by depicting an action that calls forth a certain object – so-called 'graphic gestures', ("*zeichnende Gebärden*", Wundt 1921 [1901]: 177). The latter aspect forms a category of its own in Wundt's terminology, i.e., 'co-denoting gestures' ("*mitbezeichnende Gebärden*", Wundt 1921 [1901]: 177), by which an object is "not represented by means of a direct picture, but by incidental characteristics – a man, for example, is expressed by lifting the hat" (Wundt 1916: 63). A recollected

---

17 The case cited refers to the process of nominalization, meaning a noun is derived from a verb. Many cases of deriving verbs from nouns are accompanied by the addition of conceptual content. Langacker (1991b: 25) points out that "common values for denominal verbs include 'add N' [. . .], 'remove N' [. . .], and so on."
18 See Müller (2010a, 2014a) for a discussion of the term "*Gebärden*" ('signs of sign language') deployed by Wundt (1921 [1901]).

picture is evoked through association processes (Wundt 1921 [1901]: 175).[19] The most natural and simplest way to depict actions and processes, both assigned to the category of states, is, according to Wundt, to perform an action preferably by using imitating gestures. Interestingly, he argues that this gesture type has a spoken-language equivalent in verb forms (Wundt 1921 [1901]: 172).

Although Wundt is often inconsistent in his terminology, his elaborations are a first approach to describe techniques of gestural sign creation that was later defined more clearly by Müller's notion of "gestural modes of representation" (Müller 1998, 2010a, 2014a, 2016; see also "processes of signification" [Kendon 1980a]). They are pivotal for tackling the issue of how the manual movements turn into communicative signs and for describing gestures as motivated semiotic signs. Two basic modes are distinguished, referred to as "acting" and "representing." The former is derived from everyday actions which are, in most cases, instrumental. The hands mime actions without objects, such as waving, only in a few cases. Hence, the hands reenact actions (with object) and are, thus, motivated by as-if actions (and not by images; see Müller 2018: 12; see also Kendon 1980a). Acting gestures comprise two further categories, namely "drawing" and "molding." When outlining a 2D-shape with the index finger into the air, the mode of drawing is deployed. A drawing gesture can depict either a geometric shape, such as a circle, or an object exhibiting the form outlined. However, shapes and figures can also be depicted in a three-dimensional way by using the whole hand. In the latter, the molding mode is recruited. The emerging ephemeral forms show selected properties of the entity depicted (see also Kendon 1980a). Representing gestures incorporate properties of objects. Consequently, the hands are "transformed" into sculptures. Examples are walking legs, opening windows, or flying airplanes. Objects only or motions only are mimed only in a very few cases (examples are given in Müller 2014a: 1697). The majority of representing gestures mimes objects in motion (see the discussion in Section 3.3.3).

---

[19] As becomes noticeable, the categories applied by Wundt (1921 [1901]) are not clearly defined. In his examples for co-denoting gestures, Wundt refers to different semiotic processes involved in the sign creation, such as the construal of an object by the drawing hand, the reference to an object by association, or the reference to an object that is involved in a particular action. His category of graphic gestures is also not stipulated clearly and precisely. Whereas Wundt defines them in his introduction of graphic gestures as being performed with the index finger that leaves sketches in the air, his examples describe the reenactment of actions (e.g., hammering) or even the representation of an object (e.g., "imitating the movements of walking with the index and middle fingers of the right hand upon the left arm which is held out horizontally," Wundt 1916: 62).

Note that the terms "representing gestures" or "modes of representation" do not refer to the mental representation of objects and actions but are based on the concept "*Darstellung*" as proposed by Bühler (1934: 28).

> [T]he German word *Darstellung* entails the idea of presentation or depiction, it does not imply the idea of re-presentation. Bühler's organon model of lan- guage as use conceptualizes the speaker and addressee as active participants shaping and understanding language in a communicative event. The three functions of language are conceived as fundamentals for language and they are co-present in every speech-sign. Also Bühler uses the term appeal in very idiosyncratic way. For him it captures the fact that every verbal sign that is used is addressed to somebody. Language is rooted in a speech-event and cannot be thought of other than being directed to an addressee. (Müller 2013: 204)

In a nutshell, both semiotic techniques of gestural sign creation differ in how the hands are involved to depict entities, actions, or events: In acting gestures, the hands mime mundane actions the hands themselves are engaged in. The objects manipulated by the hands need to be inferred from the mimed action through metonymy (see Mittelberg 2006; 2010b; see Section 3.3.3 for further information). The hands mime entities other than themselves in representing gestures. They are transferred into objects. The motions depicted by the hands are not the movements performed by the hands but by the embodied objects.

Considering the different ways of gesturally embodying actions and entities, as captured by the gestural modes of representation, it appears reasonable to assume that acting gestures preferably realize syntactic slots of verbs, whereas representing gestures preferably realize nouns. This semiotic distinction realized in different modes of representation could be regarded as an answer to the question: Why are gestures capable of replacing nouns and verbs of spoken language? Yet, when considering the distribution of the gestural modes of representation over the syntactic slots identified, the insights emerge that such a correspondence cannot be proven empirically. In fact, as Table 6 demonstrates, the acting mode was most often identified in both the noun and verb positions.

Accordingly, 61 % of the gestures realizing a nominal syntactic slot were executed in the acting mode, while 39 % of the gestures showed the representing mode. In the case of verb positions, 77 % of the gestures reenacted an action, whereas only 23 % represented an object. Hence, the hypothesis that the two modes of representation can be allocated to the different syntactic positions is only partly corroborated. Verb positions show a higher number of acting gestures, whereas representing gestures realize nouns more often than verbs. Yet, when taking the whole distribution into account, it becomes more than obvious that acting gestures dominate both syntactic positions.

The conclusions drawn from these findings are twofold. First of all, the distribution of the modes of gestural sign creation does not tackle the issue of why

Table 6: Distribution of modes of representation over preferred syntactic positions.

Mode of representation	Syntactic position	
	Noun	Verb
Acting	61 %	77 %
Molding	13 %	3 %
Drawing	6 %	3 %
Acting only	6 %	10 %
Acting with an object	33 %	61 %
Representing	39 %	23 %
Object in motion	39 %	20 %

gestures preferably realize nouns and verbs and not adverbs, for instance, which are often found in utterance-final position in German. Yet, the semiotic techniques of sign creation reveal semiotic properties of gestures which are essential for the construal of meaning, namely their capability to embody objects and actions in different ways. This discovery is not trivial, because it uncovers an important point of intersection of spoken and signed languages and gestures, because all of them express the conceptual archetypes of nouns and verbs.

3.3.3 Conceptual archetypes in gestures

Scholars of gestures and of signed languages have acknowledged the potential of gestures to create complex meaning, which is why the hands are considered as potential candidates for developing a linguistic system (see Armstrong and Wilcox 2007; Müller 2013). As Müller (2013: 203) points out convincingly, the hands are the "only organ apart from the vocal tract that have developed a capacity for flexible and variable movements with a high degree of articulatory precision." This means that due to their medial properties, the hands are the bodily techniques *par excellence* that can create and communicate complex information. They exhibit "a highly flexible articulation (the capacity for a high differentiation of movements is a prerequisite for a complex sign system) and [are engaged in] a manifold instrumental use of the hands, which provides the functional grounds (and infinite sources) for the creation of gestural meaning" (Müller 2013: 203).

It goes without saying that the depictive potential of gestures is the most fundamental property speakers exploit to convey meaning and replace linguistic units. As will be argued in the pages to follow, it is their potential to embody actions and objects – the conceptual archetypes of nouns and verbs – that enables gestures to substitute nouns and verbs of spoken utterances.

The previous section demonstrated that gestures can represent objects and mime actions. Objects and actions are embodied differently with both techniques. The movements performed in acting gestures are derived from the movement the hands executed in the original action. In representing gestures, the hands transform into entities and mime the movements of these objects and not of the hand themselves. In other words, whereas an action *with* an object is mimed by acting gestures,[20] the action or motion *of* an object is depicted with representing gestures. However, the link between both cases is that complex meanings are conveyed in which both an object *and* an action is embodied. The emerging semiotic pattern reflects the basal clause structures realized by a noun and a verb. As such, manual movements "are diagrammatically iconic with syntactic relations. They are objects that move about and interact with other objects. Hands are prototypical nouns, and their actions are prototypical verbs" (Armstrong and Wilcox 2007: 66). To put it differently, what is transmitted linearly in spoken language can be transferred simultaneously by one gesture in which object information is conveyed by the hand shape and action information is expressed by the movement of the hand (see also Armstrong and Wilcox 2007; Ladewig 2014a; Mittelberg 2006; Wilcox 2004a). Different inferential processes are responsible for construing objects and actions. First of all, gestural movements depict temporal relationships and, thus, processes. The movements are dependent on autonomous hand shapes, which embody things. This holds for both acting and representing gestures.

> Like signs, manual gestures consist of handshapes, locations, orientations, and movements. Handshapes are autonomous physical entities composed of material substance residing in space. In a specific gestural construction the hands occupy a location in space and an orientation (the direction in which the palm faces). Hand location and orientation are dependent properties requiring an autonomous hand for their manifestation. Movement is also a

---

20 Tracing and molding gestures are an exception, because, in these cases, the movement is a depictive means to create ephemeral forms of an object. Yet, considering the semiotics of such gestural forms, it becomes evident that the depictive movement is based on the mundane actions of drawing or molding.

dependent property: a movement makes schematic reference to an autonomous entity (which moves). In gesture, the autonomous entity is typically instantiated by the hand(s).
(Ruth-Hirrel and Wilcox 2018: 460)

On the other hand, different types of metonymy are activated by both gestural modes. Whereas, the entity manipulated by the hand is inferred from the hand shape via "external metonymy" (Mittelberg 2006, 2010b, 2013; Mittelberg and Waugh 2009a, 2014), in acting gestures, the object the hand transforms into in the case of representing gestures is inferred via "internal metonymy" (Mittelberg 2006, 2010b, 2013; Mittelberg and Waugh 2009a, 2014). In other words, in the former case, the object is contiguous to the hand and not represented by it. In the latter case, the hand turns into an entity and becomes a sculpture itself, portraying its salient aspects.

Entities can be distinguished further in spoken and signed languages in terms of semantic roles, such as agent, patient, or instrument. The (inter)action an entity is engaged can be specified regarding temporal relationships. The categories of agents or patients are realized by nouns. The (inter)actions an agent or patient is engaged in is expressed by verbs. Agents mark their grammatical status within a clause as subjects (tr), patients (lm), and objects (lm), and verbs as predicates.

Similar structures can be observed not only in signs but also in gestures (see e.g., Armstrong and Wilcox 2007; Wilcox 2004a). Accordingly, it can be argued that the parameters of hand shape and movement embody the conceptual archetypes of nouns and verbs, i.e., objects and actions, giving rise to the conceptual referents of a THING and a PROCESS (Figure 25).

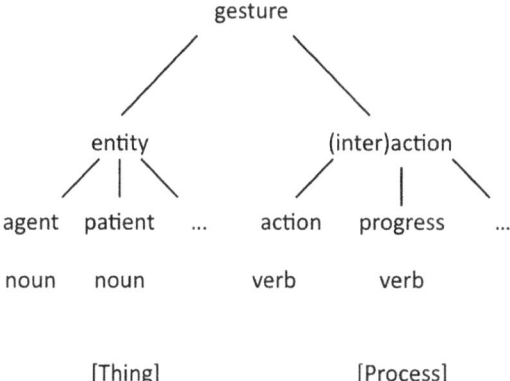

Figure 25: Gesture conceived in terms of archetypical roles, grammatical notions and schemas.

The archetypal notion defining the noun-class prototype is that of a physical object. The symbolic structure representing this prototype thus takes for its semantic pole the schematized conception of a physical object, which functions as its profile. [. . .] At the most schematic level, a noun is thus characterized as an expression that profiles a thing. [. . .] The class of verbs is comparably arranged. Its prototype is the archetypal conception of an asymmetrical energetic interaction, specifically an event in which an agent does something to a patient. Among the basic cognitive abilities that figure in this notion, two are essential for characterizing the verb-class schema: the ability to establish relationships, and to scan sequentially through a complex structure. It is claimed that every verb profiles a *process*.

(Langacker 1999: 10, original emphasis)

These considerations suggest that gestures are grounded in the same conceptual archetypes[21] that nouns and verbs forming clausal structures are based on. Archetypes and the related notion of archetypal roles (Figure 25) are deeply connected to and grounded in human action in and interaction with the world. They include notions such as physical object, physical object in motion through space, physical object in a location, participants in events, or transfer of energy between participants. Archetypes are not only instantiated verbally, but also embodied by gestures more specifically by their "*Gegenstände gestischer Mimesis*" ('objects of mimesis', Müller 2010a: 155), i.e., the entities, actions and relationships gestures mime. Similar to nouns and verbs, the conception of physical objects and (inter)actions or "force-dynamic" events (Talmy 1988) figure in a more elaborate conceptual archetype, namely the "billiard-ball model" and "the stage model" (Langacker 1987a, 1991b, 2008a). Both of them were applied to conceptualize the manual articulators of signed language (see Armstrong, Stokoe and Wilcox 1995; Armstrong and Wilcox 2007; Wilcox 2004a) and can similarly be used to conceptualize gestures. Accordingly, the billiard-ball model represents "our conception of objects moving through space and impacting one another through forceful physical contact. Some objects supply the requisite energy through their own internal resources; others merely transmit or absorb it" (Langacker 2008a: 355). It gives rise to the archetypical conception of an "action chain," representing "a series of forceful interactions, each involving the transmission of energy [. . .] from one participant to the next" (Langacker 2008a: 355–356). Objects in (inter)action are associated with "archetypical

---

21 "Archetypes, and the related notion of archetypal roles, are grounded in human action (and interaction) in and with the world. Archetypes relate to coherent experiential gestalts and include notions such as a physical object, a physical object in a location, an object in motion through space, a setting for an event, participants in an event, location, and energy transfer from one participant to another" (Evans 2007: "archetype"). As such they are reminiscent of the gestural 'objects of mimesis' ("*Gegenstände gestischer Mimesis*") introduced by Müller (2010a: 155).

roles" (semantic roles), such as "agent", "patient", "instrument", "experiencer" or "mover" (Langacker 2008a: 356; see Figure 25).

The second model proposed by Langacker, termed the stage model, brings in an external viewer who observes an event and conceptualizes it as a scene. It describes how a person construes an event: "[J]ust as actors move about the stage and handle various props, we tend to organize the scenes we observe in terms of distinct 'participants' who interact within an inclusive and reasonably stable 'setting'" (Langacker 1991a: 210). Not everything is perceived at once. Certain elements are singled out from the whole scene and focused on.

Both models provide a conceptual explanation for the interaction of entities and how they are perceived and conceived. Despite their complex structure, linguistic clauses are grounded in these very general models and archetypes, as stated by Langacker (1987a, 2008a). His approach can be applied to gestures, arguing that their complex structure of conflating object and action information is grounded in the experiences a human body makes in and with the world. However, Langacker's model focuses very much on the visual experiences that speakers draw on when construing meaning, as will be discussed in Chapter 6. The study of gestures brings in different dimensions that researchers attempted to fathom with the notion of "felt qualities" (see Johnson 2005; Kappelhoff and Müller 2011; Mittelberg 2017a; Müller and Kappelhoff 2018), for instance. However these dimensions might be framed, Cognitive Grammar should make an effort to implement them, because the human body is not only able to move through the world perceiving interacting entities or other human bodies, but it can also feel these movements and interactions.

With these lines of thought, the attempt is made to elucidate why gestures can realize nouns and verbs of spoken language. Gestures exhibit a semiotic structure which enables them to create and express complex information, similar to that transmitted by clauses in spoken and signed languages. One gesture embodies an action and object simultaneously that languages refer to by distinct notions, namely nouns and verbs. Moreover, as this section aimed to show, gestures are based on the same experientially grounded models and archetypes spoken and signed languages are rooted in. These observations provide evidence for the argument that the different modalities – spoken language, signed language, and gesture – should be integrated into one model of expression (see Wilcox and Xavier 2013).

3.4 How can gestures integrate? Gesture and speech interacting

Since the emergence of the field of modern gesture studies, scholars of gestures have worked on illuminating gestures' semantic and pragmatic potential. As has been outlined previously (Chapter 2), researchers have demonstrated that gestures interacting with speech may add, specify, or substitute semantic information and may perform (meta)pragmatic functions. Moreover, the property of realizing syntactic function has been added to the portfolio of gestural functions only recently. Yet, the research on the interaction of speech and gesture focuses predominantly on the gestural contribution to speech. Researchers point out correctly that gestures can, for instance, specify verbal information or highlight semantic information expressed in speech. Thus, it appears that the interaction of both modalities is conceived in a generally unidirectional way, in which gesture adds to speech but not *vice versa*. However, what will be discussed in the pages that follow is the process of highlighting semantic facets of the gestural modality. It is this very process which is considered pivotal for the integration of gestures into speech.

3.4.1 Simultaneous use of speech and gesture

Speakers can highlight semantic information conveyed by a multimodal utterance and do so by deploying different foregrounding techniques, one of them being the use of gestures. Gestures, so goes the argumentation, can foreground different meaning facets conveyed in speech and if they do so multiple times during a discourse, a multimodal salience structure evolves (see e.g., Kolter et al. 2012; Müller 2008b; Müller and Ladewig 2013; Müller and Tag 2010).

Consider the example illustrated in Figure 26 in which a woman in a therapeutic session is asked to improvise situations of her life. While doing so, she highlights different aspects of her description with the gestures and the other bodily movements she uses.

During the session, she conceptualizes her life as an up and down movement by using the adjectives *auf* ('up') and *ab* ('down') many times (Figure 26). While elaborating this metaphor verbally, she moves her arms repeatedly in a wave-like fashion or uses a spiral motion pattern moved up- and downwards. When examining this verbo-gestural interplay closely, it becomes noticeable that the speaker foregrounds a downward direction during the whole therapeutic session. The upward direction is foregrounded only once in the session, namely when the speaker says *geht nicht von unten nach hoch* ('doesn't go from

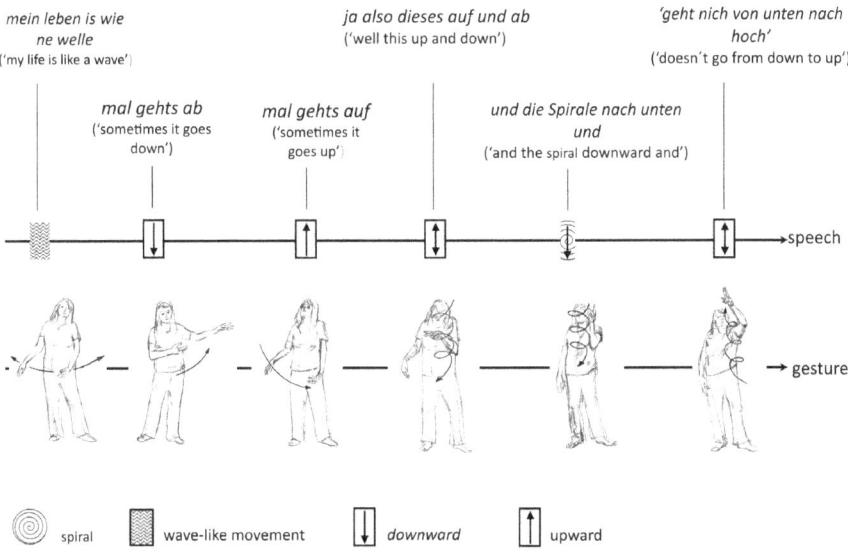

Figure 26: Foregrounding of verbal meaning through the use of gesture.

down to up') while performing a spiral movement upward. Foregrounding means precisely that; following the "Iconicity Principle," meaning is expressed in more than one modality (Müller and Tag 2010: 94). This can be observed when, in this case, a particular direction is expressed in both speech and gesture. These observations allow one to conclude that at the stage of the therapy discussed here, the patient conceives her live as a downward movement, because this direction is made salient by the speaker (see Kappelhoff and Müller 2011; Kolter et al. 2012).

In the following example, the issue of foregrounding of meaning is elaborated further but, in this case, the focus is on how speech highlights meaning aspects of the gesture – an aspect which is often neglected in the analysis of gesture–speech interaction. Moreover, it demonstrates that, picking up on the discussion led in the previous paragraph, the conceptual archetypes of nouns and verbs are embodied gesturally and are, simultaneously, highlighted by the co-occurring verbal expressions.

Figure 27 displays a sequence of gestures depicting the action of opening a window. Although an object being engaged in an action is depicted gesturally in all three examples, different semantic information is foregrounded. Consider the first gesture–speech ensemble presented in the picture on the left in Figure 27 in which the speaker represents an object with an open, flat hand oriented and moved towards her body. While performing the gesture, the speaker utters *damit*

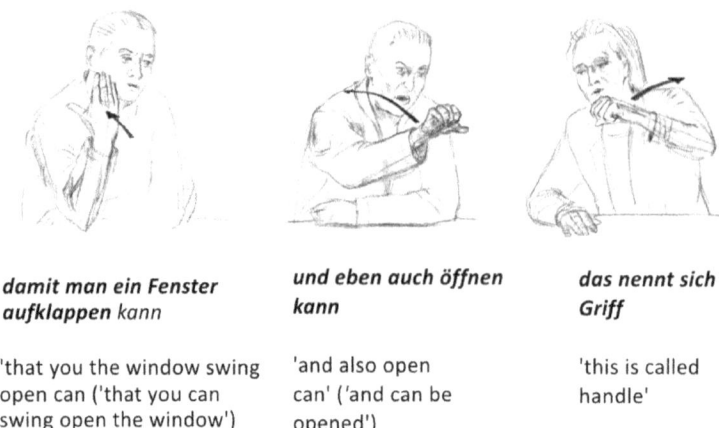

damit man ein Fenster aufklappen kann	und eben auch öffnen kann	das nennt sich Griff
'that you the window swing open can ('that you can swing open the window')	'and also open can' ('and can be opened')	'this is called handle'

Figure 27: Foregrounding of gestural meaning through the use of speech.

man ein Fenster aufklappen kann ('so that you can swing open the window'). The stroke of the gesture starts at the second syllable of the word *Fenster* ('window') and spans the rest of the utterance. By referring verbally to both the window and its movement, her verbal utterance foregrounds both conceptual archetypes – object and action – that are embodied by the gesture. As such, it can be argued, that the whole multimodal utterance profiles both a THING and a PROCESS.

In the following instance (central picture in Figure 27), the same speaker uses a gripper hand oriented downwards and moves it towards her body. In her accompanying utterance, the speaker refers only to the action of opening when saying *und eben auch öffnen kann* ('and can also open'). The stroke of the gestures accompanies the verb *öffnen* ('[to] open'). The object of a window handle that is involved in the action of opening can be inferred from the speaker's hand shape via external metonymy, yet, it remains undesignated by the verbal utterance. Hence, the conceptual archetype foregrounded in this multimodal utterance is only that of an action. The verbo-gestural ensemble profiles a PROCESS.

The final example of this gesture sequence shows a speaker who picks up the gesture performed by the woman in the previous example (right picture in Figure 27). His left hand also shows a grasping hand shape oriented down. It is moved towards his body, while he is referring verbally to a window handle (*das nennt sich Griff* ['that's called a handle']). Interestingly, although the gesture is similar to the gesture performed by the female speaker, different information is highlighted. The gestural stroke is executed on the noun *Griff* ('handle'). Moreover, the speaker does not refer to the action the object is involved in, as in the previous gesture–speech ensemble. These observations lead to the conclusion that the conceptual archetype of an object, embodied by the hand shape, is foregrounded verbally. The action of opening the window by pulling the handle, visible in the gestural movement, remains in the background. Accordingly, as the conceptual archetype of an object is construed multimodally and, thus, foregrounded, the multimodal utterance profiles a THING.

Concluding, although both conceptual archetypes object and action are mimed in all three examples discussed, this information is not set equally relevant by the speakers. Through the speakers' choices of specific lexicosyntactic units, the gestures become integrated into the utterance, while simultaneously highlighting either one of the archetypes or both. Thus, a close examination of the tight interrelation of speech and gesture provides insights into what meaning aspects are in the speaker's focus of attention (see Müller 2008b), because these aspects are singled out verbo-gesturally and made conceptually salient. In this vein, these gesture–speech ensembles make visible how a situation is construed.

3.4.2 Gestures replacing speech

The previous chapters made the case for considering gestures capable of realizing nouns and verbs both structurally and functionally. This section elaborates how speech and gestures interact in construing multimodal meaning when both modalities are not used concomitantly but sequentially. The line of thought developed subsequently is exemplified by means of the two examples introduced earlier in this chapter.

The first example shows a woman who is engaged in a discussion interrupting her utterance *Nein Staudamm. Ich wollte dieses* ('No, barrier lake. I wanted this'). A multi-stroke sequence joins in, starting on the definite determiner *dieses* ('this') and filling the subsequent pause. The gestural strokes are performed with flat hands, oriented towards the speaker's body, and moved up and down. This gesture exhibits the representing mode, depicting an object in motion, and it replaces a noun.

Following the argument developed in Section 3.3.3, the conceptual archetypes of nouns and verbs, i.e., object and action, are embodied by this gesture (and they are considered as embodied by most gestures speakers use). The hand shape invokes an object. The gestural movement mimes the object's motion. Yet, as the findings of the multimodal utterance condition revealed, the participants conceived and perceived the gesture as depicting an object only (see Section 3.2.4).

These findings lend support to the idea that the syntactic position of a noun imposes a specific view on the gestures used, namely a summary view. As has been pointed out before, the process of summary scanning results in grouping the individual states of an event so that it is apprehended as bounded and atemporal. Now, the lexical items listed in Table 2 show that the recipients of the multimodal utterances under scrutiny understood the gesture as depicting objects. Thus, it can be argued that the mode of summary scanning is imposed on the gestures realizing nouns, conceiving them as depicting objects. Moreover, because object information is embodied by the hand shape and not by the movement of a gesture, this form parameter is foregrounded by speech, more precisely by the syntactic information. Through this foregrounding, mental access to the concept of a specific object is provided. This object has been identified as that of a window, a screen, or a picture in the multimodal utterance condition. However, this does not entail that the form parameter movement is not of importance for the construal of gestural meaning. As the lexical items prove (Table 2), movement is certainly a key for the interpretation of the gestures because in some of the lexical items, the action of opening, as in the lexical item 'opening (of plates),' or the meaning of verticality, as in the item 'screen,' is construed. In the latter case, the movement is conceived as a particular type of motion, i.e., "fictive motion" (Talmy 1996). In the former case, the action an object is involved in becomes reified. Accordingly, the sequential view is not suppressed but it is not as salient as the summary view (see Langacker 2008c for a discussion of scanning modes salient in language). Therefore, when a summary view is imposed on the gesture of the first example, the whole manual movement is mentally converted into an object (Figure 28). Recipients mentally invoke the prototype of a noun, which is an object. The whole gestural depiction is not perceived in its dynamics, but it is conceived as an atemporal thing. As such, the gesture is not conceived in terms of depicting an action in the first place, but it is construed as miming an object in which the successive states are coactivated but conceived and perceived as accumulated. Accordingly, a THING is profiled in the process of summary scanning that is *not materialized by a linguistic unit but by a gesture.*

This analysis is supported by the findings of the manipulated multimodal utterance condition, in which gestures that were originally used in verb positions were inserted in noun positions and *vice versa*. Although this task appeared to be more challenging for the participants, the results give a clear picture: The gestures in noun positions were conceived as objects, in verb positions, they were considered as depicting actions.

In the second example, a woman recalls an event in which her sister tried to climb up the window to her apartment. The speaker describes the interaction

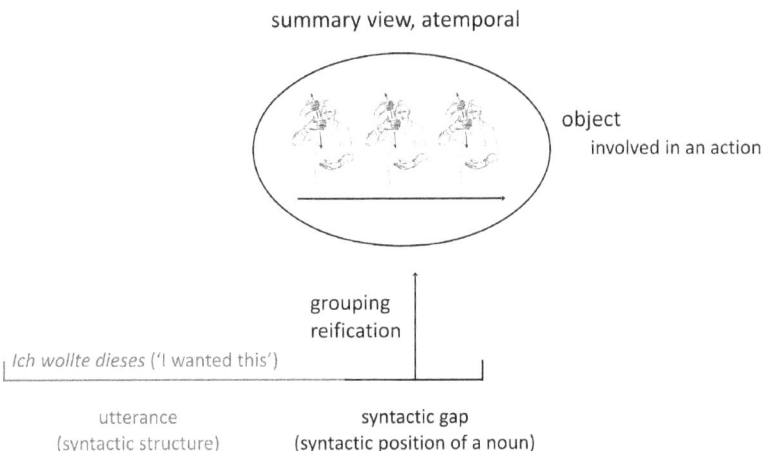

Figure 28: Summary scanning in the multimodal utterances "*Ich wollte dieses* 🖐 ('I wanted this' 🖐)".

between her, her sister, and her grandmother thoroughly. At one point of the narration, she says *die hat immer geschubst und wir hinten* ('she was pushing all the time and we from the back'), breaking off her utterance. On the second syllable of the adverb *hinten* ('from the back', literally: 'behind'), a gestural stroke joins in that realizes the verb of the subsequent syntactic slot. The gestural stroke is performed with a flat hand, oriented upwards. Additionally, the hands are moved upwards and away from the speaker's body, depicting the action of pushing an object – the conceptual archetypes of nouns and verbs. However, the results of the perception experiment reveal that the recipients of this gesture–speech ensemble consider this gesture as depicting an action only and not as miming both object and action (see Section 3.2.4). Hence, it can be argued again that the syntactic position of a verb has an impact on how gestural meaning is construed by activating the cognitive process of sequential scanning. As has been mentioned earlier, this process imposes a sequential view on a situation by scanning the successive states of an event through time mentally (Figure 29).

Accordingly, the action with its successive states, mimed by the movement of the hand, is foregrounded, which is why the whole gesture is construed as depicting an action. As such, it is argued that the syntactic position of a verb highlights the conceptual archetype of verbs, namely actions, embodied by the movement of the hands. Of course, the hands mime the action of pushing an object and information about this object can be reconstructed from the hand shape. Yet, it is argued that this information remains in the background and that the pushing movement is foregrounded by the speech. Hence, the gesture

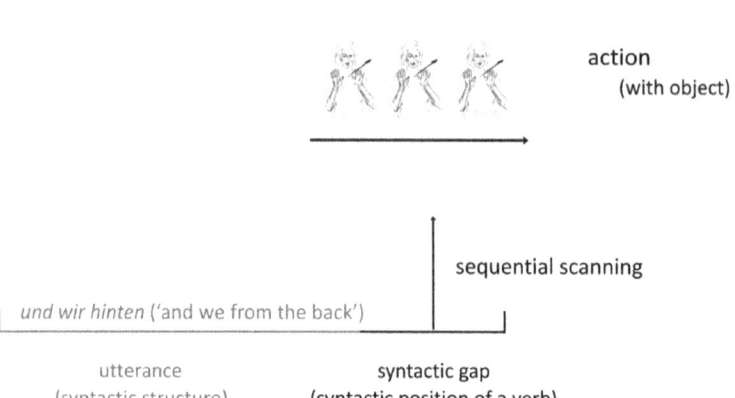

Figure 29: Sequential scanning in the multimodal utterance "*und wir hinten* 🖐 ('and we from the back' 🖐)".

profiles a PROCESS that is not materialized by a linguistic unit but by a gesture. This argument was also confirmed by the results of the third video condition in which the gestures were manipulated. In this example, the gestures were understood as designating actions.

To conclude, what the analysis of the two samples exemplified is that recipients draw on the same cognitive abilities as in the construal of verbal meaning. When creating multimodal meaning, the processes of summary and sequential scanning are held responsible for the construal of gestural meaning as objects in cases in which gestures realize the syntactic slot of nouns and as actions in cases of realizing the syntactic slots of verbs. In most cases, objects are mentally accessed by the hand shape. In other cases, the whole gestural movement is conceived as a reified event. Actions (with objects) are foregrounded by verbal syntactic slots. As such, the movement of a gesture offers access points to mentally construe an action. Moreover, the processes of summary and sequential scanning and the cognitive effort they are based on provide evidence for considering gesture and speech as integrated. In other words, the recipients were highly engaged in merging verbal and gestural information by adapting gestural meaning to verbal information. However, it is speech that "coerces" a particular reading of the gestures. In this vein, speech can be considered to trigger and impose specific mental operations on the gestures.

3.5 Summary

To sum up, this chapter presented the empirical view of gestures realizing syntactic slots of spoken utterances. Based on 2,879 lexical items that were elicited in naturalistic perception experiments this chapter showed that nouns and verbs in an utterance–final position are preferably replaced by gestures. When gestures realized the syntactic slots of nouns, they formed, together with their grounding verbal elements, multimodal nominals serving the function of an object or landmark. When realizing the syntactic slots of verbs, gestures formed multimodal clauses together with their grounding verbal constructions. Based on these findings, the question of what properties make gestures apt at realizing nouns and verbs of spoken language arises. Consequently, their semiotic structure was scrutinized, showing that gestural forms embody objects and actions which are considered the conceptual archetypes of nouns and verbs in the theory of Cognitive Grammar. When speech and gesture interact, the syntactic position realized by a gesture imposes a particular cognitive mode on the gestures. In noun position, the modes of summary scanning and conceptual reification are considered operating, leading to foreground object information embodied by the hand shape or the reification of the event embodied by the whole gestural movement. The gesture is conceived as profiling a THING. In verb position, the mode of sequential scanning is imposed on the gesture resulting in the foregrounding of action information embodied by the movement of the hand. The highlighted gestural information provides mental access to an action, the archetype of verbs. The gesture profiles a PROCESS. Hence, it is argued that the syntactic slots "coerce" a specific reading of the gestures.

Based on these findings, it is argued that the cognitive effort recipients make to interpret the multimodal utterances provides evidence that they are actively engaged in merging and, thus, *integrating* verbal and gestural information. If we observed only the switching of modalities, recipients might not be involved in the cognitive labor of "adapting" the gestures to the syntactic information exposed by the speech gap.

4 Semantic integration of gestures: constructing multimodal reference objects

The previous chapter provided empirical evidence for the structural and functional integration of gestures into linguistic structures of utterances. It was argued that gestures realizing syntactic slots are not treated as meaningless fillers by the recipients but as forming part of the utterances. Based on the observation that gestures were perceived differently when realizing nouns or verbs, it was argued that different cognitive modes are imposed on the gestures, namely summary and sequential scanning, resulting in different conceptualizations of the gestures. Accordingly, gestures were construed as depicting an object or a reified event in the case of noun positions and as miming an action when realizing a verb. In Cognitive Grammar, both are treated as the conceptual archetypes of nouns and verbs.

It goes without saying that the integrative processes on the level of syntax are only one aspect in the creation of multimodal meaning. Therefore, this chapter shifts the focus to the semantic sphere of the syntax-lexicon continuum proposed in Cognitive Grammar.

As has been pointed out previously, Cognitive Grammar conceives grammatical notions in semantic terms. This means that a strict discrimination of semantics and grammar as propagated by structuralists is not assumed. In fact, the claim that grammar and the lexicon form a continuum is fundamental for the theory of Cognitive Grammar. More precisely, both reside in assemblies of symbolic structures and it is the objective of a grammatical analysis to describe such assemblies, as Langacker (1986: 2) pointed out very early. According to him, "[l]exicon, morphology, and syntax form a continuum of symbolic units, divided only arbitrarily into separate 'components' – it is ultimately as pointless to analyze grammatical units without reference to their semantic value as to write a dictionary which omits the meanings of its lexical items." He continues to sketch out his view on grammar by stating that "formal semantics based on truth conditions is deemed inadequate for describing the meaning of linguistic expressions. One reason is that semantic structures are characterized relative to knowledge systems whose scope is essentially open-ended. A second is that their value reflects not only the content of a conceived situation, but also how this content is structured and construed" (Langacker 1986: 2).

Here, the chapter ties in by examining the semantic structure of speech and gesture in the cases under scrutiny. In doing so, the question of how speech and gesture are "structured and construed" in relation to the "knowledge systems" people ground the meaning of both modalities in. In other words, the semantics of the multimodal utterances under investigation are examined in more detail with the aim of specifying the conceptual archetypes, object and action gestures were argued to embody (see Chapter 3).

For the purpose of this investigation, the gestural forms realizing the syntactic slots are scrutinized regarding the "image schemas," "motor patterns" (see Cienki 2005; Mittelberg 2006) and 'objects of mimes' ("*Gegenstände gestischer Mimesis*", Müller 2010a: 155) they embody. The lexical items elicited in the gesture-only condition, the multimodal utterances condition and the speech-only condition are analyzed with respect to the "image schemas" (Johnson 1987), "conceptual referents" (Langacker 1987b) and semantic features they show (see Figure 30). This approach entails the analysis of both modalities, firstly, independently from each other and, thereafter, in relation to each other.

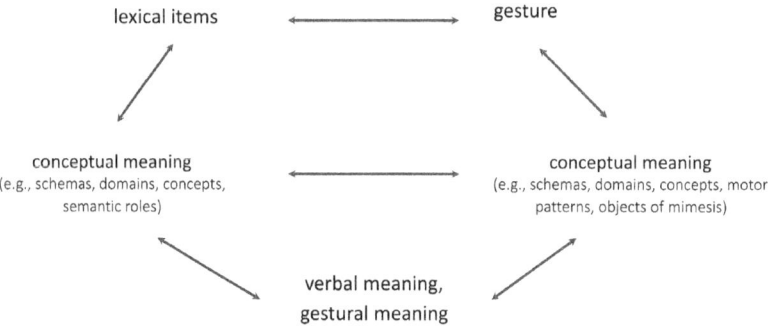

Figure 30: Schematic illustration of the comparative analysis of the lexical items and gestures.

The results of both the qualitative and the quantitative analysis will be exemplified in what follows by using the two examples introduced in the previous chapter. In doing so, the chapter assembles evidence for claiming that a) gestures contribute semantic meaning to the utterance which becomes specified as soon as they interact with speech, and b) a multimodal reference object is construed through the interaction of gesture and speech merging information from both modalities.

4.1 Do gestures integrate? Two perception experiments

This section accumulates evidence for considering gestures as integrated into speech on the level of semantics. The analysis presented in the following pages shows that gestures contribute their own meaning to that of speech and are not "overridden" by the semantics of the spoken utterances. For this reason, a comparative analysis of the lexical items elicited in both the speech-only and the multimodal utterance condition was conducted. Figure 31 lists the lexical items prompted for the example *Ich wollte dieses* ('I wanted this'), revealing interesting results. First of all, as has been shown previously (Chapter 3), the syntactic position realized by the gesture is ambiguous regarding the syntactic construction the utterance can be completed by, i.e., by either a noun or a predicate. In fact, the majority of the subjects, i.e., 13 out of 15, participating in the speech-only condition considered the syntactic position as part of a modal verb construction consisting of the verb '(to) want' and a main verb opening up the position of a noun that fulfills the function of either an accusative object (lm, in ten cases) or an adverb of time (in three cases). The multimodal utterance condition revealed the opposite, i.e., the construction of a noun was used in 14 out of the 15 cases serving the function of an accusative object (lm) of the verb '(to) want.'

Secondly, and more importantly for the analysis presented in this chapter, is the observation that the lexical items differ regarding their semantic meaning. The lexical items elicited in both conditions do not show any semantic overlaps. In other words, whereas the multimodal utterance condition creates the picture of an object being in motion or showing a vertical dimension (see Section 4.2.1 for more information), the lexical items of the speech-only condition diverge and present a rather broad range of meanings, such as concepts belonging to the domains of WATERS, VISUAL PERCEPTION, AUDITORY PERCEPTION, LOCATION, or TIME (Figure 31). Accordingly, no overlapping semantic features could be determined concerning the lexical items in both conditions.

The comparative analysis of the second example yields similar findings. Figure 32 demonstrates that while the speech-only condition prompted lexical items belonging to the domains of COMMUNICATION, POSSESSION, ITERATION, PASSIVE MOTION amongst others, actions such as pushing and pressing were elicited when recipients had both speech and gesture at hand. As a result, overlapping semantic features could only be determined in one lexical item elicited, namely the verb form *haben geschubst* ('have pushed') prompted once in the speech-only condition and eight times in the multimodal utterance condition.

In a nutshell, the semantic range of the lexical items in both examples was limited when recipients could draw on both modalities. As will be seen in the pages that follow, these meanings can be mapped onto the gestural forms. These findings furnish evidence that a) gestures contribute their own meaning to the semantics of speech and b) that the construal of meaning in the multimodal utterance condition was informed by both speech and gesture. The recipients did not focus on speech alone but also took the gestures into account when construing meaning.

Gesture-only condition | Multimodal utterance condition

Lexical items	Lexical items (translated)	Conceptual meaning	No.	Lexical items	Lexical items (translated)	Conceptual meaning	No.
Öffne das Ding doch mal.	'Just open this thing.'	process, object, motion, space	1	Ding, Gerät	'thing'	object	3
Klappe	'clapper'	surface, verticality, motion, updown, object, space	1	Ding, was sich öffnet	'thing that opens'	object, space, motion	1
senkrechte Fläche	'vertical surface'	surface, verticality, object	1	längliche Ding	'longish thing'	object, extension	1
Bildschirm, Wand, Fenster	'screen', 'wall', 'window'	surface, verticality, object	3	große Ding	'big thing'	object, size	1
wischen	'(to) wipe'	force, contact, motion, removal	1	Ding vertikal	'thing vertical'	object, verticality	1
Abgrenzung (in der Höhe)	'limits (in the height)'	bounded space, thing	1	Wandteil, Glas, Fenster, Bild, Plakat	'wall', 'glass', 'window', 'picture', 'poster'	object, surface (flat), verticality	5
hüpfend (dynamisch)	'jumping (dynamically)'	verticality, iteration, motion, enablement, up-down	2	Öffnen (Platten, die aufgehen)	'opening (panels that open)'	thing (reified motion), space	1
hoch und runter	'up and down'	up-down, verticality, motion	1	Auf- und Runterklappen zeigen	'(to) show an up-and-down flapping'	thing (reified motion), bounded space, up-down, verticality	1
auf und zu	'open and closed'	in-out, container, motion	1	vorne dran	'in front of (it)'	location, front-back	1
Sie ist irritiert. Sie aufgeregt.	'She is confused.' 'She' excited.'	emotion, affect, confusion	2				
Bist du bescheuert?	'Are you crazy?'	confusion, state	1				

Figure 31: Comparative analysis of the speech-only and multimodal utterance condition for the example "*Ich wollte dieses* 👆 ('I wanted this' 👆)".

4.1 Do gestures integrate? Two perception experiments

Gesture-only condition				Multimodal utterance condition			
Lexical items	Lexical items (translated)	Conceptual meaning	No.	Lexical items	Lexical items (translated)	Conceptual meaning	No.
hopp in die Luft	'hopp into the air'	verticality, goal, up-down, motion	1				
Sie wirft einen Ball	'she's throwing a ball'	force, object, path	1	haben gedrückt	'have pressed'	resistance, blockage, force, contact, (motion)	3
Volleyball, Basketball	'volleyball', 'basketball'	object; specific type of ball or ball game	3				
etwas hochdrücken, etwas hochschieben	'(to) press,' '(to) push something upward'	motion, object, force, contact, verticality, up-down	2	haben geschoben	'have pushed'	force, contact, motion, path, path focus	8
Ball werfen (Korb werfen)	'(to) play the ball (make a basket)'	motion; particular kind of movement	1	gegengedrückt	'have pressed against'	resistance, blockage, counterforce, contact (motion)	1
Volleyball spielen	'(to) play volleyball'	motion; particular kind of movement	2				
Tanzstil	'dancing style'	motion; particular kind of dance	1	angeschoben	'pushed start'	force, contact, motion, source-path-goal, endpoint focus	1
hochheben	'(to) lift upward'	motion force, verticality, up-down	1				
etwas schieben	'push (shove) something'	motion, object, force, contact	1	hochgedrückt	'pushed up'	force, contact, motion, path, verticality, up-down, endpoint focus	2
Bewegung (Tanz)	'movement (dance)'	motion; dance	1				
Sportübungen ausübend	'doing sport exercises'	motion; move in particular way	1				

Figure 32: Comparative analysis of the gesture-only and multimodal utterance condition for the example *"und wir hinten"* ('and we from the back').

The argument put forward is substantiated by the analysis of the whole corpus, in which the 978 lexical items elicited in the speech-only condition were compared with 975 lexical items elicited in the multimodal utterance condition. In line with the analysis presented for the two examples, a great difference between the conditions could be determined for 58 examples (88 %, Figure 33). In these cases, no or very little semantic overlap between the two conditions could be defined leading to the conclusion that a) the gestural meaning conveyed a different meaning than speech, and b) gesture was considered when interpreting the multimodal utterance. In the other 8 cases (12 %), overlapping semantic features between both conditions were identified, suggesting a strong impact of speech on the interpretation of the gesture. However, interestingly, a singular gesture was used in only two cases. Four cases showed a Palm up open hand, one showed a deictic gesture and another case showed a brushing away gesture but in referential use.

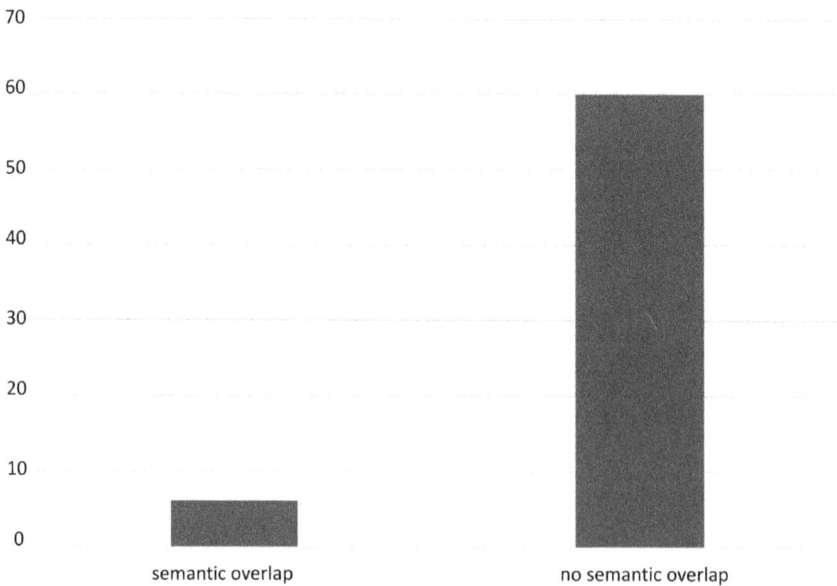

Figure 33: Comparative analysis of the speech-only and multimodal utterance condition conducted for the whole corpus.

Exemplarily, in one instance, a woman is telling a story about a visit to the Stasi Museum in Berlin. She is very affected and shocked about the documentation procedure of the Stasi and says *Da waren ja die Sachen detailliert* ('*Things there were detailedly*') and breaks off her utterance. She performs three strokes downwards with her left open hand, oriented laterally towards the center of her body, moving her arm on the horizontal axis to the right. The gesture in this example realizes the position of a main verb forming part of a multimodal clause. Notably, both the participants of the speech-only and the multimodal utterance condition chose verbs related to the domain of COMMUNICATION, such as *aufgeführt* ('noted down'), *aufgeschrieben* ('written down'), or *erklärt* ('explained'), to attach meaning to the lexical and syntactic gaps. These observations suggest that only a very few pieces of information were sufficient for the recipients to make up very similar meanings. Yet, this does not mean that the gestural meaning had no impact on the lexical items elicited in the multimodal utterance condition. On the contrary, if the gesture showed a form that would not match the meaning triggered by the syntactic and semantic structure of the utterance, the recipients would have probably adjusted their lexical items to the gestural form shown in the video conditions.

The conclusions which can be drawn from these findings are twofold: Firstly, the gestures inserted contribute their own meanings to the utterance, because the lexical items elicited in the speech-only and multimodal utterance condition differed in 90% of the cases. Hence, it can be argued that the form and meaning of the gestures are taken into account by the recipients and treated as equally strong partners in forming a multimodal utterance. Secondly, in the rare cases in which the semantics of speech has a strong impact on the perception of the gestures, i.e., in cases in which speech prompts lexical items of particular or related domains, the gestures show semantic similarities to these domains, and these resemblances are reflected in the gestural forms. These observations suggest that these cases show characteristics of constructions in Golberg's sense (1995) which lead to a high coordination of speech and gesture and an adaptation of gestural forms to the semantics of speech. Yet, more of these instances need to be investigated in order to have reliable data supporting this line of thought.

4.2 Why can gestures integrate?

The recipients responded to the multimodal utterances under scrutiny, mostly by giving feedback (16 cases) or by laughing (5 cases), in 21 cases of the data corpus. These observations suggest that recipients drew on information conveyed by both modalities – speech and gesture – and that the recipients construe meaning from the gestural forms.

The semantic information that gestures can contribute to the verbal utterance is at center stage in the following discussion. Starting from a perception experiment that reveals the complexities of gestural meaning, the idea of a gesture's inherent or context-independent meaning (see Ladewig 2010; Ladewig and Bressem

2013a; Müller 2010b) will be introduced and combined with the notion of "symbolic units" (see Langacker 1987a; for the conception of gestures as symbolic units, see Kok 2016; Kok and Cienki 2016; Ladewig 2012; Langacker 1987a; Ruth-Hirrel and Wilcox 2018; Wilcox 2002). The assumption associated with this line of thought is that gestural meaning can be conceived in terms of conceptual meaning. Based on the notion of gestural conceptual meaning, the cognitive processes held accountable for understanding the multimodal utterances under scrutiny are disentangled. For this, Langacker's (1987a) notion of symbolic units and Peirce's (1931) idea of a triadic sign relationship are linked to establish a cognitive-semiotic framework (see Daddesio 1995; Mittelberg 2006, 2013; Zlatev 2012). In doing so, special emphasis is laid on exploring Peirce's concept of an interpretant, i.e., the sense a sign carrier evokes in an interpreter's mind because it introduces a conceptual dimension crucial for the interpretation of semiotic signs.

4.2.1 Context-independent meaning of gestures

The idea that gestural meaning can be independent from speech is treated differently by gesture scholars. Whereas some researchers explicitly take a speech-independent meaning of gestures into account, others do not refer to this concept at all. The idea of a speech-independent gestural meaning is addressed implicitly when researchers, for instance, argue that gestures can fulfill an attributive or adverbial function and, thus, add to the verbal semantics (see Bressem 2012, 2014, to appear; Fricke 2012; Streeck 2002, 2016).[22] They also consider a speech-independent meaning when demonstrating that different metaphors may be expressed by speech and gestures (see Cienki 2008; Cienki and Müller 2014; Müller and Cienki 2009) or when showing that the topic of a conversation may be decoded from the gestural forms alone (see Streeck 1988: 72). The presentation of gestures without their spoken contexts was even deployed as a technique for getting "an initial indication of the gesture's independence from speech" and possible ranges of meaning (Brookes 2004: 191).

Some researchers who studied the composition of gestures out of form parameters (see Section 2.1.1) have addressed the idea of a context-independent meaning of gestures explicitly (see e.g., Cienki 2005; Kok and Cienki 2016; see also Kopp, Tepper and Cassell 2004; Ladewig 2011, 2014c; Lascarides and Stone 2009; Müller 2010b). Following Ladewig and Bressem (2013a), the determination

---

[22] Bressem (2012, to appear) discusses the idea of a context-independent meaning of gestures explicitly.

of a context-independent meaning of gestures is treated here as a separate analytical step.²³ The description of the "inherent meaning" of gestures (Ladewig and Bressem 2013a: 208) in the analysis presented below is not only based on the inferences drawn by the analyst, but, more importantly, it is grounded on a number of recipients' interpretations elicited in a naturalistic perception experiment, more precisely, in the gesture-only condition. The lexical items were analyzed regarding their semantic structures, as described above.

In what follows, the findings yielded by the analysis of the gestural forms and of the lexical items are introduced and exemplified by means of the two examples introduced in Chapter 3.

4.2.2 Context-independent meaning exemplified

The utterance *Wand, durfte man Wand sagen?* ('Wall, were you allowed to say wall?') with which a recipient responded to the multimodal utterance under scrutiny, namely *Ich wollte dieses* 👍 ('I wanted this' 👍), provides a first glance at how this multimodal utterance can be understood.²⁴ The recipient refers to a flat, upright object, extended horizontally that serves as a barrier between two spaces.

Drawing on both the recipient's response and the gestural form presented in Figure 34, we can conclude that the lexical item *Wand* ('wall'), used by the recipient in the sample, shares semantic features with the lexical items elicited in the gesture-only condition, which belong to the schemas of VERTICALITY, SURFACE, UP AND DOWN, and OBJECT (Table 7). The lexical items do not show all these schematic meanings, but 11 of them show at least one of them. Thus, overlapping semantic features can be observed when comparing the lexical items prompted in the gesture-only condition, but the range of meaning is still broader than in the multimodal utterance condition (Figure 31 and Table 9). Tying

---

23 Ladewig and Bressem (2013a: 207) posit a "3-step procedure" which is conceived of as a "discovery procedure" for the detection of patterns and structures in gestures. The first two steps aim at an investigation of gestures' forms and their possible meanings independent of speech. They comprise the segmentation of gestural movement (gesture phases), the annotation of form parameters, and the determination of the inherent meaning. In a third step, the analysis of gesture and speech is combined, focusing on the distribution of gestural forms in different contexts of use, the determination of their (sequential) positions, and the reconstruction of meaning and functions.
24 Of course, the speaker in this example had more information at hand than only the multimodal utterance. Yet, as will be argued in this and in the following chapter, the gestural form is pivotal for the construal of multimodal meaning, as it provides semantic information narrowing down the range of possible reference objects.

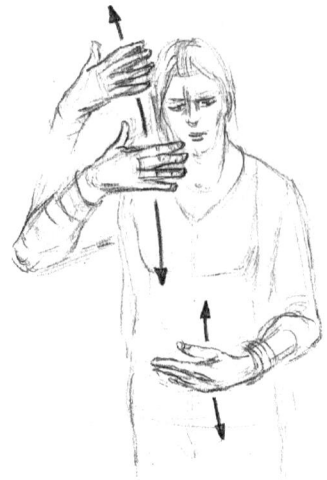

gesture phase	preparation	stroke	stroke	stroke	stroke	stroke	retraction
movement		up	down	up	down	up	
hand shape		fist	fist	fist	fist	fist	
orientation of the palm		towards body	towards body	towards body	towards body	towards body	
position in gesture space		center-upper center	center-upper center	center-upper center	center-upper center	center-upper center	

Figure 34: Gesture in the example *"Ich wollte dieses* 👋 ('I wanted this' 👋)".

in with the analysis presented in Chapter 3, this is due to the circumstance that speech did not provide an interpretative frame for the construal of gestural meaning, but the recipients were free in their interpretation and, thus, relied on their own experiences. Therefore, the gestural form clearly motivated the different lexical items (the form is illustrated in Figure 34). However, the recipients appear to have focused on different formal aspects while construing gestural meaning. They focused on single form parameters, such as the movement of the hand and its direction, as in the lexical items *hoch und runter* ('up and down'), *auf und zu* ('open and closed'), *Abgrenzung* ('limits'), *Klappe* ('clapper'), or *hüpfend* ('jumping') (Table 7). In other cases, the recipients appear to have paid particular attention to the hand configuration, i.e., the hand shape and orientation of the palm, and to the movement, as becomes observable in the lexical items *wischen* ('to wipe'), *Bildschirm* ('screen'), *Wand* ('wall'), *Fenster* ('window'), *senkrechte*

Table 7: Lexical items elicited in the gesture-only condition for the example "*Ich wollte dieses* ('I wanted this')".

Lexical items	Lexical items (translated)	Conceptual meaning	No.
Öffne das Ding doch mal.	'Just open this thing.'	action, object, space (process + thing)	1
Klappe	'clapper'	surface, verticality, motion, up-down (thing)	1
senkrechte Fläche	'vertical surface'	surface, verticality (thing)	1
Bildschirm / Wand / Fenster	'screen'/ 'wall'/ 'window'	surface, verticality (thing)	3
wischen	'(to) wipe'	force, contact, motion, removal, path; action of moving things away (process)	1
Abgrenzung (in der Höhe)	'limits (in the height)'	bounded space, verticality (thing)	1
hüpfend (dynamisch)	'jumping (dynamically)'	verticality, iteration, motion, enablement, up-down; action of moving one's own body up and down (process)	2
hoch und runter	'up and down'	up-down, verticality	1
auf und zu	'open and closed'	in-out, container	1
Sie ist irritiert / aufgeregt.	'She is confused / excited.'	emotion, affect, confusion	2
Bist du bescheuert?	'Are you crazy?'	confusion, state	1

Oberfläche ('vertical surface'), *Öffne das Ding doch mal* ('Just open this thing') (also see Chapter 3).

In the case of the lexical item *Bist du bescheuert* ('Are you crazy'), the recipients appear to have perceived the gesture as a whole, including all parameters, because these interpretations reveal an emblematic gesture. German speakers deploy the flat hand which is moved up and down in front of a speaker's face to convey the meaning of "to be a blockhead," implying that someone has a distorted vision due to a flat object located in front of the person's head. The remaining two lexical items listed in the last column of Table 7, i.e., *Sie ist irritiert/ aufgeregt* ('She is confused/excited') are based on the movement quality of the whole bodily movement and the speaker's affectual state expressed by the movement quality (see also Chapter 6).

In the second example, a woman reenacts the action of pushing when realizing the construction of a verb (Figure 35). Similar to the previous example, the recipient in this example responds to the multimodal utterance by laughing and asking *Echt?* ('Really?'). Although the second speaker does not verbally refer to the semantics of the whole multimodal utterance, such as in the previous example, her laughter and her question suggests that she has understood the multimodal contribution by merging verbal and gestural meaning.

gesture phases	preparation	stroke	partial retraction	hold
movement		straight upward		
hand shape		flat hand		
orientation of the palm		away body		
position in gesture space		upper center		

Figure 35: Gesture in the example "*und wir hinten* 👐 ('and we from the back' 👐)".

Table 8 lists the lexical items elicited in the gesture-only condition, revealing a range of different meanings designating actions, directions, or whole scenes. Similar to the previous example, these meanings can be mapped onto the gestural form, while the recipients appear to have focused on single form parameters, such as the movement direction reflected in the item *hopp in die Luft* ('hopp into the air'). In other cases, they have focused on clusters of form parameters, such as the movement, the movement direction, the configuration, and the orientation of the hand as is reflected in the items *Körbe werfen* ('play the ball'), *Volleyball spielen* ('play volleyball'), or *hochheben* ('lift upward'). In some cases, the gestural movement was conceived in general terms, as reflected by the

Table 8: Lexical items elicited in the gesture-only condition (example "*und wir hinten* 👋/ 'And we from the back' 👋").

Lexical items	Lexical items (translated)	Conceptual meaning	No.
und hopp in die Luft	'and hopp into the air'	verticality, goal, up-down	1
Sie wirft einen Ball.	'She's throwing a ball.'	force, object, path (action scheme: throw something, move arm rapidly forward, hold object-let got)	1
Volleyball, Basketball	'volleyball, basketball'	object; specific type of ball or ball game	3
etwas hochdrücken / hochschieben	'(to) press / (to) push something upward'	motion, object, force, contact, verticality, up-down; to put pressure on something with the hands and arms and move it upwards	2
Ball werfen (Korb werfen)	'throw the ball (make a basket)'	motion; throw a middle-sized round object	1
Volleyball spielen	'play volleyball'	motion; manipulate middle-sized round object	2
Tanzstil	'dancing style'	motion; particular kind of dance	1
hochheben	'lift upward'	motion force, verticality, up-down; to move something upwards	1
etwas schieben	'push (shove) something'	motion, object, force, contact, path; to put pressure on something with the hands and arms and move it upwards, use the whole body	1
Bewegung (Tanz)	'movement (dance)'	motion; dance	1
Sportübungen ausübend	'doing sport exercises'	motion; move in a particular way	1

lexical items *Bewegung* ('movement'), *Tanzstil* ('dancing style'), or *Sportübungen ausübend* ('doing sport exercises').

The insights emerging from these observations are twofold. First of all, semantic information can be drawn from gestural forms in speechless contexts and, hence, recipients are able to construe gestural meaning even if no speech, and, thus, no verbally expressed reference object is at hand. However, although recipients draw on the gestural forms, they focus on different aspects of form and, hence, conceptualize the gestures differently. They may, for instance, focus on the direction or the quality of a movement or pay attention to the bodily performance as a whole. Based on these different foci, different degrees of semantic complexity are conceived by the recipients. However, the gestural form itself sets limits on its interpretation. Though the range of meanings a gesture may convey can be multidimensional and complex, it is always constrained by the gestural form. The form, thus, reduces the variety of meanings a gesture may motivate. Exemplarily, a flat hand will most likely not be conceived in terms of depicting a roundish object, only if a roundish object is molded with flat hands.

Secondly, the fuzziness in the determination of gestural meaning is certainly due to the fact that information is missing in speech. Precisely because an external referent is not introduced verbally, recipients are free to interpret the meaning of a gestural form. Yet, they have to establish a link between a gestural form and the experiences that motivate such forms. In a second step, these experiences have to be verbalized, as was the task of the experiments. As such, the lexical items elicited here can reflect the understanding of the recipients only to a certain extent, because these meanings have already undergone processes of reflection and "translating" bodily movements into another mode of expression, i.e., language ("languaging of movement," Sheets-Johnstone 2011). However, they can give insights into the inherent meaning of gestures, which is informed by action patterns, motor experiences, schemas, or geometric patterns. When a gestural reference object is established, speakers and recipients associate the gestural form with entities, actions, events or whole scenes they have experienced. In a nutshell, gestural meanings are motivated by the form and are closely linked to the experiences that recipients have had when interacting with and in the world. As these experiences differ, a gesture may convey varying meanings, but these are always within the confines of its form.

The argumentation that was followed ascribes a particular role to the inherent meaning of gestures in the whole process of interpretation, namely that of a mediator between the gestural form and gestural reference object. For this reason, the inherent meaning will be set center stage in the following section.

4.2.3 The relationship between form and meaning in gestures

Before dwelling on the meaning-making processes of gesture, the relationship between the form and meaning of linguistic items is focused on. Its nature has intrigued scholars of language since antiquity.

> In Plato's *Cratylus*, the oldest documented of these debates, Socrates is asked to contemplate the question of whether names belong to their objects 'naturally' or 'conventionally.' The

latter of these two possibilities, namely that form and meaning are linked by convention and tradition alone, has come to dominate our modern thinking about language. Words, and more generally language as a symbolic system, are conceived of as being arbitrarily related to the world. (Perniss, Thompson and Vigliocco 2010: 1)

Accordingly, the relationship between a form and meaning in spoken languages is conceived of in terms of arbitrariness, i.e., form and material are not motivated and do not show any similarities to the entity signified. It is, furthermore, characterized by conventionality, which is an important prerequisite for the recurrent deployment of a (semiotic) sign and for being shared among speakers of a speech community (see de Saussure 1916). Hence, a natural (iconic) connection between an acoustic pattern and its meaning is not assumed. The acoustic image of the lexeme *Wand* ('wall'), for instance, does not reflect any properties of the object it designates, such as its flatness, vertical expansion or function of dividing spaces. Yet, the topic of iconicity in language has gained particular attention since the publication of Jakobson's (1965) seminal article *Quest for the essence of language*. It paved the way for including iconicity in functional approaches to language (see e.g., Bybee 2006; Givón 2001; Haiman 1985; Hopper 1988). Moreover, additional approaches captured under the term "natural language" originated from the 1970s onwards addressing the aspect of naturalness in phonology (see Donegan and Stampe 1979), morphology (see Mayerthaler 1981), and syntax (see Haiman 1985; for more information, see Willems and De Cuypere 2008). In these approaches, iconicity has been treated as a principle working on not only the lexical but also the structural level of language. Onomatopoeia or phonaesthemes, for instances, have been discussed regarding their iconic potential. The sequential order of events is considered as reflected in morpho-syntax or word order. Further notions discussed regarding iconicity include contiguity, repetition, quantity, complexity, or cohesion (for more information, see Perniss, Thompson and Vigliocco 2010). All these phenomena attest iconicity as a main structuring principle of language. Moreover, it is especially interesting for analyses within Cognitive Linguistics because of its potential to reveal general principles of thought (see below).

Iconicity has long been downplayed in sign language studies due to the fear of losing linguistic status (see e.g., Stokoe 1960). Consequently, the definition of structural similarities between signed and spoken languages has long dominated research within this field. Accordingly, since the rising interest of linguists in signed languages from the 1950s onwards, researchers have been preoccupied with accumulating evidence that signed languages are natural languages which can be described by adopting models from spoken language linguistics (see e.g., Klima and Beluggi 1979). This changed in the 1980s, when modality effects and, thus, the difference between spoken and signed language gained the attention of researchers. One objective was to discover modality-independent linguistic universals by comparing signed and spoken languages (see Steinbach et al. 2007: 140). Iconicity can certainly be considered as one of the effects a modality can have on language. Since the 1990s, it has moved into focus but remained a very debated issue. While some researchers consider iconicity to be a fundamental property of signed languages, others still struggle to fit it into their language models. Liddell (2002) sketches out four different approaches of dealing with iconicity in sign language linguistics. The first is to simply deny the existence of iconicity in sign language (see Frishberg 1975) by arguing "that since the signs are produced with handshapes, locations, and movements specific to ASL they are really not iconic" (Liddell 2002: 62). A second way is to recognize iconicity but to treat it as a modality effect. An example is Mandell's (1977) types of iconic devices used in the production of ASL signs. A third approach is to accept the existence of iconicity but to downplay its importance. An example is Hoemann's (1975) perception experiment conducted to test the transparency of ASL signs. He concluded that naïve hearing subjects are not able to deduce the meaning of a sign based on its form by stating that "[u]nder these circumstances, it is permissible to say that certain signs are transparent as to their meaning, but it is inappropriate to ascribe transparency of meaning to the Language Sign lexicon as a whole" (Hoemann 1975: 160).

In fact, Grote (2004) also showed that hearing persons need more time to establish an iconic relationship between the form of a sign and its meaning. However, she could also demonstrate that once this cognitive process has been entrenched by learning sign language, the denotation process based on iconicity becomes easier.

Last but not least, the fourth way of dealing with iconicity in sign language is to accept that iconicity is a crucial and fundamental means in the creation of signs. Making a case for iconicity, Liddell (2002: 65) affirms that this "approach recognizes that many signs are iconic but argues that iconicity is not an indication that the signs are somehow primitive or less precise than noniconic signs." Many other scholars have underscored their importance for grammatical processes (see Klima and Beluggi 1979; Wilcox and Wilcox 1995), metaphors (see Taub 2001; Wilcox 2000, 2006), or sign language phonology (see Brentari 2007), for instance, arguing that the "issues of iconicity and gesture should not be viewed as problems in the analysis, but as opportunities to learn something about language in general. The problem is not with ASL but with faulty conceptions of what language should look like" (Liddell 2002: 78).

Similar to signed languages, gestures are produced and perceived in the visual-spatial mode. Speakers make use of them to depict entities, actions, or whole scenes by establishing physical resemblance between a gestural form and the properties of an object or an action and, thus, draw on their iconic potential.

As Perniss, Thompson and Vigliocco (2010: 4) point out "[m]uch of what we communicate about is visually perceived (e.g., where things are, where they are going, how they are interacting, and what they look like), and the visual-spatial modality affords a visually iconic depiction of such information through the placement of the hands (as primary articulators) in the space in front of the body [. . .]."

Accordingly, gestures are motivated by the referents they aim to depict (see Müller 2014a, 2016; 2018; see also Mittelberg 2013), which are objects involved in actions, brought forth gesturally by the acting or the representing mode (see Section 3.3.2). Yet, the relationship between a gestural form and its reference object can be defined further by going beyond a gesture's aptitude to embody objects and actions. Noticeably, a gestural form may convey properties that specify the object or the action signified regarding size, shape, or movement quality. These properties drive the recipient's process of identifying the object or action a gesture depicts. Of course, speech plays a crucial role in this interpretation process, but it can be fairly unspecific regarding the properties mentioned. This cognitive process of construing gestural meaning is brought into focus in the following sections. As iconicity plays a crucial role in this mental operation, Peirce (1931) sign triad is introduced first and subsequently combined with Langacker's (1987a, 2008a) notion of symbolic units.

4.2.3.1 Iconicity in gestures

The application of Peirce's (1931) triadic sign model makes it possible to disentangle the different (cognitive) processes of gestural, verbal, and multimodal meaning construal, which is why it has inspired gesture scholars from many different disciplinary perspectives, including linguistics (see Andrén 2010; Bressem 2012; Fricke 2007, 2012; Mittelberg 2006, 2008, 2013), psycholinguistics (see McNeill 1992; Sowa 2006), and anthropology (see Enfield 2009; Haviland 2000). His theory aims to account for processes of meaning-making, i.e., representation, signification, and referencing, revealing the complexities of signification and interpretation. The implementation of his theory, therefore, acknowledges gestures' potential for making reference to the world and, thus, its status as a medium of expression. Moreover, its application to gestures approves the breadth and complexities of gestural and multimodal meaning construal.

> Peirce's semiotics by its very nature *includes* a theory of meaning. But semiotics is not about meaning in the ordinary way of taking it. It is about meaning engendered when signs are in their act of becoming signs, a becoming that includes sign interpreters as participating agents in the very *semiosic* process of becoming. I cannot overemphasize my

contention that meaning is not in the signs, the things, or the head; it is in the processual rush of *semiosis*; it is always already on the go toward somewhere and somewhen.

(Merrell 1997: xi, original emphasis)

The semiotic sign triad comprises three relationships, namely the Representamen, i.e., the material form of a sign, such as a sound chain or a movement, which may refer to an idea, a feeling, or a real entity, described as the Object. The third relationship, the Interpretant, is conceived as the sense evoked in the interpreter's mind which mediates between the Representamen and the object signified (Figure 36). It creates an additional sign in the interpreter's mind and can, thus, become a Representamen itself (see Chandler 2002).

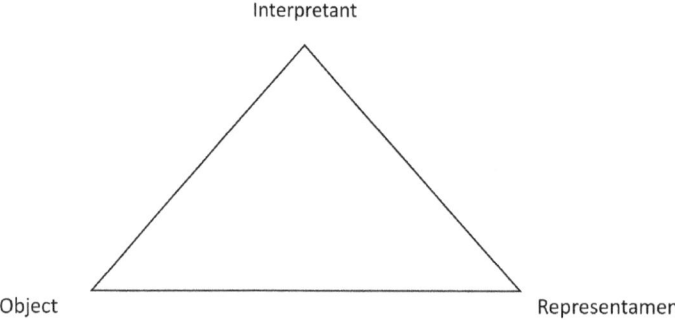

Figure 36: Peirce's (1931) triadic sign relationship.

With this third relationship, the recipient of a semiotic sign, termed the interpreter, is considered an important cornerstone in the process of meaning construal, because "without an interpreting mind there is no sign, that is, no semiosis and no meaning" (Mittelberg 2013: 759–760).

While no semiotician would doubt the legitimacy of the three *relata* presented, the fourth dimension, introduced as the Ground by Peirce, is very much debated.

> A sign, or *representamen*, is something which stands to somebody for something in some respect or capacity. It addresses somebody, that is, creates in the mind of that person an equivalent sign, or perhaps a more developed sign. That sign which it creates I call the *interpretant* of the first sign. The sign stands for something, its *object*. It stands for that object, not in all respects, but in reference to a sort of idea, which I have sometimes called the *ground* of the representamen. (Peirce 1931: 2.228, original emphasis)

Whereas some scholars oppose including this concept into semiotic theory (see Savan 1987; Short 1996), others affirm its significance (see Eco 1984; Liszka 1996;

Nesher 1984). Peirce himself refers to it as "an abstract quality or form of the sign" (Peirce 1960: 1.551; 2009: 552) which is conceived as a "pure form or idea" (Peirce 2009: 335).

Nesher (1984) is among the advocates of the Ground, attempting to define it within the context of cognitive theory. As such, his approach is of importance for a cognitive-linguistic perspective on the exploration of multimodal meaning construal. Building upon perception studies and the concept of schemata, as defined by Neisser (1976), he suggests that the Ground is based on a "process of *selection* [that] is called by some cognitive psychologists *filtering*, and by others, *attention*" (Nesher 1984: 312, italics in the original). Prower in Liszka (1996: 117) argues along similar lines when he describes the Ground as "a superordinate, abstractive, selective semiotic principle which regulates the valuation and selection of linguistic elements by making pertinent [. . .] only those predicates of a sign's object which are relevant to the signifier of the sign." Regarding the gestural modality, these processes have been discussed under the term abstraction or schematization (see Calbris 1990, 2003; Mittelberg 2010a, 2013; Müller 1998, 2014a, 2016) and metonymy (see Mittelberg 2006, 2010b; Mittelberg and Waugh 2009a), suggesting that the salient features of a reference object are selected and depicted by the hand. Following Mittelberg (2013: 764), the "Ground can thus be understood as a metonymically profiled quality of an Object that is portrayed by a Representamen; as such, the Ground puts the Representamen [. . .] to an interpreting mind into relation with an Object [. . .]" (Mittelberg 2013: 764).

Consider the following example of multimodal utterance in which speech and gesture are used simultaneously (Figure 37). Here, the speaker's left hand, considered as the sign carrier or Representamen, embodies properties such as flatness, horizontality, and verticality. It is related to the Object, "wall," mentioned in the verbal utterance, exhibiting the same semantic characteristics. The Ground, considered as an abstraction, exhibits these characteristics and foregrounds them. With the relationship between Representamen, Object and Ground, a sense will be evoked in the interpreter's mind, the Interpretant, which arises from our human understanding of interacting in and with the world. As such, both the Ground and the Interpretant are related to a recipient's mind and, thus, to people conceiving a gesture. The Object is the only relationship linked to the external world.

Iconicity can now be defined as "a perceived or construed similarity" between the three *relata*, including not only visual aspects, as Mittelberg (2013: 765) points out, but also as "'sensations' that cause something to feel, taste, look, smell, move, or sound like something else. This view again corresponds well with the multisensory basis of embodied image schemas and metaphors assumed in cognitive semantics [. . .]."

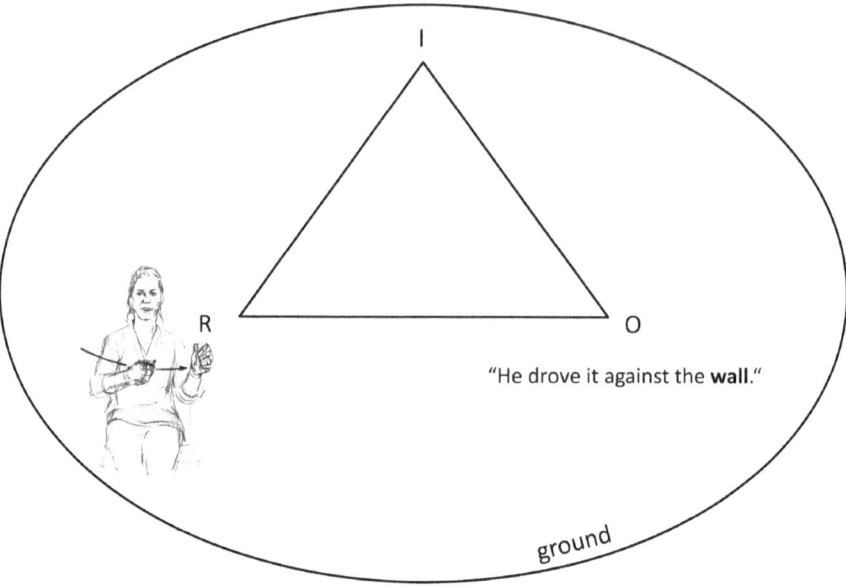

Figure 37: Example of gestures as semiotic signs.

With this conception, iconicity is not only defined in terms of a relationship between a sign carrier and its real-world reference object but is also understood as construed in the interpreter's mind. As this mental operation is essential for understanding the meaning-making process of spontaneously created, iconic gestures that form the majority of the corpus under investigation, it will now be explored.

4.2.3.2 From iconicity to cognitive iconicity

When conceiving iconicity as involving "an intimate interrelationship between form and meaning," cognitive theories, such as that of Cognitive Grammar, provide a suitable framework to describe iconic patterns as "they do not separate off linguistic form from meaning" (Taub 2001: 18). Therefore, iconicity is not treated as "an objective relationship between image and referent; rather, it is a relationship between our mental models of image and referent. These models are partially motivated by our embodied experiences common to all humans and partially by our experiences in particular cultures and societies" (Taub 2001: 19).

In order to investigate the relationship between the gestural form and its meaning, the concept of meaning construal as suggested by cognitive grammarians is essential, as it associates meaning with conceptualization and with subjectivity. Moreover, Cognitive Grammar has been described as a theory able to provide a unifying account of spoken and signed languages and gestures, because all three modalities are considered "manifestations of the same embodied conceptual system that drives the human expressive ability" (Wilcox and Xavier 2013: 90). Indeed, applying a cognitive grammatical approach to gesture makes it possible to not only explain the relationship between form and reference object but also elucidate the relationship between form and conceptual meaning, which are captured by the notions of Representamen and Interpretant in semiotic theory.

As outlined in Chapter 1 and Chapter 3, Cognitive Grammar conceives form and meaning in terms of symbolic units "consisting of a semantic pole, a phonological pole, and the association between them" (Langacker 1987a: 76). Lexicon and grammar are regarded as forming a continuum, while both are claimed to be fully describable as assemblies of symbolic structures. Langacker (1987a: 78ff.), furthermore, assumes that both the phonological and semantic structure[25] occupy different regions within the same semantic space. This claim is crucial for the exploration of iconic relationships within gestures, because it allows for a comparison of conceptual regions in the semantic space (see Wilcox 2002: 263, see also Langacker 1987a: 78). Similarity between the semantic and phonological structure is, therefore, described in terms of a distance relationship between both of them (see Wilcox 2002, 2004a). Accordingly, an iconic relationship is established between two conceptual entities, which can, thus, be conceived of in terms of "cognitive iconicity."

> [C]ognitive iconicity is defined not as a relation between the form of a sign and what it refers to in the real world, but as a relation between two conceptual spaces. Cognitive iconicity is a distance relation between the phonological and semantic poles of symbolic structures. [. . .] Iconicity is not a relation between the objective properties of a situation and the objective properties of articulators. Rather, the iconic relation is between construals of real-world scenes and construals of form. (Wilcox 2004a: 122–123)

Consider the example of the word *Wand* ('wall'), for which a great distance between the phonological and the semantic pole can be assumed as both sound and meaning have very little in common. In other words, the meaning of the linguistic item *Wand* ('wall') is not motivated and, therefore, sound and meaning are understood to reside in very different regions of semantic space, which is the typical case for spoken linguistic units (Figure 38). "This vast distance in

---

25 Semantic structure and semantic pole are differentiated as follows. A semantic structure is considered to be "a conceptual structure that functions as the semantic pole of a linguistic expression. Hence semantic structures are regarded as conceptualizations shaped for symbolic purposes according to the dictates of linguistic convention" Langacker (1987a: 98). Phonological structure and phonological pole can be conceived as corresponding to each other.

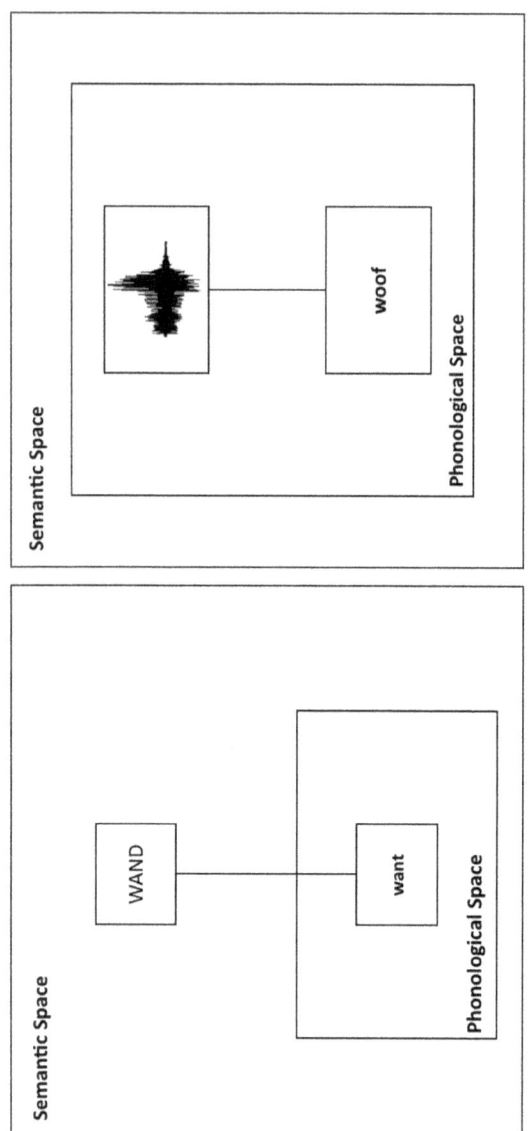

Figure 38: Distance relationships conceived for the oral-auditory mode (spoken word, onomatopoetic word), adapted from Langacker (1987a) and Wilcox (2002: 264).

semantic space, and the resulting incommensurability of the semantic pole and the phonological pole, is the basis for what linguists call the arbitrariness of the sign" (Wilcox 2002: 263).

However, as emphasized earlier, iconicity should be considered as a structuring principle in the spoken modality. Exemplary cases are the temporal order of events reflected in the linear order of linguistic units or onomatopoeia. In the latter case, the semantic and the phonological pole occupy similar regions. The onomatopoetic expression "woof," for instance, miming the sound of a dog, reflects a narrow distance between the semantic and the phonological pole, as form and meaning are similar to a certain extent. Moreover, due to their strong iconic relationship, both the semantic and the phonological pole reside in the same phonological space, which, on the other hand, occupies the semantic space (Figure 38).

Argued along similar lines, iconic relationships within the visual-spatial mode can also be conceived as symbolic units. The ASL sign for tree, for instance, "is obviously iconically motivated: the sign tree resembles the general shape of a deciduous tree" (Wilcox 2004a: 264). Thus, the relationship between its phonological and semantic pole is characterized by relative closeness. As in the case of onomatopoeia, both poles lie within the phonological space, which, on the other hand, resides in the semantic space (Figure 39).

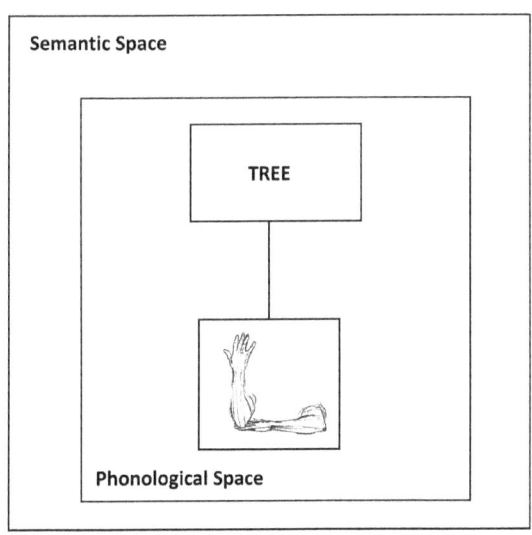

Figure 39: Distance relationships conceived for the visual-spatial mode (American Sign Language sign TREE), adapted from Langacker (1987a) and Wilcox (2002: 264).

Gestures can be conceived along similar lines, as will be exemplified in the following section. Spontaneously created gestures, characterized by relative closeness to their derivational base, are understood as showing a narrow distance relationship between form and meaning. On the other hand, recurrent gestures, which are schematized to a certain extent, show a greater distance relationship between form and meaning. Accordingly, unlike the cases discussed by Langacker (1987a, 2008a), who conceives a number of gestures as pure self-symbolization or self-reference, the approach taken in this book clearly pleads for an account of gestures that incorporates the complexity of gestural meaning creation. Accordingly, it is argued that only very few gestures can be regarded as symbolizing themselves. It is the vast majority of gestures that depict entities other than themselves. Even if a gesture represents the speaker's hand, it symbolizes the speaker's hand in a situation other than the moment of speaking and gesturing in most cases (see Wilcox 2002 for a similar argumentation of the hand presented in sign language).

4.2.4 Gestural meaning as conceptual meaning – Gestures as symbolic units

As soon as the realm of cognition is entered, the idea of conceptualization becomes an essential reference point for cognitive linguists.

> It involves imagery in the broadest sense of the word: ways of making sense, of imposing meaning. Also, the conceptualizations that are expressed in the language have an experiential basis, that is, they link up with the way in which human beings experience reality, both culturally and physiologically. In this sense, Cognitive Linguistics embodies a fully contextualized conception of meaning. (Geeraerts and Cuyckens 2007: 12)

The notion of symbolic assemblies has been introduced to grasp conceptualization processes in spoken and signed languages (see Section 4.2.3). It may very well be applied to gestures to explore their conceptual meaning and researchers have done so before (see Kok 2016; Kok and Cienki 2016; Ladewig 2012, 2014a; Ruth-Hirrel and Wilcox 2018). Accordingly, gestural forms and meanings are understood in terms of a phonological and a semantic pole residing in a semantic space. When gestural meaning is motivated by iconicity, as it is in most cases, the iconic relationship established between both poles is construed as a distance relationship between both poles. The meaning of gestures is not fixed, other than in words or signs. It is informed by the form of a gesture and can range from (image-)schematic meaning to whole action schemes. This meaning has been referred to as the inherent meaning of gestures, which can be understood as the semantics of a gesture conveyed without speech (see Section 4.2.1).

The inherent meaning of gestures is considered to inform the semantic pole of a gestural symbolic unit.

Consider again the examples introduced earlier. Based on the lexical items elicited in the gesture-only condition and on the gestural form parameters, the first example embodies the schemas OBJECT, MOTION, SURFACE, UP-DOWN, BOUNDARY, SPACE, or VERTICALITY (left picture in Figure 40). These inform the semantic pole of this gesture. The gestural form constitutes the phonological pole. Note that the gestural meanings referring to the emotional state of the speakers are not included here. These meanings would exhibit different properties.

Regarding the second example, the schemas FORCE, OBJECT, PATH, VERTICALITY, UP-DOWN, BLOCKAGE, and CONTACT, the action scheme of throwing something, or the motor pattern of moving one's arm rapidly were deduced from the lexical items and the gestural form (right picture in Figure 40). The schemas, action schemes, and motor patterns again contribute to the semantic pole. The gestural form is treated as the phonological pole of this symbolic unit.

Hence, the schematic meaning grounded in the gestural form contributes to the semantic pole of the symbolic units. Yet, gestural meaning also rests upon the felt qualities of movement experiences and on the knowledge of how the body can be used in performing actions.

> We are easily seduced into the habit of thinking only about the structural aspects of meaning and thought. This is not at all surprising, since it is principally the identification of discrete structures that allows us to discriminate features, to find meaningful gestalts, and to trace out relations among elements. But we must not mislead ourselves into thinking that this is the total content of meaning. Meaning is a matter concerning how we understand situations, people, things, and events, and this is as much a matter of values, felt qualities, and motivations as it is about structures of experience.   (Johnson 2005: 28)

Grasping these bodily feelings is not an easy task, especially when it comes to language. Yet, by taking gestures into account, we can gain a glimpse of the "flesh and blood of embodied understanding" (Johnson 2005: 27). Every gesture is performed with a specific movement quality, allowing one to draw conclusions about the felt bodily qualities. Acting gestures particularly give insights into bodily knowledge, as they originate from movements the body may perform in everyday situations. The gesture of the second example is, for instance, based on the action of pushing. This action (scheme) is not only the experiential base the schemas FORCE, BLOCKAGE or OBJECT are abstracted from, but it also grounds particular bodily feelings humans have when pushing objects of different sizes and weight. Consequently, not only the embodied schemas are represented by the semantic pole but also the action scheme of pushing a larger object, because we assume that, in addition to abstract schemas, motor experiences and the concrete bodily feelings they are connected with give rise to meaning. These different dimensions

128 — 4 Semantic integration of gestures: constructing multimodal reference objects

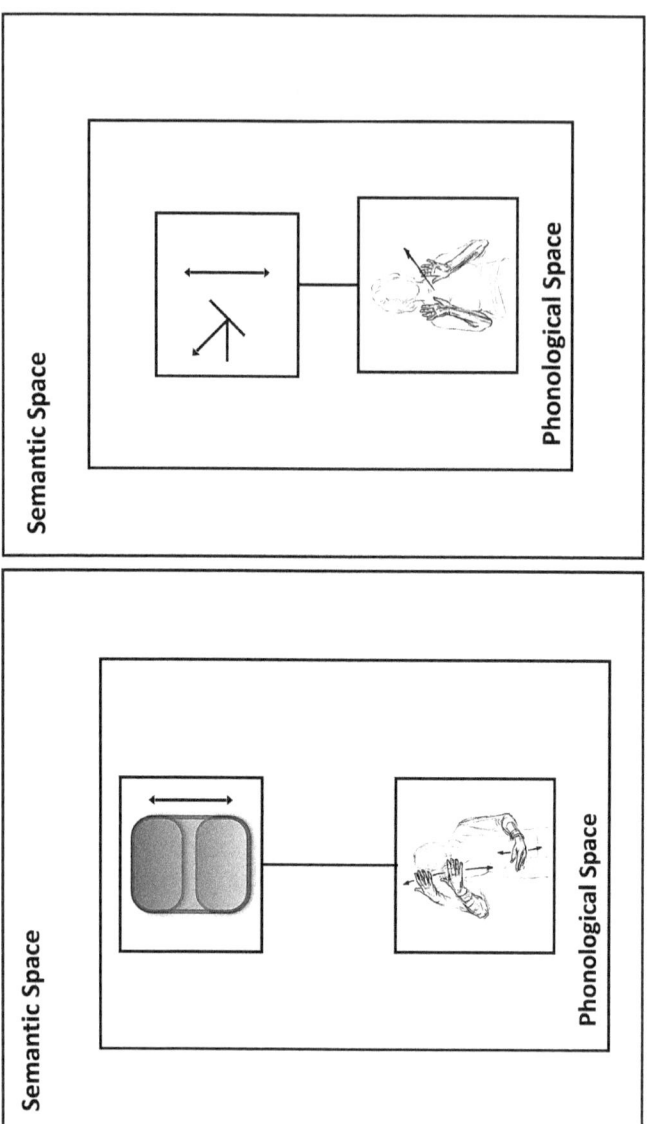

Figure 40: Cognitive iconicity in representing and acting gestures.

of meaning construal may very well comprise different levels of abstraction, yet, they are included in one semantic pole as they may all be activated to a certain extent.[26]

Based on embodied knowledge and felt bodily qualities, different distances between the semantic and the phonological poles are assumed for both examples. As mentioned before, Wilcox (2004a) captures the degrees of iconicity in terms of a distance relation between the semantic and the phonological poles. Similar observations can be made for the examples under scrutiny. A greater distance between the semantic pole and the phonological pole is assumed for the first example (left picture in Figure 40), while, for the second example (right picture in Figure 40), both poles are conceived to be relatively close to each other. These findings can be generalized for the whole corpus and for essentially every gesture. Points of departure for this argument are the different techniques of gestural sign creation referred to as "gestural modes of representation" (Müller 1998, 2014a). Accordingly, representing gestures similar to the one of the first example are grounded in the transformation of the hands into an object and in the visual perception of objects in motion from an observer's perspective (see McNeill 1992; Tuite 1993). Acting gestures, on the other hand, are grounded in the reenacting of mundane actions and, thus, in the perspective of a character's body performing the action (Müller 1998, 2014a; see second example in Figure 40). The latter addresses our em*bodied* experiences more directly than the former since motor programs and action schemes are part of our embodied knowledge. When objects in motion are observed, they are perceived only visually. Moreover, these objects cannot be felt. As human beings, for instance, we know how it feels to cut a piece of paper by using scissors. We know how to hold the scissors and how to move our fingers in order to make the blades move, and so on and so forth. Yet, we do not know how the object feels that performs the cut (if scissors had feelings). Accordingly, acting gestures are motivated by and abstracted from actions that we as humans perform ourselves and, thus, feel. Representing gestures are based on the visual perception of objects (in motion) – objects that cannot be felt in most cases (the representation of body parts form an exception). Consequently, a greater distance between the semantic and the phonological pole are assumed in the case of representing gestures. Both poles are considered as being closer to each other in cases of acting gestures. Note that feelings are experienced and

---

26 Similar to cases in which the first example conveyed the meaning of a particular emotional state of the speaker, these meaning facets would also be represented by the semantic pole. The two lexical items elicited in the gesture-only condition reflecting this meaning dimension are most probably based on processing the movement quality of the gesture and the speaker's facial expression.

construed differently than semantic or pragmatic information, because they are not considered as being cognitively represented (e.g., Horst et al. 2014; Müller and Kappelhoff 2018). However, they cannot be excluded from other processes of meaning construal, which is why they are addressed briefly in this section. This aspect is discussed in more detail in Chapter 6.

The argument put forward here provides an explanation of why the perception of acting gestures prompted a narrower range of meanings reflected by the lexical items elicited in the gesture-only condition than the perception of representing gestures. These observations are in line with Beattie and Shovelton's findings, according to which "iconic gestures shown in isolation from speech and generated from a character-viewpoint [are] significantly more communicative than those generated from an observer-viewpoint" (Beattie and Shovelton 2007: 230). With the conception of gestures as symbolic units, this chapter has, furthermore, provided means to conceive gestural meaning in terms of conceptual meaning. This notion plays an important role in the processes of elucidating the cognitive, interpretative processes activated in the recipients when encountering multimodal utterances in general and sequentially constructed multimodal utterances in particular.

4.2.4.1 Cognitive-semiotic processes of gestural meaning construal

The previous sections set out to expose what drives the construal of iconicity not only in spoken and signed languages but also in gestures. In the pages that follow, the three notions discussed, namely Peirce's triadic sign relation, cognitive iconicity (Wilcox) and symbolic units (Langacker), are combined in order to untie the cognitive processes of gestural meaning construal. This section will make a case for understanding the Interpretant of gestural forms in terms of symbolic units. As has been argued, the "interpretant gives rise to other signs, thus constituting the semiotic process of limitless circulation and interpretation of signs that derive their meaning only in the active process of *semiosis* in a given communicative act" (Mittelberg 2006: 28, original emphasis). In this way, the Interpretant is able to fulfill its role of mediating between form and reference object and, thus, is pivotal for (multimodal) meaning construal. Note, however, that the notion of symbolic units is not considered as *the* Interpretant but as a way to capture the conceptualization of gestures that informs the Interpretant and the process of semiosis it initiates.

Figure 41 shows two different triangles illustrating the cognitive-semiotic processes activated in the recipient when interpreting the gesture of the example *Ich wollte dieses* 🤚 ('I wanted this' 🤚) without its verbal context. The analysis presented is based on two lexical items elicited in the gesture-only condition. The first triangle (left picture in Figure 41) illustrates the cognitive processes

4.2 Why can gestures integrate? — 131

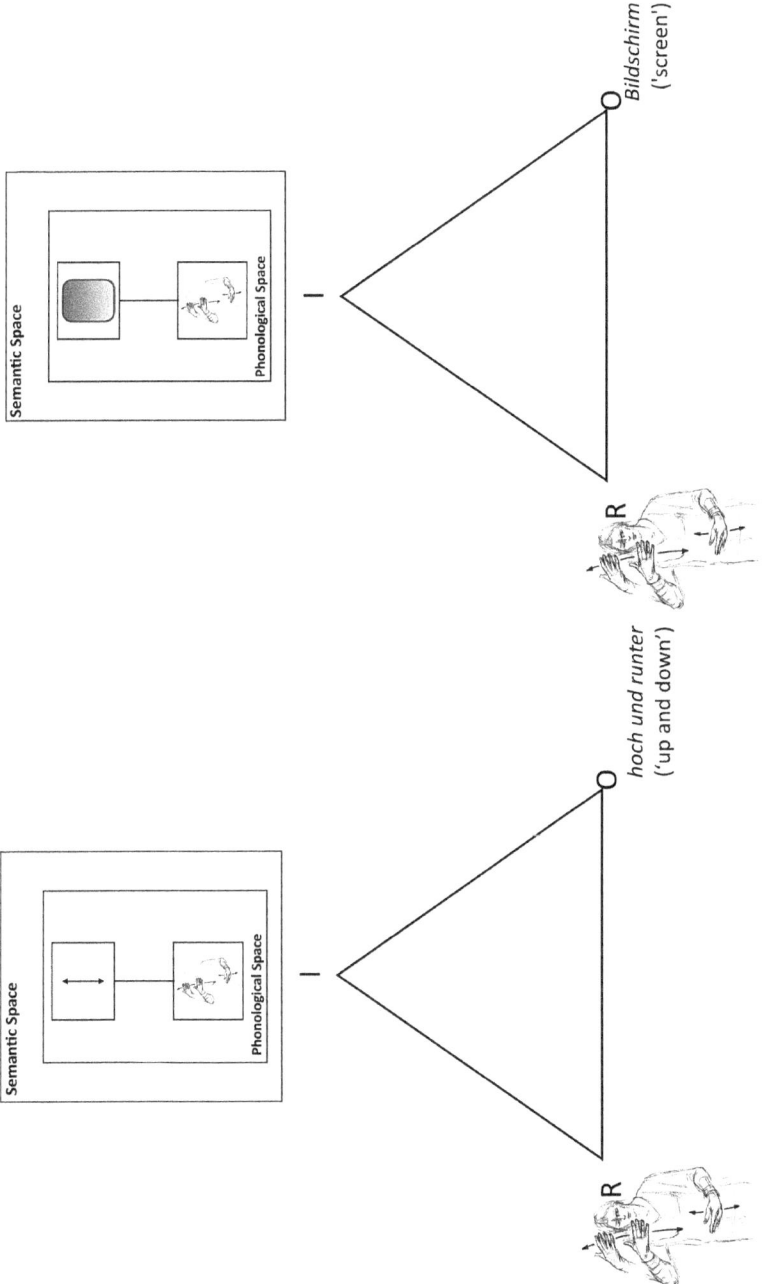

Figure 41: Processes of semiosis for the gesture of the example "*Ich wollte dieses* 👋 ('I wanted this' 👋)".

resulting in the lexical choice *hoch und runter* ('up and down'). The second triangle (right picture of Figure 41) takes the lexical items *Bildschirm* ('screen') as a starting point. Note again that the lexical items have already undergone the process of translating meaning from one modality into another. Hence, the context-independent meaning of gestures can only be captured to a certain extent, limited by the specifics of the verbal modality.

The form of the gesture, i.e., the up and down movement with flat hands, oriented towards the speaker's body, together with the lexical item 'up and down' gives reason to assume that the symbolic unit representing the gesture's meaning is informed by the schematic meaning of UP-DOWN (represented by the arrows forms in the left picture of Figure 41). Thus, in this case of gesture interpretation, the movement direction and the movement pattern were in the interpreter's focus of attention. Information of an object moving up and down was not verbalized by the recipient, which is why the flat hands remained more in the background. Based on this observation, the movement pattern and its direction are considered as forming the phonological pole coinciding with the semantic pole of UP-DOWN. The emerging symbolic unit informs the Interpretant which mediates between the gestural form, i.e., the Representamen, and its reference object (Object) identified as the direction of up and down.

In the second case (right picture in Figure 41), the symbolic unit shows a different semantic pole. If one takes both the gesture and the lexical item 'screen' into account, the schema of SURFACE (represented by the rectangular form in Figure 41) arises that forms the semantic pole of the gestural symbolic unit. Hence, in this case of gesture interpretation, the configuration of the hand and the movement pattern moved into the recipient's focus and can, thus, be considered as forming the phonological pole of the gestural symbolic units. As such, the flatness of the hands represents the flatness of the object and, thus, a SURFACE. The gestural movement represents the object's extension (and not the object's motion). This is a case in which the gestural movement is considered as a means of depiction. This symbolic unit informs the Interpretant, which establishes a link between the gestural form and its reference object, identified here as a screen.

In line with the argumentation presented above, two different semiotic triangles are presented for the second example "*und wir hinten* 👆 ('and we from the back' 👆)" (Figure 42). Based on two different lexical items, the triangles aim to illustrate the online cognitive-semiotic processes of the recipient when perceiving the gesture without sound. The first triangle is based on the lexical item *hopp in die Luft* ('hopp into the air'; see left picture in Figure 42). The second is based on the lexical item *hochheben* ('[to] lift'; see right picture in Figure 42).

4.2 Why can gestures integrate? — 133

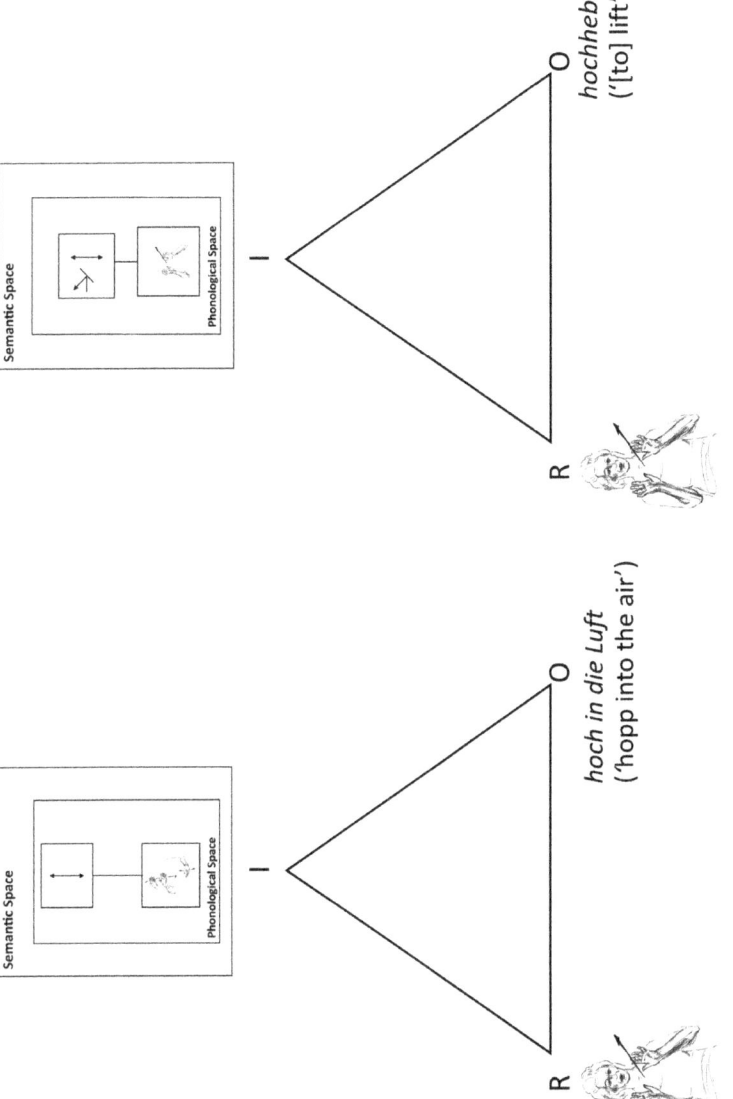

Figure 42: Processes of semiosis for the gesture of the example *"und wir hinten"* ('and we from the back' 🖐)".

When taking both the form of the gesture and the lexical item 'hopp into the air' into account, the schemas VERTICALITY and SOURCE PATH GOAL, both represented by the vertical arrow, arise (see left picture in Figure 42). In this case, the recipient conceived the meaning of the gesture only in terms of directionality, focusing on both the movement pattern and its direction. Hence, both are regarded as forming the phonological pole that coincides with the semantic pole of VERTICALITY and SOURCE PATH GOAL in the symbolic unit underlying the gestural meaning. This symbolic unit is regarded as informing the Interpretant, establishing an iconic link between gestural form and reference object, which is, in this case, a particular direction and a goal, verbalized by one recipient in the lexical item 'hopp into the air.'

The symbolic unit underlying the perception of the gesture in the second case shows a different semantic pole (right picture in Figure 42), because it includes the schemas VERTICALITY, SOURCE PATH GOAL, and CONTACT, which are represented by the different arrows. Moreover, it includes the motor pattern of lifting an entity, represented by the schematic drawing. The latter refers to the felt qualities of movement experiences and to the knowledge of bodily skills which are also considered as dimensions of meaning construal, especially in the case of acting gestures. As has been addressed earlier, this information also has to be processed when reconstructing meaning from a gestural form and, thus, is also considered as forming the semantic pole of the symbolic unit. Based on these observations, the whole gestural movement is argued to form the phonological pole of the symbolic unit, which, on the other hand, informs the Interpretant linking the Representamen, i.e., the gestural form, and the Object '(to) lift.'

To sum up, based on perception experiments, this section aimed to show that gestures can provide meaning on their own. Although it is not a usual situation (except for noisy surroundings) to perceive gestures without their verbal context, this analytical step is considered a necessary prerequisite in order to demonstrate that recipients can construe meaning from a gestural form alone, allowing them to draw information from gestures that replace speech and realize syntactic slots. Hence, the gestures under scrutiny are not considered to be fillers of speech pauses but are meaningful, providing semantic information that *integrates* with speech. This is explored in the following section.

4.3 How can gestures integrate? Construing multimodal reference objects

The previous section shed light on how gestures are construed based on a cognitive-iconic relationship between gestural form, meaning and reference object.

4.3 How can gestures integrate? Construing multimodal reference objects — 135

By pursuing a cognitive-semiotic perspective on gestures, the complex semiotic processes of interpreting gestures without their verbal context was explored, revealing that gestures are capable of transmitting meaning on their own, which allows them to replace speech. The previous section also showed that gestures without speech convey a broad range of meanings, but that this semantic range is always informed and constrained by the gestural form.

By extending the scope of investigation, this section focuses on the interaction of speech and gesture on the level of semantics, i.e., the semantic scope of the lexicon–grammar continuum assumed in the framework of Cognitive Grammar. The previous chapter has already shown that, depending on the syntactic slot realized by a gesture, different gestural information can be foregrounded that is either that of an object or an action. In what follows, it is argued that the range of meanings a gesture may convey without speech is narrowed down by the gesture's integration into speech. Based on the results of the multimodal utterance condition, it is argued that gestural meaning is specified in the interpretation process as soon as it interacts with speech. This idea does not come as a surprise. However, many gesture scholars argue from the perspective of speech, showing that gesture specifies the verbal meaning. Yet, it is argued here that in the interpreting process, recipients rely on gestural form features that are highlighted by the anteceding speech. Speech, thus, disambiguates gestural meaning and, in doing so, both modalities create multimodal reference objects.

4.3.1 Specifying gestural meaning with speech

To approach the question of how recipients merge the meaning of speech and the meaning of gestures to construe multimodal reference objects, the lexical items of the multimodal utterance condition were compared to the lexical items of the gesture-only condition in order to determine whether and, if so, how gestures are construed when realizing syntactic slots. The results of this procedure are first exemplified by means of the two video examples and, thereafter, presented in the context of the quantitative analysis.

4.3.1.1 Representation of a vertically oriented object that may create space

In the first example, the speaker is verbally reviewing her way of explaining a term to her teammates. At a certain point in her elaboration, she verbalizes the sentence *Ich wollte dieses* ('I wanted this'), interrupts her utterance and starts gesticulating. Her flat hands are oriented towards her body and moved up and down several times (Figure 34). This multimodal utterance served as the stimulus for the participants in the multimodal utterance condition, which elicited the lexical items listed in Table 9.

Table 9: Lexical items elicited in the multimodal utterance condition for the example *"Ich wollte dieses* 👇 *('I wanted this'* 👇*)"*.

Lexical items	Lexical items (translated)	Conceptual meaning	No.
Ding, Gerät	'thing'	object (thing)	3
Ding, was sich öffnet	'thing that opens'	object in motion, space (thing, process)	1
längliche Ding	'longish thing'	object (vertical or horizontal extension)	1
große Ding	'big thing'	object of a certain size (thing)	1
Ding vertikal	'thing vertical'	object, verticality (thing)	1
Wandteil / Glas / Fenster / Bild / Plakat	'wall'/ 'glass' / 'window'/ 'picture' / 'poster'	object, surface, verticality (thing)	5
Öffnen (Platten, die aufgehen)	'opening' ('panels that open')'	motion (reification), space (flat object creating space through motion) (thing)	1
Auf- und Runterklappen zeigen	'(to) show an up-and-down flapping'	motion (reification), bounded space, up-down + presentation (thing, process)	1
vorne dran	'in front of (it)'	location, front-back	1

The table shows that an object was chosen to fill the syntactic and semantic gap in 12 out of 15 cases, which make up 80 % of the lexical items gathered. A reified event (in two cases) and a location (in another case) were also chosen. Thus, most recipients interpreted the gesture as realizing nouns forming multimodal nominals (93 %). Further semantic features were determined from amongst the instances in which THINGs were perceived, such as a flat surface (five cases), a vertical dimension (six cases), or the property of creating space through motion (three cases). Speaking in terms of schematic meaning the subjects perceived the gesture in terms of OBJECT, SURFACE, SPACE, VERTICALITY, and MOTION. These are reflected in the gestural form, i.e., the flat hands oriented towards the speaker's body and moved up and down (Figure 34). Gestures used in the representing mode originate in a transformation of the hands into an object (see Section 3.3.2). The hand shape reveals that the mimed entity is flat.

4.3 How can gestures integrate? Construing multimodal reference objects — 137

Gesture-only condition

Lexical items	Lexical items (translated)	Conceptual meaning	No.
Öffne das Ding doch mal.	'Just open this thing.'	process, object, motion, space	1
Klappe	'clapper'	surface, verticality, motion, updown, object, space	1
senkrechte Fläche	'vertical surface'	surface, verticality, object	1
Bildschirm, Wand, Fenster	'screen', 'wall', 'window'	surface, verticality, object	3
wischen	'(to) wipe'	force, contact, motion, removal	1
Abgrenzung (in der Höhe)	'limits (in the height)'	bounded space, thing	1
hüpfend (dynamisch)	'jumping (dynamically)'	verticality, iteration, motion	2
hoch und runter	'up and down'	up-down, verticality, motion	1
auf und zu	'open and closed'	in-out, container, motion	1
Sie ist irritiert. Sie aufgeregt.	'She is confused.' 'She' excited.'	emotion, affect, confusion	2
Bist du bescheuert?	'Are you crazy?'	confusion, state	1

Multimodal utterance condition

Lexical items	Lexical items (translated)	Conceptual meaning	No.
Ding, Gerät	'thing'	object	3
Ding, was sich öffnet	'thing that opens'	object, space, motion	1
längliche Ding	'longish thing'	object, extension	1
große Ding	'big thing'	object, size	1
Ding vertikal	'thing vertical'	object, verticality	1
Wandteil, Glas, Fenster, Bild, Plakat	'wall', 'glass', 'window', 'picture', 'poster'	object, surface (flat), verticality	5
Öffnen (Platten, die aufgehen)	'opening (panels that open)'	thing (reified motion), space	1
Auf- und Runterklappen zeigen	'(to) show an up-and-down flapping'	thing (reified motion), bounded space, up-down, verticality	1
vorne dran	'in front of (it)'	location, front-back	1

Figure 43: Comparison of lexical items elicited in the gesture-only and multimodal utterance condition for the example "*Ich wollte dieses*👆 ('I wanted this' 👆)".

The movement either embodies the vertical dimension of the object represented (movement as depictive means, see Section 4.2.4) or shows that two parts of the reference object are moving up and down, creating an empty space between them.

The comparative analysis of the lexical items discussed to the ones elicited in the gesture-only condition reveals a great variance (Figure 43). As addressed in the previous section, a broad range of meanings is prompted when recipients perceive the gesture without its verbal context, yet, this semantic range is motivated by the gestural form. When speech and gesture intertwine, the range of meanings is reduced to a great extent. Whereas the subjects in the gesture-only condition referred to actions such as 'jumping' or '(to) wipe', to objects such as a 'screen,' a 'clapper,' or a 'window,' to directions such as 'up and down,' to states such as 'open and closed,' or to emotional states as reflected in the sentences 'She is confused,' they predominantly referred to objects or reified actions in the multimodal utterance condition. In addition, these objects show specific attributes, such as flatness, vertical expansion, or the opportunity to create space by the movable parts of the object referred to.

These observations suggest that the meaning of the gesture is specified and that the range of meaning a gesture may convey is narrowed down when gesture interacts with speech. This not only regards the construal of meaning in terms of THINGs or PROCESSes located in the grammatical sphere of the grammar-lexicon continuum, but it also concerns very specific semantic information conveyed by the different form parameters. As such, in the example observed, specific semantic attributes conveyed by the form features are highlighted by speech and made salient to a recipient. Interestingly, *few pieces of verbal information are needed to construe the gesture in a certain way* which underscores gestures' status as a medium of expression (see also Chapter 2).

4.3.1.2 Reenacting a pushing action

In the second example, a woman is telling a story about an incident in which her sister, coming home from a wedding party, is trying to enter the apartment by climbing up to the window because she has forgotten her key. Talking about her attempt to climb up to the window, the speaker uses the sentence "*und wir hinten* 👋 ('and we from the back' 👋)", breaks off her verbal utterance and starts gesticulating by reenacting a pushing action. This multimodal utterance served as the stimulus for the participants of the experiment. The lexical meanings elicited in this condition are listed in Table 10, with the conceptual meanings as reconstructed in the analysis.

As has been mentioned earlier (see the analysis presented in Chapter 3), the recipients interpreted the gestures as realizing verbs forming multimodal clause

4.3 How can gestures integrate? Construing multimodal reference objects — **139**

Table 10: Lexical items elicited in the multimodal utterance condition for the example "*und wir hinten* 👋 ('and we from the back' 👋)".

Lexical items	Lexical items translated	Conceptual meaning	No.
haben gedrückt	'have pressed'	resistance, blockage, force, contact, (motion); (to) put pressure on something with the hands, perform small movements with the hands and arms	3
haben geschoben / schieben	'have pushed' / '(to) push'	force, contact, motion, path, path focus; to put pressure on something with the hands and arms, perform larger movements with the hands or arms, use of whole body	8
haben gegengedrückt	'have pressed against'	resistance, blockage, counterforce, contact, (motion); (to) put pressure on something with the hands, perform small movements with the hands and arms	1
schoben an	'pushed start'	force, contact, motion, source-path-goal; (to) put pressure on something with the hands, perform small, abrupt movements	1
schubsten hoch	'pushed up'	force, contact, motion, path, verticality, up-down, endpoint focus; to put pressure on something with the hands, perform very small, abrupt movements upwards	1

structures. These verbs refer to pushing actions, showing different degrees of pressure exertion, body involvement, and the distance covered by the movement of the arms. These semantic distinctions are discernable in terms of the schemas RESISTANCE, BLOCKAGE, COUNTERFORCE, CONTACT, FORCE, MOTION, and PATH. In most cases, that is in 8 out 15 cases (53 %), the subjects conceived the gesture as depicting the action of pushing, exhibiting the conceptual meaning of FORCE, CONTACT, PATH and MOTION. Four subjects (27 % of the cases) conceived the gesture in terms of pressing, evoking the schemas RESISTANCE, BLOCKAGE, COUNTERFORCE, CONTACT, and MOTION. In one case, the gesture was conceived as a pushing-start action, which involves smaller and more abrupt movements. This kind of pushing action is reminiscent of the same schemas listed for the lexical item *haben geschoben / schieben* ('have pushed/[to] push'), but in this case, the GOAL of the action is emphasized rather than the PATH. In another case, the direction of the pushing movement (VERTICALITY, UP-DOWN) was mentioned.

Taking the gestural form into account, showing two flat hands, oriented and moved upwards and away from the speaker's body, it becomes noticeable that the conceptual meanings listed above are reflected in the gestural form. The acting mode indicates that the gesture originates in an action. The realizations of the parameters hand shape and orientation suggest that the speaker's hands manipulate a larger object. The movement indicates that an object not referred to by the subjects is moved upwards.

Figure 44 reveals a difference in the semantics between the lexical items elicited in the gesture-only condition and in the multimodal utterance condition. Whereas the gesture-only condition prompted items referring to actions, such as throwing or pressing, things, such as basketball or volleyball, events, such as throwing the ball, or directions ('into the air'), the items elicited in the multimodal utterance condition referred only to the actions of pushing and pressing, which show particular attributes, such as the use of the flat hands moved away from a subject's body. The objects manipulated or the directions of movement were not specified in the lexical items and can, thus, be considered as backgrounded and not in the recipient's focus of attention.

The argument put forward for the first example (Table 9) holds in fact for the second. The meaning of the gesture is specified as soon as it interacts with speech, which is, in the case under scrutiny, an antecedent verbal utterance including only a trajectory and modifier. Not only is the gesture's meaning specified regarding profiling a THING or a PROCESS or both, but it is also made more explicit in terms of particular semantic attributes allowing one to identify the PROCESS the speaker is reenacting. These attributes, motivated by form parameters, are highlighted by a very few pieces of verbal information.

The arguments developed by means of the two examples hold for all examples examined in the comparative analysis of the lexical items elicited in the gesture-only and multimodal utterance condition. Every example was specified regarding expressing verbal, nominal, or clausal information. Moreover, in the interaction of speech and gesture, kinesic and semantic features of the gestures were highlighted allowing the identification of a particular THING or PROCESS. Only in one case, that of the Ring gesture, was a specific meaning of the gesture already identified in the gesture-only condition, which is that of a positive evaluation.

To conclude, the findings reveal that speech specifies gestural meaning by narrowing down its semantic range. Moreover, fairly few pieces of verbal information are needed to not only specify gestural meaning in terms of profiling a THING, a PROCESS, or both, but also to concretize its semantic attributes necessary to identify a certain object (THING) or action (PROCESS). In a nutshell, speech and gesture together help to establish a multimodal reference object. A reference object is also construed when recipients interpret the gesture without its verbal context. Yet, when speech and gesture merge, recipients construe very similar reference objects when perceiving one and the same multimodal utterance. This process is elaborated in the subsequent section.

4.3 How can gestures integrate? Construing multimodal reference objects — 141

Gesture-only condition				Multimodal utterance condition			
Lexical items	Lexical items (translated)	Conceptual meaning	No.	Lexical items	Lexical items (translated)	Conceptual meaning	No.
hopp in die Luft	'hopp into the air'	verticality, goal, up-down, motion	1				
Sie wirft einen Ball	'she's throwing a ball'	force, object, path	1	haben gedrückt	'have pressed'	resistance, blockage, force, contact, (motion)	3
Volleyball, Basketball	'volleyball', 'basketball'	object; specific type of ball or ball game	3				
etwas hochdrücken, etwas hochschieben	'(to) press,' '(to) push something upward'	motion, object, force, contact, verticality, up-down	2	haben geschoben	'have pushed'	force, contact, motion, path, path focus	8
Ball werfen (Korb werfen)	'(to) play the ball (make a basket)'	motion; particular kind of movement	1	gegengedrückt	'have pressed against'	resistance, blockage, counterforce, contact (motion)	1
Volleyball spielen	'(to) play volleyball'	motion; particular kind of movement	2				
Tanzstil	'dancing style'	motion; particular kind of dance	1				
hochheben	'(to) lift upward'	motion force, verticality, up-down	1	angeschoben	'pushed start'	force, contact, motion, source-path-goal, endpoint focus	1
etwas schieben	'push (shove) something'	motion, object, force, contact	1				
Bewegung (Tanz)	'movement (dance)'	motion; dance	1	hochgedrückt	'pushed up'	force, contact, motion, path, verticality, up-down, endpoint focus	2
Sportübungen ausübend	'doing sport exercises'	motion; move in particular way	1				

Figure 44: Comparison of lexical items elicited in the gesture-only and multimodal utterance condition for the example *"und wir hinten 👈"* ('and we from the back' 👈).

142 — 4 Semantic integration of gestures: constructing multimodal reference objects

4.3.2 Merging verbal and gestural meaning

The cognitive-semiotic processes of creating multimodal reference objects, such as the ones listed in Table 9 and Table 10, are spelled out in what follows. Guided by the objective of exploring how recipients create meaning with different semiotic resources, Peirce's sign triangle is applied to disentangle the different semiotic steps of multimodal meaning construal. Contrary to what has often been studied, i.e., the simultaneous use of speech and gesture, it is crucial here to follow the sequential arrangement of both modalities. In other words, the starting point is the meaning of speech, which is subsequently merged with the meaning of gestures, as these are used when the verbal utterance has been broken off. Note again that the perspective of the recipient is taken when analyzing the multimodal utterances under scrutiny. The processes of establishing a multimodal reference object are exemplified by means of both samples used previously.

4.3.2.1 Process of construing a multimodal reference object in the example "Ich wollte dieses ✋ ('I wanted this' ✋)"

As has been outlined previously, the speaker in the first example is engaged in clarifying her explanation strategy. The analysis presented in the following pages focuses on the utterances *Ich wollte dieses* ✋ ('I wanted this' ✋), which is "completed" by a gesture. As was argued before, in this case, the gesture realized the syntactic slot of a noun and forms, together with speech, a multimodal nominal (see Chapter 3 for a detailed analysis). Table 9 has shown that five out of 15 lexical items (33 %) elicited in the multimodal utterance condition refer to objects showing a flat surface and a vertical dimension. This group of lexical choices serves as a sample domain for the chain of sign triads presented in Figure 45.

Accordingly, the definite determiner *dieses* ('this') following the modal verb *wollte* ('wanted') grounds a nominal slot which is realized by a gesture. The verbal utterance, more specifically the grounding element and the syntactic slot exposed, serve as the Representamen (R_1) of the first sign triad. This Representamen provides only a little information about the reference object (O_1), namely the profiling of a THING. Yet, the profiled THING not only serves as the reference object (O_1) of the first sign triad, but it is also the Object of the second triad (O_2), in which a gestural form serves as the Representamen (R_2). Hence, the verbally profiled entity is simultaneously the reference object of the gesture "filling in" for a verbal construction. Through this realization of a noun, certain formal and semantic aspects of the gesture are highlighted, namely the hand shape providing access to the construal of entities (see Section 3.4.2). Moreover, an iconic relationship between the gestural form (R_2) and its reference object (O_2) is created by way of the

4.3 How can gestures integrate? Construing multimodal reference objects

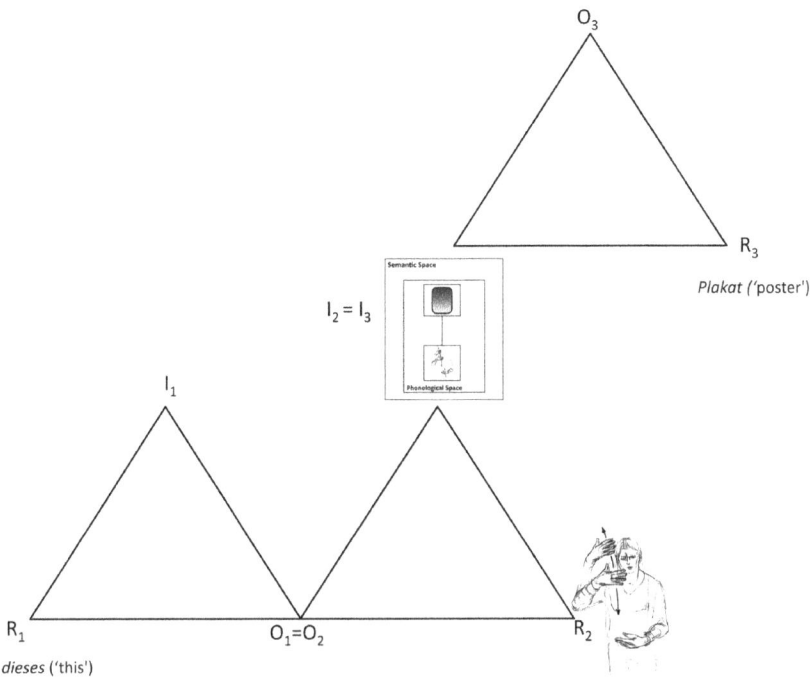

Figure 45: The construal of a multimodal reference object in the example "*Ich wollte dieses* 🖐 ('I wanted this' 🖐)".

conceptualized meaning of the gestural form – the Interpretant (I_2). In this way, form, its conceptual meaning, and the reference object of an entity are associated. The final step is to fuse these verbally and gesturally created signs into a third sign triad which is based on the Interpretant of the gesture (I_2) serving as the Interpretant of the lexical item (I_3) *Plakat* ('poster'). It associates the sound chain of this lexical item (R_3) with the object it refers to (O_3), a poster. A reference object is construed with these cognitive-semiotic steps informed by speech and a speech-replacing gesture.

4.3.2.2 Process of construing a multimodal reference object in the example "*und wir hinten* 🖐 ('and we from the back' 🖐)"

In the second example introduced, the speaker is telling a story about the attempt to climb up to a window to access an apartment. The focal utterance taken from the story is *und wir hinten* 🖐 ('and we from the back' 🖐), which the speaker herself broke off and terminated with a gesture.

144 — 4 Semantic integration of gestures: constructing multimodal reference objects

Table 10 demonstrated that the majority of the lexical items prompted in the multimodal utterance condition designate a pushing action, which varies in the degree of pressure exerted, the involvement of the whole body, and the distance covered by the movement of the arms and the rest of the body. The lexical item of *haben geschoben* ('have pushed'), as taken from the items elicited (Table 10), serves to exemplify the construal of a multimodal reference object in this example. The cognitive-semiotic process the designated action is considered to be based on is illustrated in Figure 46. It shows the first sign triad, in which the verbal utterance *und wir hinten* ('and we from the back') and the subsequent syntactic slot serve as the Representamen (R_1) The syntactic slot exposed profiles a PROCESS serving as the reference object (O_1) of not only this first sign triad but also the second (O_2), which has a gestural Representamen (R_2). With the PROCESS profiled, the movement of the gestural Representamen (R_2) is foregrounded, thus, providing access to the construal of an action. The specific action of pushing is brought forth by the Interpretant of the gesture (I_2), its symbolic unit, which mediates between the gestural Representamen (R_2) and

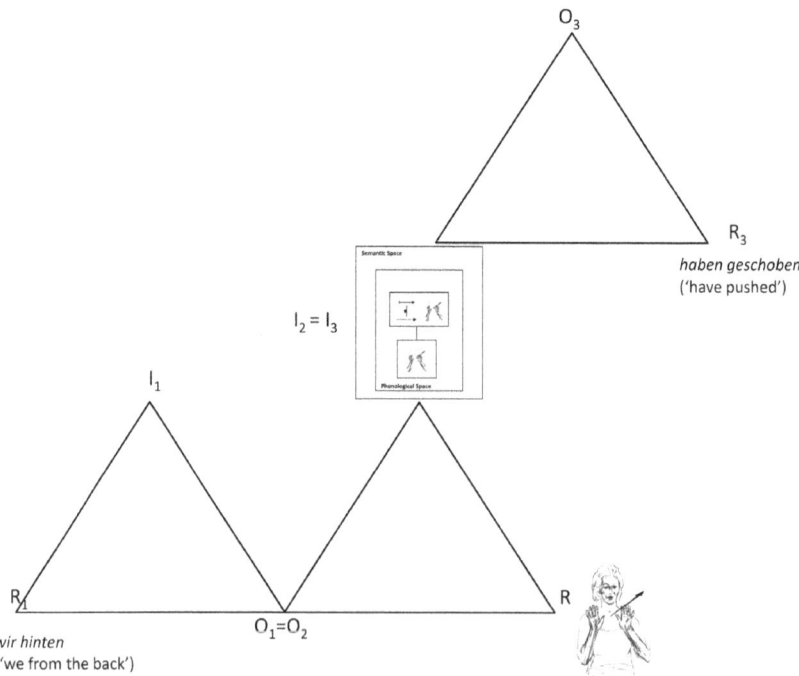

Figure 46: The construal of a multimodal reference object in "*und wir hinten* 👋 ('and we from the back' 👋)".

its reference object (O_2), thus, establishing an iconic link between them. At the same time, it informs the Interpretant of the third sign triad (I_3), which associates the verbal Representamen (R_3), *haben geschoben* ('have pushed') and the action designated (O_3). Using these cognitive-semiotic steps, a reference object is construed which is informed by both verbal and gestural information.

To sum up, two chains of sign triads were put forward (Figure 45 and Figure 46) combining Peirce's notion of a triad sign relationship consisting of the Representamen, Interpretant, and the Object, with Langacker's notion of symbolic units. The point of departure for this undertaking was the aim of elucidating the conceptualization of the semiotic resources speech and gesture and the construal of multimodal reference objects. The linear ordering of the chains aims to reflect the sequential nature of the multimodal utterances under scrutiny and, thus, to grasp the temporal unfolding of multimodal meaning as perceived by the recipients. It was argued that recipients merge verbal and gestural information to construe multimodal reference objects. The syntactic slots profiling either THINGs, PROCESSes, or both highlight kinesic and semantic features of the gestures that provide access to these mental reference objects. In other words, the syntactic information is responsible for construing a gesture either as a THING or a PROCESS (or, in a few cases, both). Moreover, the highlighted form features, i.e., the hand shape in the case of realizing nouns and the movement in the case of realizing verbs, together with their conceptual meaning help to identify a particular thing or process as the reference object of the whole multimodal utterance. To put it differently, the form of the gesture is responsible for conceiving the THING profiled by the syntactic structure as a flat object (first example) or the profiled PROCESS as a pushing action (second example). In this way, the meaning of gestures is specified and narrowed down to a small range of possible reference objects exhibiting the formal features embodied by a gesture, at least in the case of singular gestures (see Chapter 5).

4.4 Summary

The chapter's objective was to disentangle the cognitive processes operating when perceiving and interpreting the multimodal utterances under scrutiny. The chapter addressed three questions: Do gestures integrate into the semantics of spoken utterances? If so, why can they integrate into the semantics of spoken utterances and how can they do it? Based on three perception experiments, namely the speech-only condition, the gesture-only condition and the multimodal utterance condition, the chapter showed that, firstly, gestures are integrated into the semantics of the verbal utterance by contributing their own meanings to it. These observations are based on the findings revealed by a comparative analysis of the speech-only and multimodal utterance condition, showing that the semantics of the lexical items in both conditions differ in 88 % of the examples. In the remaining 12 %, corresponding to eight examples, the gestural meaning is related to the meaning prompted by speech. Secondly, the ability to contribute their own meaning, i.e., context-independent meaning, was discussed as one reason why gestures integrate into the semantics of spoken utterances. Based on the gesture-only experiment which indeed elicited a broad range of meanings, yet, meanings that are related to the gestural forms, the chapter advanced the argument that gestures can convey meaning on their own, which serves as a conceptual mediator between a gestural form and its reference object. This conceptual mediator was further investigated by drawing on Peirce's notion of the Interpretant and Langacker's concept of symbolic units, which were both fused to form one of the *relata* in Peirce's semiotic triangle. The latter were used to disentangle the cognitive-semiotic processes operating when construing multimodal reference objects, arguing, thirdly, that only a small number of verbal constructions are necessary to narrow down the semantic range of gestural meanings and to conceive a reference object belonging to a specific domain.

5 Multimodal sentences and discourse contexts: salience, attention and foregrounding

The previous chapters assembled evidence that gestures integrate into interrupted spoken utterances. This argument was based on the observation that gestures are not treated as mere fillers to create filled pauses but as contributing meaning to the semantics of the utterance. Another important observation for this argument was that speech provides an interpretative frame for the construal of gestural meaning. When recipients perceived gestures without speech, they deployed a range of meanings and syntactic constructions to refer to the gestural meaning. This changed as soon as gestures were perceived in interaction with (often very short units of) speech. In these cases, the gestures were conceived as either depicting objects or actions, depending on the syntactic slots of nouns and verbs they realized. It was further argued that through the interaction of both modalities, single kinesic and semantic features of the gestures were highlighted and moved to the recipient's focus of attention. Based on this foregrounding process, the recipient conceptualized the gestures in a specific way which reduced the range of possible reference objects the gestures are associated with. These findings allow one to conclude that speech guides the conceptualization of a gesture to a certain extent, at least in the cases under scrutiny (see Chapter 6 for a discussion of this aspect).

It goes without saying that speech events are situated in an ongoing conversation, embedded in a social situation. Discourse is "thus essential for understanding grammar" (Langacker 2008a: 457). This topic deserves an extended treatment of its own, which is why the multimodal utterances under scrutiny situated in broader discourse contexts gain this chapter's attention. With this exploration, the dynamics of multimodal meaning construal, i.e., multimodal meaning as it unfolds over time, is illuminated, thereby, addressing two research questions:
1. How are the multimodal utterances integrated into the ongoing discourse?
2. How is multimodal meaning construed in the flow of discourse?

In order to answer these questions, a qualitative analysis of all examples identified in the data was conducted by applying the methods developed within the field of "dynamic multimodal communication" (see Müller 2008a, 2008b; see Section 5.2). In a later analytical step, the qualitative analysis was combined with perception experiments testing the understanding of the multimodal utterances under scrutiny in their broader discourse context.

The chapter starts by presenting the outcome of two perception experiments which addressed the first question raised above: How are the multimodal utterances under scrutiny integrated into the ongoing discourse? Thereupon, the field of dynamic multimodal communication will be introduced from both a theoretical and methodological perspective. By applying this approach to the corpus gathered, it will be demonstrated that (a) the speakers of a conversation create a "multimodal salience structure" (Müller and Tag 2010: 5) by foregrounding and backgrounding information, and (b) the meaning of the speech-replacing gestures is specified by the unfolding discourse, and this is done by means of the semantic strategies of intension and extension.

5.1 How are multimodal sentences integrated in the discourse? Two perception experiments

Departing from the hypothesis that gestural meaning becomes specified in the unfolding discourse context, two perception experiments were conducted and the findings compared. The first experiment tested the comprehension of the multimodal utterances only (see Chapter 3 and Chapter 4). The second experiment investigated the comprehension of the utterances embedded in their larger discourse context (discourse condition). The procedure was the same as in the multimodal utterance condition introduced in Section 3.1. A total of 15 subjects (ten female, five male) participated. The average age was 27 years. The lexical items elicited were analyzed semantically applying the notions presented in Chapter 4. Thereafter, the findings gleaned from the discourse condition were compared with the results gained from the multimodal utterance condition. Consider Figure 47 for an illustration of the comparative analysis using the example *Ich wollte dieses* 🖖 ('I wanted this' 🖖).

The comparison of the items listed in Figure 47 reveals that the reference objects conceived by the recipients in the discourse condition are more specified, to a certain extent. Although we find objects such as wall, glass or poster, most of the lexical items elicited in the multimodal utterance condition for this example are fairly unspecific, referring to objects that can move in a certain way or have a vertical orientation (8 out of 15). The objects in the discourse condition are specified regarding belonging to certain domains, that of vertical objects, fulfilling the function of blockage (12 out of 15), and that of water objects (nine 9 of 15).

Similar findings are gained when looking at the second example (*und wir hinten* 🖖 / 'and we from the back' 🖖), revealing that the gestures are conceptualized differently in both conditions.

As shown in Figure 48, most lexical items elicited in the multimodal utterance condition, i.e., 12 out of 15 cases, focused on the act of pushing only. Yet, additional characteristics of the mimed action were conceived in its original context of narrating a story (discourse condition). Two-thirds of the 15 lexical choices include

5.1 How are multimodal sentences integrated in the discourse?

Discourse condition

Lexical items	Lexical items (translated)	Conceptual meaning	No.
Dammwand, Dammding	'dam wall', 'dam thing'	object, surface, verticality, blockage, WATER	7
Wand	'wall'	object, surface, verticality, expansion, blockage	2
Absperrung	'barrier'	object, surface, verticality, blockage	1
Brett davor	'shelf before'	object, surface, blockage	1
Ding das sich öffnet (besteht aus Platten die sich öffnen)	'thing that opens (consists of plates that open)'	object, space, motion	1
Schleuse	'water gate'	object, surface, blockage, WATER	1
Ufer	'shore'	surface, expansion, WATER	1
Ding dort beschreiben	'thing there describe' ('[to] describe that thing there)'	object	1

Multimodal utterance condition

Lexical items	Lexical items (translated)	Conceptual meaning	No.
Ding, Gerät	'thing'	object	3
Ding, was sich öffnet	'thing that opens'	object, space, motion	1
längliche Ding	'longish thing'	object, extension	1
große Ding	'big thing'	object, size	1
Ding vertikal	'thing vertical'	object, verticality	1
Wandteil, Glas, Fenster, Bild, Plakat	'wall', 'glass', 'window', 'picture', 'poster'	object, surface (flat), verticality	5
Öffnen (Platten, die aufgehen)	'opening (panels that open)'	thing (reified motion), space	1
Auf- und Runterklappen zeigen	'(to) show an up-and-down flapping'	thing (reified motion), bounded space, up-down, verticality	1
vorne dran	'in front of (it)'	location, front-back	1

Figure 47: Comparative analyses of the lexical items elicited in the discourse condition and in the multimodal utterance condition for the example "*Ich wollte dieses* 👆 ('I wanted this' 👆)".

Discourse condition

Lexical items	Lexical items (translated)	Conceptual meaning	No.
gegengehalten	'resisted'	resistance, blockage, counterforce, contact	1
gegengedrückt, drücken dagegen	'pressed against'	resistance, blockage, counterforce, contact	3
dagegen	'against'	blockage, counterforce, resistance	1
haben sie hochgedrückt, hochgeschoben, nach oben geschubst	'pushed up'	blockage, force, contact, verticality	5
geschubst	'pushed'	force, contact	1
geschoben	'pushed'	force, contact	4

Multimodal utterance condition

Lexical items	Lexical items (translated)	Conceptual meaning	No.
haben gedrückt	'have pressed'	resistance, blockage, force, contact, (motion)	3
haben geschoben	'have pushed'	force, contact, motion, path, path focus	8
gegengedrückt	'have pressed against'	resistance, blockage, counterforce, contact, (motion)	1
angeschoben	'pushed start'	force, contact, motion, source-path-goal	1
hochgedrückt	'pushed up'	force, contact, motion, path, verticality, up-down, endpoint focus	1

Figure 48: Comparative analysis of the lexical items elicited in the discourse condition and in the multimodal utterance condition for the example *"und wir hinten* 👇*"* ('and we from the back' 👇)".

the characterizations of directionality and resistance. In five cases, the recipients focused on the vertical direction of the movement, and in another five cases, they focused on the additional meaning of blockage or resistance. Thus, when embedded in its original context of use, the gesture is still conceived as belonging to the domain of pushing someone or something, however, it was specified regarding its function and the direction of the pushing movement.

What can we conclude from these observations? First of all, when gestures are perceived in their original discourse context, their meanings are enriched, which means that the gestural reference objects are either reduced to a particular domain, as shown in the first example, or they are specified regarding specific semantic aspects which are, and this is an important observation, embodied by the gestural form, as demonstrated in the second example.

These observations are substantiated by the whole corpus, i.e., gestural meaning was specified in 11 cases regarding particular semantic aspects embodied by gestural form parameters. For the process of interpretation, this means that specific gestural form parameters on which recipients focused in the flow of discourse are highlighted. Gestural meaning was specified regarding the gestural reference objects in 26 examples.[27] The semantic domain already observable in the lexical items elicited in the multimodal utterance condition became more specified in the discourse condition. Both the focus on gestural parameters and the reduction of the semantic domain was observable in four cases. Thirteen examples did not show a change of meaning from the multimodal utterance to the discourse condition. Interestingly, five recurrent gestures and four emblems here are involved in the realization of the syntactic slots, suggesting that their meanings are stable enough not to undergo a specification process in the discourse context. From the eight cases in which the meaning of the syntactic slots was determined verbally (see Section 4.1), six gestures were recurrent gestures and, thus, similarly, show a stable form-meaning relation. Moreover, these gestures are understood to work on the level of pragmatics and metacommunicative actions rather than on the level of semantics.

However, these findings do not come as a surprise. Sure enough, meaning becomes much more specific when more information is at hand to interpret a gesture, a spoken item or a multimodal utterance, regardless of whether it is construed simultaneously or sequentially. Yet, what remains unclear is how the meaning of a gesture and, thus, of a multimodal utterance becomes enriched

---

27 Of course, a specification of the semantic domain can also be determined, to a certain extent, in the first case, i.e., the focus on gestural form parameters. Yet, specific form and meaning aspects of the gestures are highlighted in the flow of discourse in these cases, whereas a set of members exhibiting certain features beyond form are defined in the 26 cases referenced here.

and specified. This issue is tackled in the following section by arguing that meaning becomes specified through the foregrounding and backgrounding of information in the flow of discourse.

5.2 Dynamic multimodal communication

Gestural meaning is not only shaped by the syntactic and semantic structure of a spoken utterance it interacts with, but is also, of course, embedded in a process of meaning unfolding. This insight does not come as a surprise nor is it debatable. Yet, scholars of gestures have taken a "static" perspective on multimodal phenomena for a long time by describing either the wide functional range of gestures or the many facets of gesture–speech interaction in producing multimodal utterances (see Chapter 2). One impetus for this narrow scope was to show clearly that gestures are equal partners in the creation of meaning, capable of contributing meaning on their own and adding meaning to speech. Another reason was to conduct basic research on gestures to document its forms and functions and, thus, give insights into the semiotic properties of gestures as a medium. Now that researchers have provided a complex picture of the gestural modality, which is by no means complete, we are able to zoom out and look at the orchestration of gesture and speech in the unfolding discourse.

Scholars of gestures already explored the level of multimodal discourse very early in the history of gesture studies, i.e., in the phase of its emergence. Kendon (1972) was amongst the first to show that "locution groups," distinguished by a particular intonation pattern or tempo, may be held together by particular movement patterns of the arms or head. Taking up his idea, McNeill (1992) argued that gestural forms recurring over a flow of discourse may be generated by a specific mental image. Together with prosodic features, gestures, thus, "offer clues to the cohesive linkages in the text with which it co-occurs" (McNeill et al. 2001: 10). His observations, first captured by the term "cohesive gestures" (McNeill 1992), inspired his notion of "catchments," that was explored in many of his publications (e.g., McNeill et al. 2001). Accordingly, a "catchment is a kind of thread of visuo-spatial imagery that runs through a discourse to reveal the larger discourse units that emerge out of otherwise separate parts" (McNeill et al. 2001: 11). In this way, so goes the argumentation, thematic cohesion is achieved in the discourse.

Recent studies within this field have focused on how multimodal meaning emerges over the discourse and how it is interactively construed by focusing on temporality, dynamics and multimodality. Temporality embraces the observation that meaning evolves in time, which results in the fundamental claim that meaning is a process and not a product (see Cameron 2002; Müller 2008a). Moreover, aspects may be highlighted or hid in the process of meaning creation by means of different modalities, thus, creating a dynamic network of different meaning dimensions expressed with different modalities.

The investigation of metaphors set the starting point for researching temporal, dynamic and multimodal processes of meaning creation and, thus, became a major subject in this field. Grounded in the observation that metaphors can be expressed in one or more than one modality (see e.g., Cienki and Müller 2008; Cienki and Müller 2014; Müller and Cienki 2009), and that meaning is not stable but changes in the flow of discourse, Müller (2007, 2008a, 2008b; Müller and Tag 2010) made a compelling case for conceiving metaphoricity as embodied, dynamic and gradable. She put forward the challenging idea that metaphoricity can be activated to different degrees by speech and gesture over the discourse. Her argumentation is based on the observation that speakers apply different multimodal devices to highlight metaphoric meaning. "Examples include the following: prosodic marking of a verbal metaphor, semantic oppositions, gaze to gesture, enlarging and extending gestures, repeating gestures, holding gestures, or moving gestures into the visual center of attention. These devices are salience markers for metaphoric meaning, and the ways in which they are used and combined reveals degrees of salient metaphoricity" (Müller 2017b: 301–302).

Based on these observations, two different ways of profiling metaphoricity are distinguished: "(a) *[M]ultiple instantiations* of an experiential source domain and (b) *salience markers*, operating upon and highlighting metaphoric expressions," such as prosodic features or gestures (Müller 2017b: 302, original emphasis). These modes of profiling metaphoric meaning have been accounted for in terms of foregrounding techniques (see Müller and Tag 2010), co-participants apply to move metaphoric meaning dimensions into the focus of attention. Three foregrounding techniques have been identified, subsumed under the "Iconicity Principle," the "Interactive Principle" and the "Syntactic and Semantic Principle," which were sketched out by Müller and Tag (2010: 94) as follows:
1. Expressing metaphoricity in more than one modality foregrounds metaphoricity: This foregrounding strategy follows an Iconicity Principle.
2. By using salience markers, a verbal, gestural or verbo-gestural metaphor is additionally foregrounded. These salience markers follow Interactive, Semantic and Syntactic Principles.

In addition to exploring the dynamic and multimodal nature of metaphoric meaning, researchers have also gained knowledge about the unfolding of metaphoricity throughout the discourse. This regards the temporal dimension of meaning creation. By conceiving metaphoric meaning as a process and not as a product, different stages in the development of metaphoric meaning can be identified. This was done for different media, including film, speech and gestures, and framed under the notion of metaphor emergence (see Horst 2018; Kappelhoff and Müller 2011; Kolter et al. 2012; Müller and Ladewig 2013; Müller and Schmitt 2015).[28] Regarding multimodal interaction, it was shown (a) that the source domain or the vehicle of a metaphor is often first expressed in the gesture, whereas the target domain or the topic becomes verbalized at a later stage of a discourse; (b) that the emergence and negotiation of metaphoric meaning "includes successions, simultaneities and alternations of metaphoric expressions in speech, body, and hand gesture" (Müller and Ladewig 2013: 315); and (c) that meaning is negotiable, in that speakers may align their conceptualizations which become visible in the gestures (see Boll 2018; Feyaerts, Brône and Oben 2017). Based on these observations, we can conclude that the creation of meaning should be regarded as an interactive process that unfolds over time and is expressed in different modalities.

A dynamic approach to attention (see Chafe 1994), which connects well with a dynamic approach to multimodal communication, is another frame of reference pivotal for understanding why gestural, verbal and multimodal meaning becomes enriched and specified in the flow of discourse. It starts from the premise that attention flows selectively from one focus to another. Through this shifting of attention, only a small subset of information is selected and processed and is, thus, moved into the "center of attention" (see Chafe and Li 1976), which is essential for keeping information in mind and for conveying meaning as Chiarcos (2011: 106) states:

> The flow of attention is a key mechanism controlling any kind of mental activity. It is motivated by a "bottle-neck effect": The world surrounding us (and even our internal world) is far too rich to be realized, understood, or described as a whole. Rather, just relevant or especially significant elements are chosen to build up a finite symbolic representation describing the situation sufficiently but sparsely enough to be held in mind or to be communicated.

The approach of attentional flow is in harmony with an interactive approach to communication, arguing that speakers organize their multimodal contributions for an attending co-participant ("recipient design," Garfinkel 1967). Accordingly, information relevant for the speaker is made relevant or foregrounded by the speaker to share this information.

---

28 See Cameron (1999); Cameron et al. (2009); Fiumara (1995); Gibbs (1993) for the processual nature of metaphoric meaning expressed verbally.

Now, how can these foregrounding activities be uncovered and described in both their temporal structure and their simultaneous and linear arrangements? For this purpose, the linguistic Metaphor Foregrounding Analysis (MFA) has been developed (Müller and Tag 2010), aiming to make the foregrounding techniques speakers use in the flow of discourse visible. Accordingly, the simultaneous or adjacent employment of different modalities, such as speech and gesture, is regarded to reflect the Iconicity Principle, because semantic information can be considered highlighted in these cases. The Interactive Principle operates if interactive techniques, such as eye gaze, are used by the participants to achieve shared attention (see e.g., Gullberg and Kita 2009; Streeck 1988, 2009). The Syntactic and Semantic Principle covers the integration of gestural meaning into spoken utterances by way of deictic particles or by filling in syntactic gaps.

The Metaphor Foregrounding Analysis (MFA) is combined with the Keynote-based Timeline Annotation (KeaTa) (see Müller 2017b; Müller and Ladewig 2013),[29] to document the temporal unfolding of meaning. This annotation system was originally developed for the annotation of multimodal metaphors and expressive movements in audiovisual media (see e.g., Kappelhoff et al. 2015; Kappelhoff, Bakels and Greifenstein 2019; Kappelhoff and Greifenstein 2015; Müller and Schmitt 2015) and later applied to the analysis of verbo-gestural metaphors in manual and full-body gestures (see Kolter et al. 2012; Müller and Ladewig 2013). Both methods were combined in the "CineMet" method (see Müller and Kappelhoff 2018) to analyze film and face-to-face interaction. This

> transdisciplinary method (CineMet) [was] designed to capture dynamic structures specifically in relation to affective processes and the flow of metaphorical meaning-making. Film studies and linguistics have both contributed to its development. Note, that CineMet is not just a combination of two sets of methods coming from different disciplines, rather, it further develops and sometimes alters methods that were developed earlier. The method addresses the temporality of meaning-making as a specific mode of perceiving, sensing, and feeling, and offers different forms of visualizations of this temporal affectivity and the dynamics of metaphorical meaning. Our starting point is the temporality of experiencing which characterizes film-viewing as much as face-to-face interaction.
> (Müller and Kappelhoff 2018: 227)

The annotation visualized in Figure 49 documents the repeated use of a particular metaphor and its distribution over different modes of expression on a timeline. The different monomodal and multimodal metaphoric expressions are shown as boxes on a timeline. The graphic patterns of the boxes correspond to the different meanings conveyed by speech and gesture. The size of the boxes corresponds roughly to the duration of the monomodal and multimodal metaphoric expression

---

[29] See also www.hermann-kappelhoff.de/node/24.

identified in the part of the interaction displayed. This procedure results in a visualization of activated metaphoric meaning and the attentional flow of both speaker and co-participant, thus, creating "an interactive salience profile of waking metaphors" (Müller 2017b: 313).

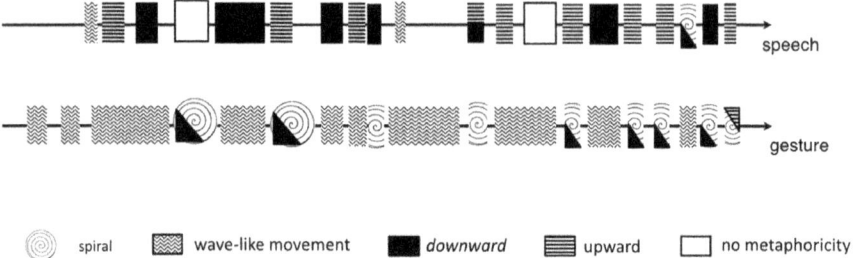

Figure 49: Timeline annotation in Keynote (Müller and Ladewig 2013: 305).

What has been assumed for metaphors, can be claimed for all processes of meaning creation. Accordingly, meaning in general, be it literal or metaphoric, has the potential for being construed multimodally, elaborated, negotiated, and foregrounded or backgrounded. Hence, meaning should generally be considered as dynamic, to a certain extent. This means for the study of sequentially constructed multimodal utterances that not only metaphoric expressions, but every verbal or gestural expression assessed retrospectively to create a particular conceptual space is documented.

5.3 Salience and attention – foregrounding of meaning

With the focus on the dynamic processes of meaning creation, the scope of analysis is expanded from investigating single utterances to examining longer stretches of discourse. The key question of this chapter is how multimodal meaning becomes specified by discourse and, thus, how multimodal utterances are integrated into the discourse space. To tackle these issues, the findings of the qualitative analyses, which combined the Metaphor Foregrounding Analysis and Keynote-based Timeline Annotation method, are presented and exemplified by means of the two examples introduced earlier.

5.3.1 An emerging barrier located at a lake

When zooming out onto a larger stretch of discourse, the discourse topic of the first example under scrutiny can be identified which centers around waters and objects located in and around them. Its unfolding is visualized in Figure 50, showing that a multimodal salience structure emerges through the simultaneous and sequential relationships of the information expressed verbally and gesturally, directing the attentional flow of the co-participants. What becomes noticeable, furthermore, is that the participants are engaged in two different speech activities. The first one is predetermined by the parlor game whose goal is to guess a particular term. It is characterized by the exchange of spoken items belonging to a specific domain, namely that of waters. The subsequent speech activity is a discussion which is, of course, based on the previous game turn. Both speech activities are the subject of the analysis presented now.

As shown in Figure 50, the speech activity of collectively guessing a word starts with the game leader's expression of *ein Meer in klein* ('a small sea,' literally: 'a sea in small'), followed by a sequence of listing various bodies of water, including *See* ('lake'), *Teich* ('pond'), *Tegernsee* ('Lake Tegern') or *Fluss* ('river'; see the appendix for the whole transcript). The sequence ends by naming the object of a *Seerose* ('water lily'). Notably, the focus of attention in the course of this game turn shifts from larger to smaller bodies. Moreover, the domain WATERS is profiled and activated through the close temporal proximity of the different items expressed by different speakers. Speaking in terms of Müller and Tag (2010), the Iconicity Principle is operating here. The domain of waters is construed and elaborated interactively because more material is considered to convey more meaning.

Speaker 1, with her utterance *also dieser See* ('well this lake'), shifts the focus of attention to the concept of a lake. This shifting of attention or refocusing is carried out by expressing the German particle *also* ('well'), marking a break between the previous and the subsequent part of the game turn. The thematic shift is performed by expressing the concept of a lake, which is, simultaneously, highlighted by being accentuated verbally and accompanied by an accentuated gesture. Hence, this specific body of water is brought into the center of attention by means of the Iconicity Principle, establishing a reference frame for the subsequent part of the guessing round because immediately afterwards, an object related to this referential frame is designated, namely a dock (*Steg*). In the following sequence, the speaker specifies the guessing term by mentioning a building located at the lake she mentioned before and by vaguely addressing its function: *da ist so ne Art Gebäude damit dort das* ('there is such a kind of building in order that there'). In doing so, she moves the focus of attention further towards the concept of objects, which is taken up and elaborated instantaneously by one of the co-participants.

158 — 5 Multimodal sentences and discourse contexts

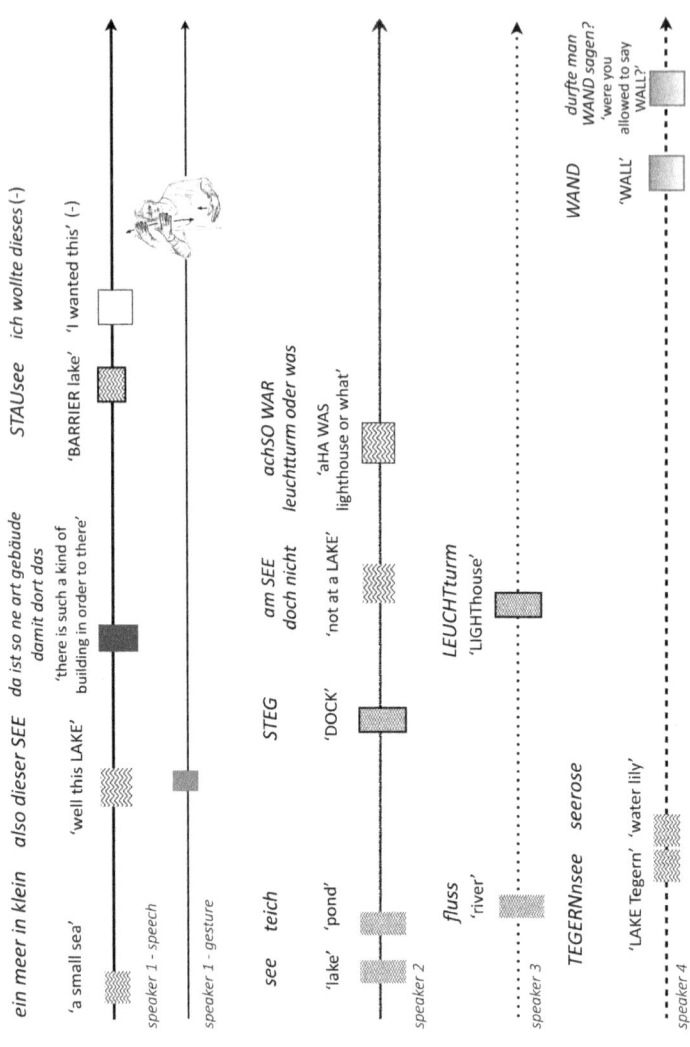

Figure 50: A multimodal salience structure evolving for the example *"Ich wollte dieses* 👋*"* ('I wanted this' 👋")".[30]

---

30 The annotation of speech follows roughly GAT2 (Selting et al. 2011). Hence, capital letters mark accents in speech.

Speaker 2 specifies the general concept of an object by naming a particular entity situated at waters, namely a *Leuchtturm* ('light house'). The domain of WATER OBJECTS is foregrounded by means of the Iconicity Principle through the close temporal relationship of both utterances and the stressing of the first syllable of *Leuchtturm*. The second speaker's lexical choice is challenged by the third speaker who refocuses on the concept of a lake again with the following utterance: *am See doch nicht* ('not at a lake'). This domain of WATERS is highlighted and moved into the co-participants' attention as the noun "lake" is stressed (Iconicity Principle). At this point, the game turn is finished, yet, the co-participants do not terminate the semantic elaboration of the guessing term but become engaged in a discussion. This second speech activity is initiated by the first speaker who reacts to the previous utterance by indicating that she understands it as a critique of her explaining strategy (*Mann ich wusste nicht wie ich's beschreiben soll* / 'Man I didn't know how to describe it').[31] Based on her complaint, speaker 3 asks whether the concept of lighthouse was the correct choice (*achso war Leuchtturm oder was* / 'aha was it a lighthouse or what'). Speaker 1 negates strongly and focuses again on the domain of WATERS by specifying it in terms of a barrier lake (*Nein Stausee* / 'No barrier lake'). This attentional shift is again foregrounded by stressing the first syllable of the noun *Stausee* (Iconicity Principle). Shortly afterwards, she expresses the multimodal utterance under scrutiny, i.e., *Ich wollte dieses* ('I wanted this'), followed by a gesture performed with flat hands which moved contrarily up and down. Following the Semantic and Syntactic Principle, it can be argued that this gesture is foregrounded and moved into the focus of attention as it fills a syntactic and semantic gap by realizing a noun. Thus, the gesture is the only modality in which the co-participants find information grounded by the definite determiner 'this.' Moreover, together with the verbally expressed idea of an artificial lake used to keep water, a *Stausee* ('barrier lake'), the information of a flat object serving the function of a barrier is evoked. The following utterance by speaker 4 substantiates this interpretation, because he refers to the object as a *Wand* ('wall') twice, thus, ratifying the first speaker's *multimodal* utterance.

The multimodal salience structure created interactively by the co-participants, visualized in Figure 50, reflects how meaning evolves dynamically in the interactive process of guessing a word in a parlor game situation. However, it not only reflects the process of multimodal meaning making, it also guides the participants' flow of attention, thus, shifting the co-participants focus of attention to the gesture under scrutiny at the end of the whole sequence, because this gesture is filling a syntactic and semantic gap and, thus, is highly activated. Moreover, the inherent

---

31 This utterance is not included in Figure 50 as it does not profile a specific concept.

meaning of the gesture under scrutiny is enriched through the foregrounding and backgrounding of information (for more information see Chapter 4 and Section 5.4), evoking the idea of a flat object serving as a barrier at a lake.

This analysis is supported not only by the recipient's response in the example analyzed but also by the findings yielded in the discourse condition. As has already been pointed out (see Section 5.1 and Figure 47), the lexical choices elicited in the discourse condition designate objects exhibiting a flat surface, often with a vertical orientation. Moreover, in most cases, i.e., in 12 out of 15 cases, these objects fulfill the function of a barrier and/or are considered to be situated in or at waters (nine cases).

5.3.2 A scenario of pushing downward and upward
Meaning was created interactively in the previous example by basically exchanging a range of words in order to guess a particular lexical item. The next example focuses on a narration about a specific event. In this example, the speaker is telling a story about a woman who has forgotten the key to her apartment and, therefore, tried to climb up to the window. The story culminates in describing how the narrator tried to help her sister, while her grandmother aimed at preventing her from climbing up to the window. Figure 51 illustrates the dynamic evolvement of meaning in this example.

We are entering the scene when the story is reaching its climax, i.e., when the grandmother tries to push her grandchild away from the window grill. At this point of the narration, the speaker starts imitating the characters of the story. Firstly, she mimes her grandmother's voice and bodily actions by saying *und Oma immer. Was willst denn du?* ('and grandma always. What are you doing?; see Appendix C for the whole transcript). When uttering the personal pronoun *du* ('you'), she performs a gesture, reenacting the action of pushing something or somebody forward. Subsequently, the gesture is held, while the speaker looks at it, represented by the arrow leading from the timeline "gaze" to the timeline "gesture" in Figure 51. At this moment, the Interactive Principle is operating because gazing at one's gestures is considered as one strategy to foreground information and make it relevant for the ongoing discourse (see also Streeck 2009). Hence, the gestural hold is moved into the speaker and recipient's focus of attention. Afterwards, the speaker continues to imitate her grandmother's actions by quoting her, *Geh du runter* ('You get down'), speaking with a particular voice, and by miming her gestures again. She reenacts a second pushing movement accompanying the adverbial modifier *runter* ('down'), however, in this case, the gesture is performed with a downward movement. As downwardness is expressed both verbally and gesturally, it can be considered as foregrounded (Iconicity Principle).

5.3 Salience and attention – foregrounding of meaning

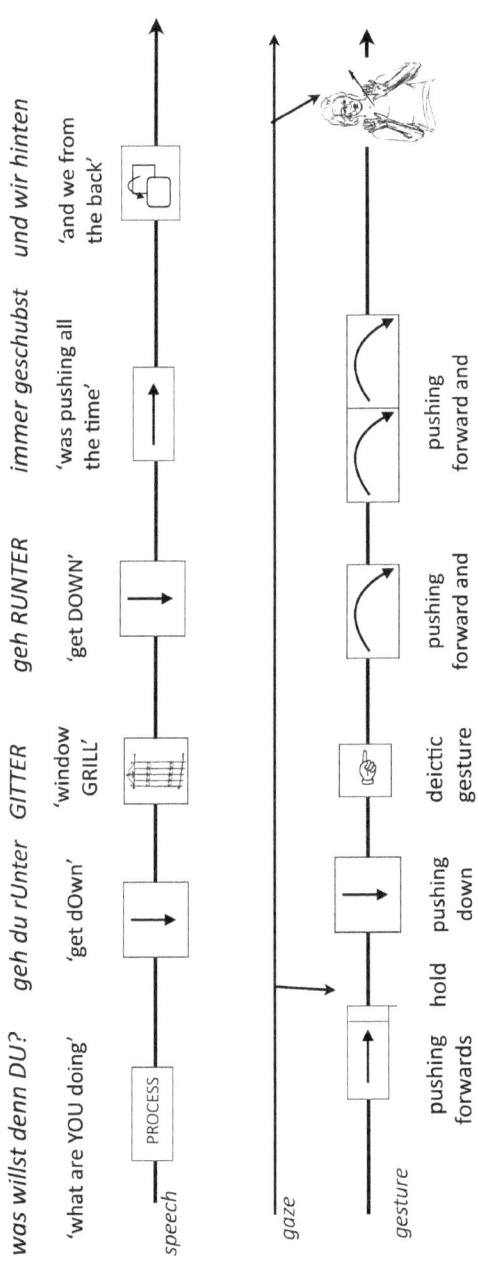

Figure 51: A multimodal salience structure evolving for the example "*und wir hinten* 👇 ('and we from the back' 👇)".

More material, i.e., more modes of the expressions used, are considered to convey more meaning. Accordingly, downwardness is made salient in this specific moment of speaking and gesturing.

The story continues with a side sequence, clarifying what kind of apartment her sister tried to enter: *es war sone Zweiraumwohnung hier mit som Gitter* ('it was such a two-room apartment here with such a window grill'; see Appendix C for the whole transcript). The utterance is accompanied by a deictic gesture referring to an apartment across the street. After the return to the story line, the speaker is relating that her sister tried to justify her actions, miming her sister's voice and way of speaking (*Oma sie hat doch n Schlüssel vergessen* / 'Grandma she has forgotten the key'), but her grandmother did not stop from holding her off from climbing up the window. The scenario of the grandmother pushing her grandchild off the window grill is then reactivated by miming her grandmother's speech and actions again. In the multimodal utterance *Geh runter* ('Get down'), the speaker is stressing the adverbial modifier *runter* ('down') and accompanies it by a pushing gesture, showing an arced movement pattern oriented downward. Downwardness is again foregrounded with this multimodal utterance and made salient for the discourse as the Iconicity Principle is operating here. The story culminates in the reenactment of several pushing actions which were originally executed by the grandmother and by the speaker herself. At first, the speaker performs two pushing movements which show the same form as the one performed before. These gestures are accompanied by the utterance, *und die hat immer geschubst* ('and she was pushing all the time'). The third pushing action directed upward fills a syntactic and semantic gap by realizing a verb grounded by the verbal construction *und wir hinten* ('and we from the back', Syntactic and Semantic Principle) and is made salient and relevant by the speaker's gaze at her gesture (Interactive Principle).

Similar to the previous example, a multimodal salience structure emerges in which the actions depicted by the protagonists of the story are foregrounded. First of all, all actions performed by the grandmother are expressed both verbally and gesturally, which means that the Iconicity Principle is operating in these depictions. Secondly, the speaker's own actions embodied gesturally fill a syntactic gap, thus, making the gesture salient for both the speaker and recipients (Semantic and Syntactic Principle). Additionally, the speaker looks at her gesture, making it even more salient (Interactive Principle). Moreover, and this is an interesting observation, thirdly, a semantic opposition between the two directions is created. The speaker foregrounds the direction of downwardness many times during the course of her storytelling (Figure 51). By miming a pushing-upward action at the end of the story, an opposition is created between the downward and upward directions. Although this aspect is not included in

Müller and Tag's (2010) differentiation of foregrounding strategies, it is subsumed under the Iconicity Principle (see Ladewig 2012; Ladewig and Hotze in press/2020; Müller and Kappelhoff 2018, ch. 10). In doing so, the upward direction is singled out and made salient.

The inherent meaning of the gesture under investigation becomes enriched and specified through the foregrounding and backgrounding of information and, thus, through the multimodal salience structure that is emerging. The gesture is still considered as a pushing action, but now, through the situatedness in the ongoing discourse, it is conceived as an antagonistic force to the pushing movement downward performed before. Thus, upwardness is made salient by being "staged" as the opposite of downwardness, which has been foregrounded throughout the discourse.

This analysis is not only supported by the lexical items elicited in the discourse condition (see Section 5.1 and Figure 48), according to which two-thirds of the 15 lexical choices include the characterizations of directionality and resistance, but also by the co-participant's response. The recipient sitting at the right-hand side of the speaker looks at the storyteller throughout the story. Immediately after the multimodal utterance under scrutiny was performed, she asks *echt* ('really'), thus, ratifying the sequentially constructed utterance by displaying her understanding. Afterwards, her question is affirmed by the storyteller and both start laughing. This observation allows one to conclude that the co-participant has understood the gestural meaning as a pushing upward action which is used as an antagonistic force against a pushing downward action.

As has been pointed out previously, the multimodal utterances presented in more detail throughout the book serve as exemplary cases for the whole corpus. This means that not only the two examples presented show the specification of multimodal meaning through the flow of discourse but that the majority of the examples of the corpus do (i.e., 81 %; see Table 11). The next section will illuminate the ways in which multimodal meaning becomes specified to complete the picture of how the sequentially constructed multimodal utterances are integrated into the discourse. Based on the analysis presented in this paragraph, it will be shown that the sequence of attentional foci described here create complex conceptual spaces in which the gestures are situated.

5.4 Multimodal semantic strategies: intension and extension

The previous section assembled evidence that multimodal meaning evolves dynamically over the course of a discourse and interactive meaning-making. It was argued that gestural meaning becomes highly specified through the interactive

Table 11: Enrichment of meaning determined in the discourse condition for all syntactic positions realized by gestures.

Focus on gestural form parameters	Reduction of semantic domain	Reduction of semantic domain of gestures based on focus of form parameters	No change in meaning	Becoming more heterogenous	Very heterogenous meanings	Meaning determined verbally	Total
11	26	4	13	1	3	8	66

5.4 Multimodal semantic strategies: intension and extension

negotiation and the dynamic flow of information. Taking up this idea, this section illuminates the processes of gestural meaning specification in more detail, attending again to the examples described above.

When looking at both examples again, one aspect becomes evident: Gestures in noun position and verb position undergo different processes of specification. Whereas the recipients of the first example appear to have focused more on the matching of gestural form and reference object, the recipients of the second example seem to have focused more on specific form aspects of the gesture. In other words, whereas in the first example, the range of possible reference objects was reduced by connecting gestural form and meaning developed in the discourse, the inherent meaning of gestures (see Chapter 4) became specified in the second example. These observations give reasons to assume that two different processes are active in the interpretation of gestures when situated in the flow of interactive meaning-making. Based on and regarding the analysis of spoken language, these processes have been referred to as "extension" and "intension" (see Carnap 1947) or "reference" and "sense" (see Frege 1892). The extension of a lexical item is understood as a set of things that may apply to the item. The intension of a lexical item encompasses its set of properties. To be more precise:

> [a] concept's intension is the set of attributes defining its members, while its extension comprises its actual members. Thus the intension of *bachelor* might include characteristics such as male, unmarried and adult, making its extension the set of male, unmarried adults in the world, which would mean that both the Pope and an unmarried man cohabiting with the same partner for 25 years are bachelors. (Ramscar and Port 2015: 79)

The problem with these notions is that reference in philosophy or linguistics is often understood as a relationship between an expression and an entity existing in the real world. These kinds of relationships certainly exist, but this is not always the case. Some referents of nominals, for instance, may be either abstract or problematic regarding their objective existence. Moreover, many situations talked about might be virtual, at least to some extent, due to subjective construal of meaning by the participants of a conversation (see Langacker 2008a: 271). This entails that it is very likely that participants in a conversation have different ideas about the situation, object or event being talked about. Even when speaking about an object that exists in the real world, they may still construe it in very different ways based on both their own embodied experience with this particular object and their memory of it. Thus, while lexical units may undoubtedly refer to objects in the real world, we have to acknowledge that each time a lexical item is used it is associated with a particular conceptualization based on individual experiences, and it is, thus, subject to meaning construal.

> An expression's meaning is not just the conceptual content it evokes – equally important is how that content is construed. As part of its conventional semantic value, every symbolic structure construes its content in a certain fashion. It is hard to resist the visual metaphor, where content is likened to a scene and construal to a particular way of viewing it. Importantly, CG does **not** claim that all meanings are based on space or visual perception, but the visual metaphor does suggest a way to classify the many facets of construal, if only for expository purposes. In viewing a scene, what we actually see depends on how closely we examine it, what we choose to look at, which elements we pay most attention to, and where we view it from. (Langacker 2008a: 55, original emphasis)

Resting upon these reflections, Langacker (2008a) introduces the notions of "type" and "instantiation" and brings in the observation that people are capable of construing virtual entities or situations – another aspect of meaning construal. Nominals, for instance, are considered to be referential

> as they single out a grounded instance of a type as their referent. Their special property is that they profile a **virtual** instance rather than an **actual** one. [. . .] They do so by designating virtual situations that constitute the abstracted commonality of actual situations. Being part of these virtual situations, the things referred to (hub, wheel, hobbit, and unicorn) are virtual instances of their types – the abstracted commonality of actual instances. (Langacker 2008a: 271, original emphasis)

According to Langacker, the virtual objects, virtual situations, virtual actions or events referred to are found in mental spaces representing these objects, situations, actions or events.

Similar processes can and should be assumed for gestures. The reasons are twofold. First of all, the majority of gestures do not have a particular meaning that can be extended to particular class of reference objects due to their nonconventional character. As shown in Chapter 3 and Chapter 4, a range of different meanings is ascribed to the gestures when being perceived without speech. Secondly, gestural meaning is still construed individually, depending on how information is interpreted, even when used in the context of speech, which certainly provides information for establishing a link between a gestural form and a reference object. Although speech specifies the meaning of gestures in many cases and vice versa, the degree of specification is subjective and remains "located" in the mind and body of a speaker and recipient. Gestures may become the subject of negotiation, however, it will never be the case that participants have exactly the same meaning in mind. This holds true for both verbally and gesturally expressed meaning.

In a nutshell, speakers and recipients construe meaning constantly. By definition, if meaning is considered conceptual, it needs to be regarded as construed. Moreover, as a matter of fact, we cannot assume that people have identical meanings in their minds when communicating with each other.

5.4 Multimodal semantic strategies: intension and extension — 167

In what follows, the idea of meaning construal of multimodal meaning is taken up again and elaborated from a discourse perspective. It will be argued that processes of meaning specification can be described by applying the notions of intension and extension introduced earlier. Discussing these from a discourse perspective entails treating these notions as processes and not as products that can be observed as the discourse proceeds. Accordingly, two processes are differentiated, namely such processes that primarily reduce the extensional meaning of multimodal utterances or gestures and processes that modify the proposition or intensional meaning of multimodal utterances or gestures. Interestingly, these two processes of semantic specification distribute over the different syntactic positions realized by gestures, as will be exemplified in the following pages.

5.4.1 The extensional meaning of a surface

When resting upon the speech activity of designating various bodies of water and water objects in the first example, the emergence of different conceptual spaces (see Langacker 1987a, 1991b) situated in a larger conceptual space, can be reconstructed (Figure 52). The different conceptual spaces are defined here regarding the conceptualizations expressed both verbally and gesturally that belong to a specific domain, such as BODIES OF WATER and WATER OBJECTS.

The first conceptual space is activated by the utterance *ein Meer in klein* ('a small sea'). Based on the conceptualization of a small sea, the game partners started immediately to name small bodies of water, such as "lake," "pond," "river" or "lake Tegern." The item "water lily" then shifts the focus of attention to objects located in or around water. This is visualized by the overlapping sphere of the first and the second circle in Figure 52, representing that this conceptualization has emerged from the previous elaboration and frames the upcoming talk by (a) referencing to a particular body of water, i.e., a lake (note that *Seerose* literally translates into 'lake lily') and (b) designating an object residing in a lake, a lily.

The interactants refer in what follows both to the concept of a lake ("this lake," "not in a lake") and to objects located in or at lakes ("dock," "building," "lighthouse"). Note that the generic noun "building" is brought in by the game leader with the attempt to specify the meaning of the guessing word. The attempt can be considered successful, as one of the game partners specifies its meaning regarding situating this concept within the conceptual space of water established previously. This process becomes evident in the utterance "light house." When the game turn is finished and all participants start the discussion, the game leader brings her conceptualization of a lake up again by referring to a lake not

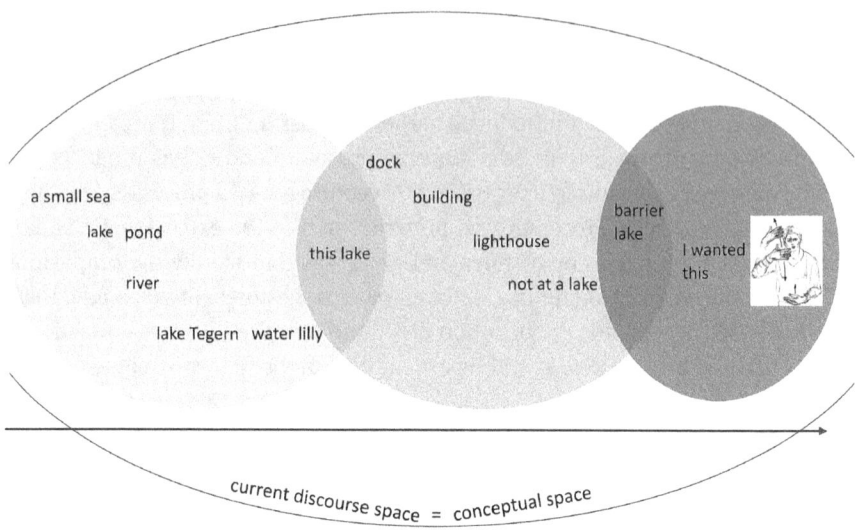

Figure 52: Process of specifying the extensional meaning in the example *"Ich wollte dieses 👆* ('I wanted this' 👆)".

mentioned before (probably because she was not allowed to due to the rules of the game), which is a "barrier lake." This item marks the transition of the second to the third conceptual space, represented by the overlapping sphere in Figure 52, because it has emerged from the first two spaces and now frames the third one by combining the notion of a particular body of water, an artificial lake, and objects situated around water. That is to say, an intrinsic part of barrier lakes is an object functioning as a barrier which is specified by the game leader in her next multimodal utterance, which is the one under scrutiny, *Ich wollte dieses* 👆 ('I wanted this' 👆). As the analyses presented in Chapter 3 and Chapter 4 demonstrate, this utterance multimodally designates an object with a flat surface, a vertical orientation and/or movable (flat) parts.

What does this admittedly schematized account of the process of meaning evolution show? The instance discussed serves as an example for the stepwise specification of conceptual meaning during the flow of discourse and the interactive negotiation. The multimodal utterance under scrutiny is situated in the third conceptual space (Figure 52), which is informed by and related to the conceptual spaces established before. The extensional meaning of the guessing word negotiated by the participants, i.e., a specific object at a particular body of water – a barrier lake – is merged with the inherent meaning of the gesture, i.e., a flat and vertical surface which profiles a THING through the interaction with speech. Accordingly, the THING profiled multimodally is retrospectively defined as a flat, vertically extending object situated at a barrier lake. The lexical items elicited in the discourse condition substantiate this interpretation, as 12 out of 15 items refer to objects fulfilling the function of a barrier and/or considered to be situated in or at water (nine cases).

The stepwise reduction of extensional meaning is certainly inherent to the type of the parlor game discussed here. However, the process of reducing the extensional meaning has been observed for other examples as well (Table 11).

5.4.2 The intensional meaning of pushing

A different process of meaning specification is observable in the second example, namely that of specifying the intensional meaning of the gesture by constantly foregrounding formal properties of the gestural modality.

The conceptual space illustrated in Figure 53 is created mainly by the narrator. Yet, it can be considered as shared, at least to a certain extent, as it is part of an interactive process of storytelling, situated in an ongoing flow of discourse.

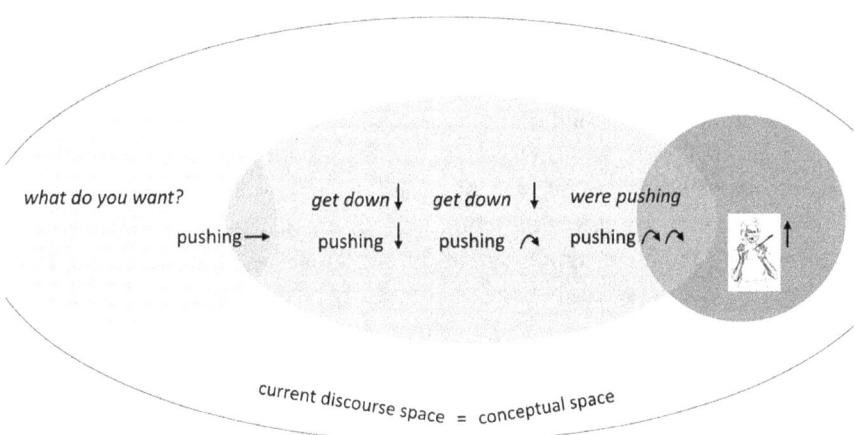

Figure 53: Process of specifying the intensional meaning for the example "*und wir hinten* 👋 ('and we from the back' 👋)".

As the whole narration cannot be constructed here (but see Ladewig and Hotze in press/2020), the account of the dynamic process of meaning-making starts with the narrator's first instance of imitating her grandmother (*was willst denn du?* / 'what do you want?'). While saying this, the narrator uses a gesture, reenacting the action of pushing forward (first smaller conceptual space in Figure 53). The pushing movement used here for the first time is repeated multiple times in the following discourse. Yet, the direction of the pushing movement changes in the following gestures, meaning that the next four gestures are directed downward (one showing a straight and three an arced movement pattern) and the fifth gesture is directed upwards. As argued in Section 5.3, the direction of movement is highlighted in the first two pushing gestures through the interplay with speech because they are verbally accompanied by the modifier *runter* ('down'). The action itself is not designated verbally but is in the next two multimodal utterances. However, the direction of movement can also be regarded as foregrounded, because the gesture is used twice. Based on these observations, it is argued that the notion of pushing downward emerges, creating the second smaller conceptual space. The multimodal utterance of *und wir hinten* ✋ ('and we from the back' ✋) closes this part of the narration. In this case, the gesture is directed upwards and, thus, as argued in Section 5.3, establishes an opposition between downwardness and upwardness, foregrounding the upward direction and creating the third conceptual space.

Based on this schematic account of the process of meaning creation in the flow of discourse, we conclude that the properties of the gestural movement are moved in the speaker's and, thus, recipients' foci. The action of pushing frames the whole sequence, but it is the direction that is made salient. Accordingly, the intensional meaning is elaborated in this example, which is why the lexical items of the discourse condition focused mainly on the action of pushing *and* the direction of movement (in 10 out of 15 cases). But the recipient's reaction of saying *Echt?* ('Really?'), followed by cheerful laughter also substantiates this interpretation. The climax of the whole story visualized in Figure 53 can only be understood if the opposition between the two movement directions and, thus, the absurdity of the whole action, i.e., one party pushing a person upward and the other pushing her downward, is recognized.

Interestingly, the analysis of the corpus confirms that the two processes of specifying the extensional and the intensional meaning are operating when the multimodal utterances are perceived in the discourse. It is noticeable that both processes distribute over the different positions realized by the gestures (Table 11). Accordingly, most gestures realizing nominal slots are embedded in a process of specifying the extensional meaning of a conceptualization that is materialized by a gesture. In the case of the gestures realizing verbal slots, the intensional meaning was often specified. Table 12 gives an overview of the processes of specification determined for the whole corpus.

Accordingly, as already addressed in Section 5.1, the analysis of the sample reveals that gestural meaning becomes enriched and specified when perceived

Table 12: Processes of specification determined in the discourse condition for the syntactic positions of nouns or verbs realized by gestures.

	Intension	Extension	Extension/ Intension	No change in meaning	Becoming more heterogenous	Very heterogenous meanings	Meaning determined verbally	Total
Noun	/	18	2	5	/	/	5	30
Verb	11	5	2	7	1	3	3	32

in its original discourse context (see Table 11 for the whole corpus including clause positions). The set of members showing the attributes foregrounded in the flow of discourse are defined in 18 cases of noun positions realized gesturally. Thus, the range of possible gestural reference objects is reduced in the flow of discourse. This process has been referred to here as that of extension. When gestures realize verbal slots, the intensional meaning or inherent gestural meaning tends to become specified (11 out of 32 cases). Accordingly, particular semantic aspects embodied by gestural form features become highlighted in the process of discourse unfolding. The extensional meaning was refined in five cases. In two cases of gestures realizing nominal slots and two cases of gestures realizing a verbal slot, both possible reference objects of gestures were reduced based on the foregrounding of gestural form parameters in the flow of discourse. In five cases of noun positions and seven cases of verb positions, no change of meaning was observable, as shown in the lexical items. As was addressed earlier, five recurrent gestures and four emblems were used here, suggesting that these do not undergo any processes of specification because their meaning is fairly stable. In one case of a gesture realizing a verb, the meaning became more heterogenous and in three cases of gestures realizing verbs the meaning of the lexical items was heterogenous in both the multimodal utterance and the discourse condition. In the cases in which the meaning was determined verbally to a great extent, i.e., in five gestures realizing nominal slots and three gestures realizing verbal slots, a high number of conventionalized gestures was determined as well. Recurrent gestures were used which worked on a pragmatic rather than a semantic level of meaning creation in six out of eight cases.

In a nutshell, what was demonstrated here from a retrospective point of view is how the recipients of the multimodal utterance, situated in the flow of a discourse, specify the meaning of the gestures and, thus, of the multimodal utterances. It was shown that the sequence of attentional foci creates different complex conceptual spaces integrated in a larger conceptual and discursive space. Within these spaces, gesture becomes specified regarding its extensional or intensional meaning. The set of members showing the attributes foregrounded through the flow of discourse are defined in the case of gestures realizing nouns. Hence, the range of possible objects profiled gesturally and, thus, the extensional meaning of gestures becomes specified. In the case of gestures realizing verbs, a tendency towards the opposite can be observed, meaning that gestural properties and, thus, the gestures' intensional meaning is specified in the flow of discourse.

What is concluded here for the experimental condition also holds true for the prospective processes of meaning-making that took place in the original conversational situations. That is to say, meaning is negotiated and elaborated, foregrounded and backgrounded in the flow of discourse, thus, creating complex and rich conceptual spaces which specify the meaning of the gestures in such a way that they can replace speech. Let us make this argument more explicit. First of all, it is certainly not surprising that discourse specifies meaning. Even the distribution illustrated in Table 11 may not surprise linguists given that nouns refer to entities and verbs predicate about the entities referred to. This functional difference has been labeled "reference" and "predication." However, the interesting aspect with the multimodal utterances investigated here is that gestures are used to realize the syntactic slots of nouns and verbs and are, hence, treated as conveying sufficient information to substitute for the meanings of nouns and verbs of spoken language. This "sufficiency" is grounded in the rich discourse contexts the gestures are embedded in, which provides enough information to replace a noun or a verb by a gesture. It can be further assumed using this argument that the multimodal utterances of the kind investigated here are not observable in the beginning of a new discourse unit but at moments of speaking and gesturing when complex meanings have been created. Pantomimic gestures may form an exception due to their "high degree of semiotic complexity" (Bressem, Ladewig and Müller 2018: 234) but this remains a matter of speculation.

Consequently, as has been mentioned earlier, the gestures investigated in this study should not be considered as mere compensation for expressing meanings a speaker is not able to verbalize. As shown before, they are always foregrounded, as they fill a syntactic and semantic gap. Yet, saliency is not solely achieved by such an integration but also by the performance of a gesture. If we take notice of the first example again, it becomes evident that this gesture is performed with a large movement size and that it is positioned in the central gesture space. Moreover, while the speaker is gesturing, she leans forward and, thus, addresses her recipients bodily. Taking these properties into account, the gestures are made to be seen and, hence, *made (relevant) for a co-participant*. Therefore, these gestures must be considered as equally relevant as speech.

To conclude, when the subjects perceived the gestures in their larger discourse context, the meanings proved to be much more specified than when perceived in their utterance context only. These observations are anticipated, given that speech specifies the meaning conveyed by the gestural form. However, the systematicity in meaning specification is interesting, as different steps can be observed based on the size of a discourse. That is to say, the context of an utterance specified the meanings of the gestures regarding the depiction of objects or actions. In their larger discourse context, the gestures were specified in their extensional or intensional meaning, i.e., with respect to their reference objects or their inherent meaning.

5.5 Summary

The point of departure of this chapter was the observation that a) "[d]iscourse is in fact the very basis for language structure and is thus essential for understanding grammar" (Langacker 2008a: 457) and b) like spoken words, gestures are embedded in an unfolding process of meaning-making. For this reason, the dynamic processes of meaning creation as they unfold over time were elucidated.

By and large, the findings presented above advance the argument that the meanings of gestures perceived in their "natural" environment, i.e., spoken discourse, are specified in the context of an utterance. Needless to say, these findings are anticipated and any other outcome of the analysis would have been fairly surprising. Yet, the question arising from these observations is how gestures are specified through the flow of discourse. This issue was tackled by applying a dynamic approach to multimodal discourse, allowing one to illuminate the orchestration of multimodal meaning as it unfolds in time. Analyzing discourse from such a dynamic perspective revealed that some aspects of meaning, more precisely, certain conceptualizations or their properties, are foregrounded and others are backgrounded, thus, creating a multimodally construed and interactively negotiated salience structure which guides the co-participants' flow of attention. Moreover, through this salience structure, meaning is elaborated in such a way that the gestures under scrutiny, embedded in an enriched local context of use, are specified in their meaning for which different semantic processes are regarded as responsible. One of the two processes is that of specifying the extensional meaning of a gesture by reducing the reference objects that can be profiled by a gesture. A second process is that of defining the intensional meaning of gestures and, thus, their formational and semantic properties. These two processes of semantic specification distribute over the different syntactic positions realized by the gestures. The process of extensional meaning specification was observed in cases of gestures realizing the syntactic slot of nouns and that of intensional meaning precision was identified in gestures realizing the syntactic slot of verbs. Although the study presented in this book aims at elucidating the interpretation of gestures and is, thus, conducted from the perspective of the recipient, an interesting observation is that the gestures investigated here are considered as conveying sufficient information to replace nouns and verbs in the ongoing discourse. The reason for this conceived "sufficiency" is grounded in the rich context in which the gestures are embedded. To put it differently, the discourse has provided ample information for the gestures to replace a noun or verb. As such, the gestures not only profile a particular reference object elaborated by the participants of a conversation, but, in a way, they embody the whole conceptual space created previously. That is why the speech replacing gestures investigated here are always used towards the end of a particular discourse space and not at the beginning of a new discourse unit.

To conclude, the aspects discussed in this chapter show that gestural meaning is not only specified by the meaning of its accompanying utterance but is also detailed by the flow of information which is, simultaneously, a flow of meaning construal and, thus, a flow of conceptualization.

6 Conclusion

The point of departure for the investigation of sequentially constructed multimodal utterances was an empirical question brought forth by an examination made in the data where a woman explaining her playing strategy produces the utterance *Ich wollte dieses* ('I wanted this'), interrupts it and performs a gesture (flat hands, oriented towards her body, moved antagonistically up and down). Thereupon, a co-participant responds to her multimodal utterance by saying *Wand. Durfte man Wand sagen?* ('Wall. Were you allowed to say wall?'). This observation raised many questions including why does the recipient respond to the utterance and not ask for clarification? And why does he refer to an object and not to an activity that exhibits certain form features? These questions could be answered in the analysis presented here by looking at both speech and other modalities, i.e., gesture, and by analyzing the tight interrelatedness of such modalities. Accordingly, we found that the subsequent pause is "filled" by a gesture, and this gesture is not treated as a mere filler, but the second speaker draws information from the gestural form, namely flatness and vertical dimension. Moreover, the syntactic structure of the interrupted utterance grounds or projects a noun that is realized by a gesture representing flatness, vertical dimension and vertical movement. This very condensed presentation of the findings allows one to conclude that the recipient of the multimodal utterance merged both verbal and gestural information in a particular way which led him to refer to the object of a wall in his response.

The study presented in this book analyzed such examples by combining a qualitative and quantitative approach. The 66 examples identified in the data were analyzed on semantic, syntactic and cognitive-semiotic levels and they served as stimuli for naturalistic perception experiments. The findings demonstrate that, first of all, recipients of such utterances treat the gestures as forming part of the verbal utterance and conveying semantic information that interacts with speech. Secondly, nouns and verbs are preferably realized in utterance-final position. When gestures realized nouns, they formed multimodal nominals together with their grounding verbal elements. This multimodal unit served the function of an object or landmark (lm) in the majority of cases. When realizing verbs, gestures formed multimodal clauses together with their grounding verbal constructions.

Thirdly, the syntactic position "coerces" a specific view on gestures by imposing particular cognitive scanning modes onto them. The modes of summary scanning and conceptual reification operate in noun positions, leading to the foregrounding of object information embodied by the hand shape of a gesture (or, in some cases, to the reification of the event embodied by the whole gestural performance). The highlighted gestural information provides mental access to an object – the archetype of nouns – and profile a THING. When realizing verbal slots, the mode of sequential scanning is imposed on the gesture, resulting in the foregrounding of action information embodied by the movement of the hand. The highlighted gestural information provides mental access to an action, the archetype of verbs. The gesture profiles a PROCESS.

Fourthly, gestures contribute their own meaning to the interpretation of the whole utterance. Their inherent or context-independent meaning can be conceived as symbolic units in which a cognitive-iconic relationship between the semantic and phonological pole is established. This conceptual meaning of gestures serves as a mediator between the gestural form and the object it depicts, which forms a multimodal reference object in the interaction with speech. Moreover, in this process of multimodal meaning construal, speech narrows down the semantic range of gestural reference objects and helps conceive a multimodal reference object belonging to a specific conceptual domain.

Finally, the meaning of gestures is specified in their "natural" environment, i.e., interaction. Certain conceptualizations or their properties are foregrounded through the temporal unfolding of meaning, thus, creating a multimodally construed and interactively negotiated salience structure which guides the co-participants' flow of attention. Moreover, this salience structure creates an enriched local context of use which specifies the gestures that replace speech. These processes have been identified as extension and intension. Specifying the extensional meaning of a gesture means that their range of possible reference objects motivated by the gestural form is reduced. Specifying the intensional meaning of gestures means that their formational and semantic properties are defined. These two processes of semantic specification are distributed over the different syntactic positions realized by the gestures. The process of extensional meaning specification was observed in the majority of gestures realizing the syntactic slots of nouns; that of intensional meaning precision tended to occur more often in gestures realizing the syntactic slots of verbs.

All these findings allow one to conclude that the gestures under scrutiny should be considered as *integrated* into the verbal utterance. The cognitive effort recipients make to interpret the multimodal utterances provide evidence that they are actively engaged in merging and, thus, integrating verbal and gestural information. What the condensed presentation of the findings shows is that gestures are conceived differently depending on the position they realize, i.e., they are conceived as objects, reified events or actions. Furthermore, the range of semantic meanings motivated by gestural form is reduced in the interaction with speech, which provides further evidence that recipients construe gestural meanings very differently depending on the syntactic slot realized. Hence, as has been argued in the pages before, speech provides an interpretative frame for the gestures that realize syntactic slots.

Consequently, gestures are considered as forming part of the utterance investigated here and not as a mode a speaker may merely "switch" to for different communicative purposes. This by no means neglects that different communicative purposes are expressed with speech-replacing gestures. Speakers may, for instance, perform highly pantomimic gestures combined with the expression of *be like* (see Streeck 2016) in particular communicative settings, such as talk shows, to achieve a humorous effect. The introductory example of this book created such a humorous effect (Figure 1). Yet, on the level of multimodal utterance formation and, thus, on the level of gesture–speech interaction, it is not in any way different from the other examples gathered in the corpus, because it shows that gestures are another bodily resource speakers naturally and deliberately make use of to express information at certain moments in the flow of discourse and interactive meaning-making. Hence, as the gesture-only condition of the study has demonstrated, without being integrated into a verbal utterance providing, *to some extent*, a frame for interpreting a gestural form, certain communicative purposes might simply not be communicated due to the multiple meanings one gestural form can convey.

6.1 Cognitive grammar multimodal?

The findings yielded by the study presented here lend support to the idea that gestures realizing syntactic slots should be considered as integrated into the verbal utterance. Integration, thereby, means that gestural and verbal information are merged, and the interpretation of gestural meaning is, to some extent, framed by the syntactic and semantic meaning conveyed by speech. But can and should we speak of a multimodal conception of Cognitive Grammar based on these findings? The approach advocated here suggests a positive answer to this question, yet, a clarification of the term "multimodal" is needed.

The study of multimodality attracts an increasing number of researchers from very different fields, including linguistics, semiotics, film studies, art and image science. However, whereas many researchers consider multimodality as the combination of different semiotic resources, such as "facial expressions and gestures – or technologically – pen and ink, or computer hardware and software" (van Leeuwen 2005: 3), and, thus, adopt a wider conception of the term, this book advances the idea of "linguistic multimodality," advocating that linguistic notions are modality-independent and can, therefore, be expressed in different modalities even if these modalities have not reached the status of a fully-fledged linguistic system.

Therefore, two readings of the term "multimodal" are associated with a linguistic approach to multimodality exemplified by the phenomenon scrutinized in this book. First of all, the phenomenon offers empirical evidence that an utterance can be composed of two modalities ("composite utterances," Enfield 2009) and that gestures can become an integral component of an utterance. Integration is essential for the formation of multimodal syntactic structures. Yet, it is by no means defined in terms of obligatoriness (see e.g., Ningelgen and Auer 2017) but rather as a specific way of gesture–speech interaction. Contrary to the idea of gestures adding information to speech, suggesting that speakers merely switch modes, the notion of integration entails that both gestural and verbal information are merged to form one multimodal gestalt (or "expressive movement," Kappelhoff and Müller 2011). As has been pointed out previously, although the analysis presented here pursued an analytic approach to illuminate the semiotic scaffold of gestures, they are not perceived in their single form parameters but as "weak Gestalten" (Köhler 2007 [1938]: 29). This notion implies that gestures are holistic in nature but that we as recipients "are not completely blind for [their] 'parts', i.e., the move(s) and hand-shape(s) and so forth that make up gestures as acts, even though we tend to see 'through' them, to the overall acts as intentional wholes" (Andrén 2010: 84). Following this idea, the integration of speech and gesture means that the different modalities are not different meaning layers, where one adds one meaning on top of the other, but they form an integrated whole, where the modalities are interrelated and coordinated. This is done by specifying each other, for instance. Gesture specifies speech, as many studies have demonstrated (see e.g., Bressem 2012, to appear), but speech can also specify gesture, as elaborated in the previous pages. Accordingly, gestures do not simply replace verbal constructions, "filling" the gap exposed, but are actively, cognitively "adjusted" to the syntactic information provided by speech. In a nutshell, the question of "whether integration can take place across linguistic and gestural systems" (Wilcox and Xavier 2013: 92) is answered positively here. The notion of a "cognitive grammar multimodal," therefore, refers to the integration of speech and gesture on a syntactic and semantic level of utterance production.

The second reading of multimodal in the notion of "cognitive grammar multimodal" relates to the realization of grammatical structures in different modalities, such as spoken and signed languages and gestures. These structures can but do not have to be realized in two modalities simultaneously (such as in speech–gesture or sign–gesture ensembles). The idea behind it is to consider these three modalities as "manifestations of the same underlying conceptual system that is the basis for the human expressive ability" (Wilcox and Xavier

2013: 95). Gestures embody a variety of grammatical notions (see Chapter 2), including the conceptual schemas of THINGs and PROCESSes underlying nouns and verbs. It is noteworthy that this is one reason why gestures are so special, allowing them to integrate into verbal utterances and to develop into language systems themselves. They do so not only because they can fulfill depictive functions (like other semiotic resources including pictures or memes), but because they are most probably the only modality (besides language) that can embody a variety of grammatical notions. This potential is grounded in their "capacity for a high differentiation of movements [which] is a prerequisite for a complex sign system" (Müller 2013: 203). Integration, to the extent described here, can only take place if structural similarities are observable, which is the case with gestures replacing nouns and verbs of verbal utterances.

The observation of a gestural embodiment of grammatical structures fits in well with the theory of Cognitive Grammar, because it makes their embodied roots visible. The conceptual archetypes of nouns and verbs, i.e., objects and actions, are considered as deeply rooted in the body, because the human body has become expert in the handling of objects. Gestures, on the other hand, emanate from such actions and reactivate this knowledge whenever they are performed. As such, they are not only good candidates for replacing nouns and verbs but also for developing these linguistic concepts themselves. As a matter of fact, their basic semiotic structure of embodying object and action information (see Chapter 3) is recruited for the production of many signs of signed language (see Armstrong and Wilcox 2007), regardless of whether they are used as nouns or verbs or other linguistic constructions in a signed utterance. Signed languages can even be distinguished based on how they embody these information. Whereas British Sign Language signs, for instance, strongly prefer "instrument" patterns (Padden et al. 2013), New Zealand Sign Language prefers "handling" forms (Haviland 2013b: 5). Interestingly, both forms have also been identified for gestures and were discussed under the notion of "gestural modes of representation" (Müller 1998, 2009; 2014a, see Chapter 3) or "processes of signification" (Kendon 1980a). Instrument patterns are equivalent to the mode of "representing" (Müller 2014a), while the handling forms are equivalent to the "acting mode" (Müller 2014a). Following Müller (2009: 275), we can, thus, conclude that "[g]estures and signs of signed languages are both ultimately based on mimesis: they share the *material* and also the basic mimetic *modes* and the cognitive-semiotic processes of sign-formation" (Müller 2009: 275, original emphasis; see also Kendon 1988b: 175). We may even assume, as was done in this study, that these different processes of sign creation are recruited as a phonological distinction between nominal and verbal information in gestures or evolving signed languages. Haviland (2013b: 6), for instance, hypothesized recently that

> the profiling of action inherent in Padden's 'handling' pattern might be appropriate to verbs, whereas the profiling of the object invoked by the 'instrument' pattern might be more appropriate as a formal means of specifying nouns. Such a hypothesis seems to be confirmed in much of the Z signers' descriptions of stimuli designed to elicit either nominal or verbal expressions, but the distinction is sometimes too subtle (and not always consistent enough) to be considered grammatically robust.

Although Haviland (2013a: 87ff.) points out that this "distinction is sometimes too subtle (and not always consistent enough) to be considered grammatically robust", it is confirmed, to some extent, by the Z homesign system. A similar hypothesis was addressed in the study presented here regarding the use of gestures in nominal and verbal slots, however, it could not be corroborated at all. The empirical findings presented in Chapter 3 rather demonstrated that the gestural mode of acting ("handling") was preferably used regardless of whether the gestures realized nouns or verbs of spoken utterances. Accordingly, gestures used in speech pauses do not show any phonological distinction in the depiction of objects or actions, as evolving signed languages may show. Yet, this observation confirms the idea proposed earlier, namely that gestures are grounded in the manipulation of objects. They depict the *handling* of objects rather than their visual perception (see Chapter 3 for more information), which explains why the acting mode is used preferably to convey meaning gesturally. Interestingly, these different techniques of symbolizing and, thus, of creating semiotic signs are processed in different hemispheres as neurological studies have shown. According to Lausberg et al. (2003), representing gestures ("body part as object") are processed in the right hemisphere, while acting gestures ("pantomime") are processed in the left hemisphere, where language is processed as well.

It appears noteworthy that gestures are not generally considered as "part of" grammar but that grammatical notions can be embodied gesturally, and they can do so to different degrees. Therefore, the approach advocated here can be connected to Cienki's (2012, 2013a) idea of a "flexible model of grammar," in which speech and gesture converge at particular points in time and on different time scales, forming either monomodal or multimodal entrenched units (see Chapter 2) or serve as bodily resources in the process of utterance formation. This flexible model of grammar suggests variable degrees and ways in which gesture can become linguistic (Cienki 2015: 508). The gestures under scrutiny are certainly different from those embodying grammatical notions such as aspect, negation or plural, because they replace linguistic (lexical) units and do not show stabilized movement patterns, for instance. However, because they can embody the conceptual schemas underlying nouns and verbs, which allows them to create not only multimodal semantic but also syntactic structures, the phenomenon discussed here is considered to belong to the realm of multimodal cognitive grammar.

To conclude, with the view developed here, the *acting* body rather than the visually perceiving body is emphasized to develop a theory of multimodal cognitive grammar and embodied language in general. Embodied meaning which gives rise to linguistic meaning does not only emerge from seeing objects moving through space, captured by notions such as the "billiard-ball model" and "the stage model" (see Langacker 1987a, 1991b, 2008a). Embodied experiences comprise sensorimotor experiences of the body and our associated knowledge of how we can move and use our bodies. Following this argument, humans not only conceptualize things and processes by observing them visually but, first and foremost, by experiencing them with and in the body. This becomes particularly visible when we look at gestures. As such, the book argues that grammatical categories embodied gesturally are not only embodied instantiations of grammatical concepts. They (also) come from the hands.

6.2 Beyond the approach advocated here

Two final points should be addressed briefly to come full circle. First of all, as pointed out throughout this book, the approach advocated here combines with a specific perspective on gesture and language, as it observes gestures as a medium of expression and their linguistic potential (see Armstrong and Wilcox 2007; Müller 2013). Accordingly, their representational function ("*Darstellungsfunktion*", Bühler 1934) and the issue of how it materializes in the gestural modality was set center stage in this book. The study presented was undertaken in an attempt to determine the gestural (semiotic) properties, allowing them to provide access to mentally construed reference objects and, thus, replace speech. These properties have the potential to develop into linguistic structures when considering stabilization processes in gestures (see above).

However, only one facet of gestural meaning creation could be illuminated with this focus of the book, which, on the other hand, is considered as fundamental when we aim at understanding gestures as a separate modality. As a matter of fact, meaning has very different dimensions, including affective, semantic, pragmatic or social ones. Moreover, interaction is the *locus communis* where meaning evolves and is elaborated. Yet, interactive processes of meaning negotiation have only been addressed to some extent in the view developed here, namely regarding the foregrounding of meaning (Chapter 5). The study, therefore, offered a glimpse into how meaning evolves and yet does not reconstruct the processes of how conversing bodies reach mutual understanding. Cognitive Grammar certainly considers language as grounded in and guided by social interaction, however, the latter is always related to the knowledge of individual speakers. Langacker (2008a: 7–6) points out that "[w]ithin functionalism, cognitive linguistics stands out by emphasizing the semiological function of language. It fully acknowledges the grounding of language in social interaction, but insists that even its interactive function is critically dependent on conceptualization."

With this take on language, the approach certainly served the research question addressed here. Moreover, it goes without saying that conceptual meaning, i.e., the *what* of multimodal meaning construal, plays a pivotal role when tackling the issue of intersubjectivity. Because when we speak, "we conceptualize not only what we are talking about but also the context in all its dimensions, including our assessment of the knowledge and intentions of our interlocutor. Rather than being insular, therefore, conceptualization should be seen as a primary means of engaging the world. And empty heads cannot talk, interact, or negotiate meanings" (Langacker 2008a: 29).

Acknowledging that meaning construal on a conceptual level plays an important role when establishing intersubjectivity does not mean that the *how* of verbal and gestural performance is less important. However, tackling this issue goes beyond the approach advocated in this book, as it leaves the realm of conceptual representations to open the door to the affective dimensions of speaking and gesturing. Following the body of research developing a phenomenological perspective to affect (e.g., Greifenstein 2019; Horst 2018; Horst et al. 2014; Kappelhoff 2004; Kappelhoff and Müller 2011; Müller and Kappelhoff 2018), affect and emotions are not conceived of as being symbolized, displayed and, thus, as being represented. Quite the contrary, affective meaning is understood as being "intermingled with the structure of the world outlined by [a] gesture" and a verbal expression (Merleau-Ponty [1962] 2005: 216). Thus, affect is not represented by a gesture, it is *in* the gesture itself.

Consider the following observation made by Merleau-Ponty ([1962] 2005: 214, emphasis in the original), which, among others, has inspired researchers to develop a different view on gestural expression of affect.

> Faced with an angry or threatening gesture, I have no need, in order to understand it, to recall the feelings which I myself experienced when I used these gestures on my own account. I know very little, from inside, of the mime of anger so that a decisive factor is missing for any association by resemblance or reasoning by analogy, and what is more, I do not see anger or a threatening attitude as a psychic fact hidden behind the gesture, I read anger in it. The gesture does not make me think of anger, it is anger itself.
> (Merleau-Ponty [1962] 2005: 214, original emphasis)

Put more generally, the affective dimension of a gesture is not represented in a single form parameter, but it is embodied by the whole gestural *gestalt*. It is most prominent in the movement quality associated with the *how* of a gestural performance (see Müller 2013: 202). A speaker's affective involvement in a conversation expressed by gesture and speech "calls up bodily resonances in the *perceiving* interlocutor" creating a "constant affective exchange between interlocutors" (Horst et al. 2014: 2116, original emphasis; see also Kappelhoff and Müller 2011; Müller and Kappelhoff 2018). This exchange is not conceived as an affect expression of individual speakers but as "inter-affectivity," which forms the very basis of human interaction, meaning creation and, thus, establishes intersubjectivity (see Horst et al. 2014; Müller and Kappelhoff 2018).

Connecting this brief excursion with the study advocated in this book shows once more how complex human interaction is and that different approaches can illuminate different dimensions of the human ability to express and interact. Different perspectives open up the scene for different ways of theorizing and empirically investigating multimodal meaning-making. The approach presented in this book offers a way to examine the conceptual construal of speech and gesture, shifting the attention to gestures' capacity to convey meaning and, thus, integrate by realizing verbal constructions.

Appendices

In this section, the qualitative analysis of the data will be illustrated briefly by supplying information on the data and coding system and by providing longer transcripts and a table listing of the examples. It is noteworthy that this section should not be understood as a coding manual but as an opportunity to address methodological issues that have not been discussed in the previous chapters. The methodological approach applied here and its theoretical implications are discussed elsewhere in more detail (see Müller, Bressem and Ladewig to appear). If a reader is interested in a more systematic account of a linguistic coding system, s/he is referred to the Linguistic Annotation System of Gesture Analysis ("LASG", Bressem, Ladewig and Müller 2013). A sketch of the quantitative analysis can be found in Chapter 3, Chapter 4 and Chapter 5.

Appendix A: Sample and phenomenon defined

The study presented in this book is based on 20 hours of naturalistic German data covering different discourse types, including everyday conversations, TV shows, and parlor games collected during 2004–2010. In these data, the phenomenon under scrutiny was identified by applying the following criteria:

- An interrupted utterance is identified by means of syntactic and prosodic devices involved in the production of utterances (see e.g., Selting 1995; Selting 1998, 2001). Syntactic constructions are interrupted and the intonation remains constant. The latter observation is of crucial importance as it differentiates cataphoric reference from integration into nominals. An utterance such as "I wanted this," where the definite determiner is used with a focus accent, can be considered as a self-contained unit, at least on the level of spoken language. Yet, it cataphorically integrates a gesture which serves to add information missing in speech (see Chapter 3)
- Gestures join in interrupted utterances. The spoken utterances are not continued after the deployment of (a) gesture(s).
- No dysfluency markers which document lexicalization or verbalization problems are produced by the speakers.
- The utterances are interrupted by the speaker and not by a co-participant.

The single clips created from the data base were imported as audio video interleave files into the annotation software *Elan* (see Wittenburg et al. 2006).

Additionally, wave files exported from the clips were imported to determine the exact position where speech is broken off and the pause begins.

Appendix B: Coding scheme

Different tiers were set up in Elan (a) to transcribe and annotate speech and b) to annotate gesture for each articulator. Figure 54 visualizes the different coding categories applied and the corresponding tiers. Additionally, the speaker's gaze was annotated and the co-participants' utterances transcribed.

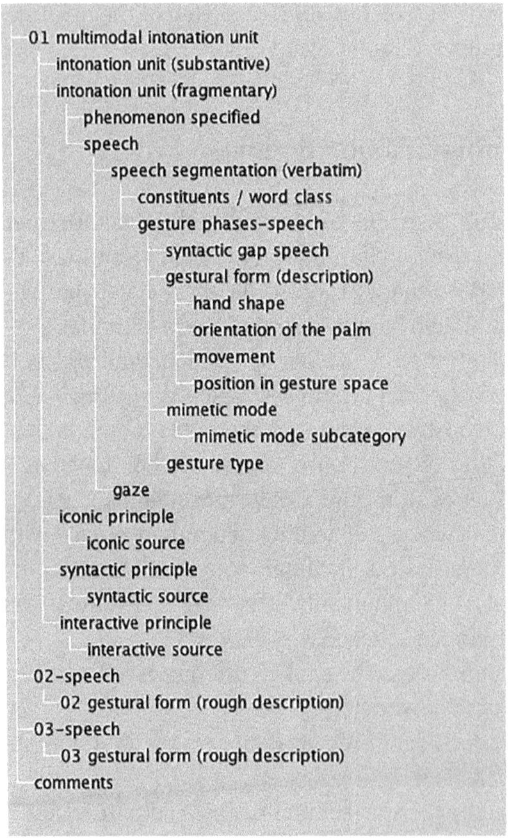

```
01 multimodal intonation unit
    intonation unit (substantive)
    intonation unit (fragmentary)
        phenomenon specified
        speech
            speech segmentation (verbatim)
                constituents / word class
                gesture phases-speech
                    syntactic gap speech
                    gestural form (description)
                        hand shape
                        orientation of the palm
                        movement
                        position in gesture space
                    mimetic mode
                        mimetic mode subcategory
                    gesture type
        gaze
    iconic principle
        iconic source
    syntactic principle
        syntactic source
    interactive principle
        interactive source
02-speech
    02 gestural form (rough description)
03-speech
    03 gestural form (rough description)
comments
```

Figure 54: Coding scheme (Elan window showing tier dependencies). Sequential integration of gestures into speech.

The parent tier of all dependent tiers includes the whole multimodal utterance unit. The tier "monomodal units" separates the verbal and the gestural modality, which are transcribed and annotated on the subsequent tiers. Speech was first transcribed following GAT2 (Selting et al. 2011) and segmented verbatim afterwards. The verbal constructions were determined based on the linguistic segmentation. Gestures were annotated on speech-dependent tiers observable as hierarchies in Figure 54. The reason for implementing a speech-dependent hierarchy of gestures was to determine the exact position of the gestural stroke in relation to the verbal constructions. This procedure allowed one to distinguish between the simultaneous usage of gesture and speech and the sequential use of both modalities. Such a distinction could, in many cases, not be made from merely watching a video clip. On the following tiers gestures were annotated regarding their gestural form parameters (see Bressem 2013; Ladewig and Bressem 2013a), modes of representation (Müller 1998, 2014a), and gesture type (singular, recurrent, emblematic; see Ladewig 2010, 2014c; Müller 2010b, 2017a). The foregrounding principles introduced by Müller and Tag (2010) were incorporated and annotated on separate tiers to trace the emergence and activation of meaning. These tiers are linked directly to the parent tier ("multimodal utterance"), because they are based on the information annotated for speech and gestures.

The co-participants' utterances were transcribed separately for each speaker. Their gestures were described roughly on separate tiers.

Appendix C: Transcripts

Longer transcripts of the two examples introduced in Chapter 3 are provided in this section.

Appendices

Transcript of example "Ich wollte dieses 👆 ('I wanted this' 👆)"[32]

		und zwar ä::h	(-)	n meer in: klein	ja/	und da is denn quasi	nein	also dieser	SEE	da is so ne art ä::h	
1	S1. speech	und zwar ä::h	(-)	n meer in: klein	ja/	und da is denn quasi	nein	also dieser	SEE	da is so ne art ä::h	
2	S1. speech translated	*and well e::h*	(--)	*a sma:ll sea*	*yes/*	*and there is so to speak*	*no*	*well this*	*LAKE*	*there is a kind of e::h*	
3	S1. gesture	rh, touches her head					bh, sweeping away (twice), periphery		bh, flat hand, AB, straight downwards		
4	S1. gaze					gaze at the computer screen					
5	S2. speech			see							STEG
6	S2. speech translated			*lake*							*DOCK*
7	S3. speech			fluss							
8	S3. speech translated			*river*							
9	S4. speech						TEGERNsee				
10	S4. speech translated						*TEGERN lake*	*water lily*			
11	S1. speech	gebäude?			(.h) damit dort dis		mann ich wusste nicht wie ichs beschreiben soll				
12	S1. speech translated	*building?*			*(.h) that there this*		*man I didn't know how to describe it*				
13	S1. gesture	rh, Cyclic gesture, PD, if stretched, right periphery									
14	S1. gaze	gaze at computer screen					gaze towards speaker 3 and 4				

32 rh = right hand, lh = left hand, bh = both hands.

#	Tier								
15	S2. speech	tÜ::t	am SEE doch nicht					achSO WAR leuchtUrm oder was?	
16	S2. speech translated	tOO:t	not at a LAKE					aHA WAS lighthouse or what?	
17	S3. speech	LEUCHTturm							
19	S1. speech	NEI::N	StAUsee = ich	wollte	dieses-				
20	S1. speech translated	NO::	BARRIER lake I	wanted	this-	(-)			Nein.
21	S1. gesture phases			preparation	stroke	stroke	stroke	stroke	stroke	stroke	stroke	retraction
22	S1. movement				up	down	up	down	up	down	up	
23	S1. hand shape				flat	flat	flat	flat	flat	flat	flat	
24	S1. orientation				towards body	towards body	towards body	towards body	towards body	towards body	towards body	
25	S1. gesture space				center center to upper per center	upper center to center center	center center to upper per center	upper center to center center	center center to upper per center	upper center to center center	center center to upper per center	
26	S1. gaze				towards speaker 2 and 4							
27	S4. speech								toward speaker 4	at the computer	WAND? Durfte man WAND sagn?	
28	S4. speech translated										WALL? Were you allowed to say WALL?	

Transcript "und wir hinten 👆 ('and we from the back' 👆)"

1	S1. speech	und Oma imma	was WILLst dEnn DU?		GEH DU RUnta	s war sone zweiraumwohnung hier mit sonem gitter
2	S1. speech translated	*and GRAndma always*	*what do YOU WANT?*		*YOU GET DOwn*	*it was such an apartment here with such a window grill*
3	S1. gesture		pushing forwards	hold	pushing down	
4	S1. gaze			towards her hands		
5	S2 speech					(laughing)

6	S1. speech	und Hanne imma	oma ich hab doch n schlÜSsel vergessn	gEH Runta	und die hat imma geschUbst
7	S1. speech translated	*and Hanne always*	*granny I've forgotten the KEY*	*gET down*	*and she was pUshing all the time*
8	S1. gesture			pushing forward + down	pushing forwards twice
9	S1. gaze				
10	S2 speech			laughing	

11 S1. speech	und	wir	hin	tn-	(0.5s)	Ja	(lacht)
12 S1. speech translated	*and*	*we*	*from the*	*back-*	*(0,5sec)*	*Yes*	*(laughing)*
13 S1. gesture phases	preparation		stroke			partial retraction	hold
14 S1. movement				straight upward			
15 S1. hand shape				flat hand			
16 S1. orientation				away body			
17 S1. gesture space				upper center			
18 S1. gaze	forward					towards Sp.2	forward
19 S2. speech					ECHT?	(lacht)	
20 S2. speech translated					REALLY?	(laughing)	

Appendix D: Tabulation of examples

No.	Example	Utterance	Translation (transliteration)	Gesture type	Mode of representation	Syntactic position determined in the multimodal utterance condition
1	there is a	man sagt = man sagt irgendwie am meer gibts ne-	'one says = one says on the beach there is a-'	referential	representing	noun
2	I wanted this	StAUsee = ich wollte dieses-	'barrier lake = I wanted this-'	referential	representing	noun
3	with these	Ach hier mit diesn-	'Ah I see, here with these-'	referential	acting	noun
4	it runs on a	und es läuft auf einem	'and it runs on a-'	referential	representing	noun
5	it has this strange	hat nur vorne drauf dIEsn s'Elts'Amen-	'only in the front it has this strange-'	referential	acting	noun
6	a little	ich glaub ich lass mein kulturwisschenschaftstutorium son bisschen-	'I think I set my tutorial for cultural studies a little-'	referential	acting	verb
7	I just wanted	ich wollt einfach mal-	'I just wanted-'	referential use of recurrent gesture	acting	verb
8	are detailed(ly)	da sind jA: die s'achn detailliert-	'well there, the things are detailedly-'	referential	representing	verb

Appendix D: Tabulation of examples — 195

9	he had a	*der hatte da einen-*	'there he had a-'	referential	acting	noun
10	have a particular	*müssen eine bestimmte KOnfektiOn haben eine bestimmte-*	'must have a particular size have a particular-'	referential	acting	noun
11	my nose	*dass ich meine nase-*	'that I my nose-'	referential	acting	verb
12	my nose	*dass ich meine nase-*	'that I my nose-'	referential	acting	verb
13	in the rooms	*(-) dass wir nicht in den zimma:n-*	'that we do not in the rooms-'	referential	representing	verb
14	all of a sudden	*stEll da mal vor du stEhst da in inna Umkleide of Eenmal-*	'just imagine you are in the changing room and all of a sudden-'	referential+ referential	acting	clause
15	and we from behind	*und die hat immer geschubst und wir hintn-*	'and she was pushing all the time and we from behind-'	referential	acting	verb
16	had in the little bed	*hast im bettchen-*	'had in the little bed-'	referential	acting	verb
17	and there was	*wie war so offmachen und da war-*	'as we opened and there was-'	referential	acting	noun
18	in the same	*die vierte war aber im hinterhof im 'selbn-*	'but the fourth was in the court in the same-'	recurrent (pointing)	representing	noun
19	(that is) this	*(S1: das is) dieses-*	'(that is) this-'	referential	acting	noun
20	of course with the	*(S1: beim maln bin ich auch) natürlich bei dem-*	'when painting I'm also of course with the-'	referential	acting	noun
21	they just have their	*nee die haben nur ihre-*	'no they just have their-'	referential (pantomime)	acting	noun

(continued)

(continued)

No.	Example	Utterance	Translation (transliteration)	Gesture type	Mode of representation	Syntactic position determined in the multimodal utterance condition
22	and there and	und haben uns gleich die jacken abgenommen und hingehangen und-	'and immediately took our jackets and went there and-'	referential	acting	verb
23	was in the	das war ja och in dem-	'well it also was in the-'	recurrent (pointing)	representing	noun
24	we looked	ham wa geg'Uckt irgendwann-	'we looked. At some point-'	referential	acting	clause
25	one needs a little	man muss ein bisschen-	'one needs a little.'	recurrent	acting	verb
26	overall had these	und hatte aber überall diese-	'but overall had these-'	recurrent (pointing)	representing	noun
27	and they down	Oh und dIE Untn-	'well and they downstairs-'	emblem	acting	verb
28	would it rather	so würd ich denn nich plan=ich würd es denn ebnd-	'I wouldn't plan like this I would it rather-'	referential	acting	verb
29	well this is still	KarlHheinz dis is ja noch	'Karl Heinz well this is still-'	referential	acting	noun
30	and recorded and	wie dis denn = Überall gings denn ab und aufgezeichnet und-	'how this then = it went off everywhere and recorded and-'	referential	acting	verb

31	there was	und denn war dis fernsehteil = da war-	'and then the TV thing = there was-'	referential	acting	noun
32	could have the curtain	und drum rum wies och schon aussah. Da hättste die gardine-	'and how it looked everywhere you could have the curtain.'	recurrent (Throwing away)	acting	verb
33	had of course	haste natürlich-	'you had of course.'	recurrent (Throwing away)	acting	noun
34	you were then	nee du bist ja denn-	'no you were the-'	referential	acting	verb
35	tried a little to	die ham o noch versucht son bisschen-	'well they also tried a little to-'	referential	acting	verb
36	and she	ich hab meine schokolade weggehabt und she-	'my chocolate was all gone and she.'	referential (pantomime)	acting	verb
37	and then it is like a	der farbkleks und dann wird das zusammgefaltet (.) dann macht mans auf und dann ist es wie ein-	'the blur of color and then it is folded (.) then you open it is and then it is like a-'	referential	acting	noun
38	think about	aber = aber denkt ma-	'but = but think-.'	recurrent (bimanual asynchronous Cyclic gesture)	representing	Verb (adverb)
39	across a	poltern = man poltern auf einmal über eine-	'rumble = suddenly one rumbles across a-'	referential	representing	noun

(continued)

(continued)

No.	Example	Utterance	Translation (transliteration)	Gesture type	Mode of representation	Syntactic position determined in the multimodal utterance condition
40	you need	wenn das so große fleischmassen sind dann braucht man-	'if these are huge masses of meat then you need-'	referential (pantomime)	acting	noun
41	and he had up there	der stand die ganze zeit off de hinterbeene (.h) und hat obn-	'all the time she was standing on her back limb (.) and had up there-'	referential (pantomime)	acting	verb
42	before he then	wie son baseballschläger der vorher die füße so in den sand gräbt bevor er dann-	'like a baseball player who digs his feet in the sand before he then-'	referential (pantomime)	acting	verb
43	I walk on the	ja (. . .) das nennt man laufen deswegen läuf ich auf den-	'yes (. . .) you term it walk that's why I walk on the-'	referential	representing	noun
44	any further	wir wollen das thema nicht weiter-	'we do not want this topic any further-'	recurrent (Sweeping Away)	acting	verb
45	that you	wo da wo dat tropfding dranne hängt (-) die du-	'where where the drip thing hangs on (-) that you-'	referential (pantomime)	acting	verb
46	don't think again that I	denk wieda nich dass ich-	'don't think again that I-'	emblem	representing	verb + pred.noun

Appendix D: Tabulation of examples — 199

#							
47	and then he	was meintn das kind damit/ (..) und denn-	'what does the child mean by that/ (..) and then-'	emblem	acting	verb
48	actually was hidden	das war eigntlich och versteckt-	'actually it was also hidden-'	emblem	acting	verb
49	then they were	ja dann sind se-	'yes then they were-'	recurrent (Throwing away)	acting	noun
50	normal citizens or	es gibt ja glob=ich mEhr dumme als es normalbürger gibt oder-	'I think there exist = more dumb than normal citizens or-'	referential	representing	noun
51	but all of it is	die hat zwar och ne weiße rauhfaser aber is ja alles-	'it also had a white ingrain wallpaper but all of it is-'	emblem	acting	noun
52	and then he	die türe ging off und dann hat=er-	'the door went open and then he-'	recurrent (Sweeping Away)	acting	verb
53	then he was	denn war=er-	'then he was-'	recurrent (Sweeping Away)	acting	noun
54	he already had her	also die hat quasi wahrscheinlich den kinderwagen nehm ich an runter und denn hatter sie schon-	'well she probably had the baby buggy, I assume, down and then he already had her.'	referential	representing	verb
55	to what extent all this	die frage is ja inwieweit dis alles-	'the question is to what extent all of this-'	referential	representing	verb

(continued)

(continued)

No.	Example	Utterance	Translation (transliteration)	Gesture type	Mode of representation	Syntactic position determined in the multimodal utterance condition
56	a child there	*ich mein wie kommt man denn off die idee (-) son kind da-*	'I mean how do you come up with such an idea (-) a child there-'	referential	acting	verb
57	she wanted once more	*die wollte noch mal-*	'she wanted once more-'	emblem	acting	verb
58	and white but	*wenn ich mal nich: schwarzweiß haben will sondern-*	'if I don't want black and white but-'	recurrent (PUOH)	acting	noun
59	you just want	*aba manchma haste willste halt-*	'but sometimes you have you just want-'	referential (pantomime)	acting	verb
60	then there emerges a	*wenn ich irgendwo was verfärbe dann entsteht ein-*	'if I stain something somewhere then there emerges a-'	recurrent (PUOH)	acting	noun
61	I give him my	*ich möchte dass er mich ä::hm dass er mich kontaktiert dann geb ich ihm meine*	'I want that e:::m that he contacts me and then I give him my -'	recurrent (PUOH)	acting	noun
62	antenna or	*man hat entweder ne antenne oder-*	'you either have an antenna or-'	recurrent (PUOH)	acting	noun

Appendix D: Tabulation of examples — 201

63	words and then just	*merk dir dit und dann sagt er genau die ersten beiden wörter und du genau die letzten beiden wörter genommen und dann einfach mal-*	'remember this and then he said just the first two words and you just the last two words and then just -'	referential	acting	verb
64	but there will	*landebahn drei wunderba: (..) da werdn aba-*	'landing runway three great (..) but there will-'	referential	acting	clause
65	and on the	*die haben ja ziemlich viele beinchen (...) ja so lobster und an den-*	'they have quite a few little legs (...) yes such a lobster and on the-'	referential	representing	noun
66	and wants to know	*du hast gesagt kommt aus bonn und möchte wissen-*	'you said comes from Bonn and wants to know.'	referential	representing	clause

References

Andrén, Mats. 2010. *Children's Gestures from 18 to 30 months*. Lund: Lund University.

Andrén, Mats. 2014. Multimodal constructions in children: Is the headshake part of language? *Gesture* 14(2). 141–170.

Arciuli, Joanne & Louisa M Slowiaczek. 2006. What does Dichotic Listening Reveal about the Processing of Stress Typicality? *11th Australasian International Conference on Speech Science and Technology 2006*, ASSTA Inc. 1–6.

Armstrong, David F., William C. Stokoe & Sherman Wilcox. 1995. *Gesture and the Nature of Language*. Cambridge: Cambridge University Press.

Armstrong, David F. & Sherman Wilcox. 2007. *The gestural origin of language*. Oxford & New York: Oxford University Press.

Auer, Peter. 2005. Projection in interaction and projection in grammar. *Text-Interdisciplinary journal for the study of discourse* 25(1). 7–36.

Auer, Peter & Stefan Pfänder. 2011. *Constructions, Emerging and Emergent*. Berlin & Boston: De Gruyter.

Barske, Tobias & Andrea Golato. 2010. German so: managing sequence and action. *Text & Talk* 30(3). 245–266.

Battison, Robin. 1974. Phonological deletion in American Sign Language. *Sign Language Studies* 5(1). 1–19.

Bavelas, Janet B., Nicole Chovil, Douglas A. Lawrie & Allan Wade. 1992. Interactive Gestures. *Discourse Processes* 15. 469–489.

Beattie, Geoffrey & Heather Shovelton. 2007. The Role of Iconic Gesture in Semantic Communication and its Theoretical and Practical Implications. In Duncan, Susan D., Justine Cassell & Elena Tevy Levy (eds.), *Gesture and the dynamic dimension of language* (Gesture Studies 1), 221–241. Philadelphia: J. Benjamins Pub. Co.

Birdwhistell, Ray L. 1970. *Kinesics and context*. University of Pennsylvania press Philadelphia.

Bohle, Ulrike. 2007. *Das Wort ergreifen-das Wort übergeben: explorative Studie zur Rolle redebegleitender Gesten in der Organisation des Sprecherwechsels*. Berlin: Weidler.

Boll, Franziska. 2018. *Multimodalität und Interaktion im Prozess konsekutiven Übersetzens*. Frankfurt (Oder), European University Viadrina: Dissertation thesis.

Boutet, Dominique, Aliyah Morgenstern & Alan Cienki. 2016. Grammatical Aspect and Gesture in French: A kinesiological approach. *Russian Journal of Linguistics* 20(3). 132–151.

Brentari, Diane. 2007. Sign language phonology: Issues of iconicity and universality. *Verbal and Signed Languages, Comparing Structures, Constructs and Methodologies*. 59–80.

Bressem, Jana. 2012. *Repetitions in gestures: Structures and cognitive aspects*. Frankfurt (Oder): European University Viadrina: Dissertation thesis.

Bressem, Jana. 2013. A linguistic perspective on the notation of form features in gestures. In Müller, Cornelia, Alan Cienki, Ellen Fricke, Silva H. Ladewig, David McNeill & Sedinha Teßendorf (eds.), *Body – Language – Communication. An International Handbook on Multimodality in Human Interaction* (Handbooks of Linguistics and Communication Science 38.1.), 1079–1098. Berlin & Boston: De Gruyter Mouton.

Bressem, Jana. 2014. Repetitions in gestures. In Müller, Cornelia, Alan Cienki, Ellen Fricke, Silva H. Ladewig, David McNeill & Jana Bressem (eds.), *Body – Language – Communication. An International Handbook on Multimodality in Human Interaction* (Handbooks of

Linguistics and Communication Science 38.2.), 1641–1649. Berlin & Boston: De Gruyter Mouton.

Bressem, Jana. 2015. Repetition als Mittel der Musterbildung bei redebegleitenden Gesten. In Dürscheid, Christa & Jan Georg Schneider (eds.), *Satz, Äußerung, Schema* (Handbücher Sprachwissen 4), 421–441. Berlin & Boston: de Gruyter.

Bressem, Jana. to appear. *Repetitions in gesture: A cognitive-linguistic and usage based perspective*. Berlin & Boston: De Gruyter Mouton.

Bressem, Jana & Silva H. Ladewig. 2011. Rethinking gesture phases – articulatory features of gestural movement? *Semiotica* 184(1/4). 53–91.

Bressem, Jana, Silva H. Ladewig & Cornelia Müller. 2013. A linguistic annotation system for gestures (LASG). In Müller, Cornelia, Alan Cienki, Ellen Fricke, Silva H. Ladewig, David McNeill & Sedinha Teßendorf (eds.), *Body – Language – Communication: An International Handbook on Multimodality in Human Interaction* (Handbooks of Linguistics and Communication Science 38.1.), 1098–1125. Berlin & Boston: De Gruyter Mouton.

Bressem, Jana, Silva H. Ladewig & Cornelia Müller. 2018. Ways of expressing action in multimodal narrations – The semiotic complexity of character viewpoint depictions. In Hübl, Anika & Markus Steinbach (eds.), *Linguistic Foundations of Narration in Spoken and Sign Languages*, 223–249. Amsterdam: Benjamins.

Bressem, Jana & Cornelia Müller. 2014a. The family of AWAY gestures. Negation, refusal and negative assessment. In Müller, Cornelia, Alan Cienki, Ellen Fricke, Silva H. Ladewig, David McNeill & Jana Bressem (eds.), *Body – Language – Communication. An International Handbook on Multimodality in Human Interaction* (Handbooks of Linguistics and Communication Science 38.2.), 1592–1605. Berlin & Boston: De Gruyter Mouton.

Bressem, Jana & Cornelia Müller. 2014b. A repertoire of German recurrent gestures with pragmatic functions. In Müller, Cornelia, Alan Cienki, Ellen Fricke, Silva H. Ladewig, David McNeill & Jana Bressem (eds.), *Body – Language – Communication. An International Handbook on Multimodality in Human Interaction* (Handbooks of Linguistics and Communication Science 38.2.), 1575–1592. Berlin & Boston: De Gruyter Mouton.

Bressem, Jana & Cornelia Müller. 2017. The "Negative-Assessment-Construction" – A multimodal pattern based on a recurrent gesture? *Linguistics Vanguard* 3(s1).

Broccias, Cristiano & Willem B. Hollmann. 2007. Do we need summary and sequential scanning in (Cognitive) grammar? *Cognitive Linguistics* 18–4. 487–522.

Brookes, Heather. 2004. A repertoire of South African quotable gestures. *Journal of Linguistic Anthropology* 14(2). 186–224.

Brugman, C. 1984. The very idea: A case study in polysemy and cross-lexical generalizations. *CLS XX, Papers from the Parasession on Lexical Semantics*. 21–38.

Bühler, Karl. 1934. *Sprachtheorie. Die Darstellungsfunktion der Sprache*. Stuttgart & New York: Fischer.

Butterworth, Brian & Uri Hadar. 1989. Gesture, speech, and computational stages: A reply to McNeill. *Psychological Review* 96 (1). 168–174.

Bybee, Joan. 2006. From usage to grammar: The mind's response to repetition. *Language*. 711–733.

Calbris, Geneviève. 1987. Geste et motivation. *Semiotica* 65(1/2). 57–96.

Calbris, Geneviève. 1990. *The semiotics of French gestures*. Bloomington: Indiana University Press.

Calbris, Geneviève. 2003. From cutting an object to a clear cut analysis. Gesture as the representation of a preconceptual schema linking concrete actions to abstract notions. *Gesture* 3(1). 19–46.
Calbris, Geneviève. 2008. From left to right … : Coverbal gestures and their symbolic use of space. In Cienki, Alan & Cornelia Müller (eds.), *Metaphor and Gesture*, 27–53. Amsterdam: Benjamins.
Calbris, Geneviève. 2011. *Elements of meaning in gesture*. Amsterdam: John Benjamins Publishing Company.
Cameron, Lynne. 1999. Identifying and describing metaphor in spoken discourse data. In Cameron, Lynne & Graham Low (eds.), *Researching and applying metaphor*, 105–132. Cambridge: Cambridge University Press.
Cameron, Lynne. 2002. *Metaphor in educational discourse*. New York: Continuum.
Cameron, Lynne, Robert Maslen, Zazie Todd, John Maule, Peter Stratton & Neil Stanley. 2009. The discourse dynamics approach to metaphor and metaphor-led discourse analysis. *Metaphor and Symbol* 24(2). 63–89.
Carnap, Rudolf. 1947. *Meaning and necessity: A study in semantics and modal logic*. Chicago: University of Chicago Press.
Casasanto, Daniel & Kyle Jasmin. 2012. The hands of time: Temporal gestures in English speakers. *Cognitive Linguistics* 23(4). 643–674.
Chafe, Wallace L. 1994. *Discourse, consciousness, and time: the flow and displacement of conscious experience in speaking and writing*. Chicago: University of Chicago Press.
Chafe, Wallace L. & Charles N. Li. 1976. Givenness, Contrastiveness, Definiteness, Subjects, Topics, and Point of View in Subject and Topic.
Chandler, Daniel. 2002. *Semiotics: The Basics*. Hoboken: Taylor & Francis.
Chiarcos, Christian. 2011. The Mental Salience Framework: Context-adequate generation of referring expressions. In Christian Chiarcos, Berry Claus, Michael Grabski (eds.), *Salience: Multidisciplinary Perspectives on its Function in Discourse*, 105–142. Berlin & New York: De Gruyter Mouton.
Chui, Kawai. 2005. Temporal patterning of speech and iconic gestures in conversational discourse. *Journal of Pragmatics* 37(6). 871–887.
Cienki, Alan. 1998a. Metaphoric gestures and some of their relations to verbal metaphorical expressions. In König, Jean-Pierre (ed.), *Discourse and Cognition: Bridging the Gap*, 189–204. Stanford, CA: Center for the Study of Language and Information.
Cienki, Alan. 1998b. Straight: An image schema and its metaphorical extensions. *Cognitive Linguistics* 9(2). 107–149.
Cienki, Alan. 2005. Images schemas and gesture. In Hampe, Beate (ed.), *From perception to meaning: Image schemas in cognitive linguistics*, 421–442. Berlin & New York: Mouton de Gruyter.
Cienki, Alan. 2008. Why study metaphor and gesture. In Cienki, Alan & Cornelia Müller (eds.), *Metaphor and gesture*, 5–25. Amsterdam & New York: John Benjamins.
Cienki, Alan. 2012. Usage events of spoken language and the symbolic units we (may) abstract from them. *Cognitive processes in language*. 149–158.
Cienki, Alan. 2013a. Gesture, space, grammar, and cognition. In Auer, Peter, Martin Hilpert, Anja Stukenbrock & Benedikt Szmrecsanyi (eds.), *Space in Language and Linguistics Geographical, Interactional, and Cognitive Perspectives*, 667–686. Berlin: De Gruyter.

Cienki, Alan. 2013b. Image schemas and mimetic schemas in cognitive linguistics and gesture studies. *Review of Cognitive Linguistics. Published under the auspices of the Spanish Cognitive Linguistics Association* 11(2). 417–432.

Cienki, Alan. 2015. Spoken language usage events. *Language and Cognition* 7(4). 499–514.

Cienki, Alan. 2017. Utterance Construction Grammar (UCxG) and the variable multimodality of constructions. *Linguistics Vanguard* 3(s1). 3–10.

Cienki, Alan & Olga K. Iriskhanova (eds.). 2018. *Aspectuality across Languages: Event construal in speech and gesture*. John Benjamins Publishing Company.

Cienki, Alan & Cornelia Müller. 2008. Metaphor, Gesture, and Thought. In Gibbs, Raymond W., Jr. (ed.), *The Cambridge handbook of metaphor and thought*, 483–501. Cambridge: Cambridge University Press.

Cienki, Alan & Cornelia Müller. 2014. Ways of viewing metaphor in gesture. In Müller, Cornelia, Alan Cienki, Ellen Fricke, David McNeill, Silva H. Ladewig & Jana Bressem (eds.), *Body – Language – Communication. An International Handbook on Multimodality in Human Interaction* (Handbooks of Linguistics and Communication Science 38.2.), 1766–1781. Berlin & Boston: De Gruyter Mouton.

Clark, Herbert H. 1996. *Using language*. Cambridge: Cambridge University Press.

Clark, Herbert H. 2016. Depicting as a method of communication. *Psychological review* 123(3). 324–347.

Condon, William C. & Richard Ogston. 1966. Sound film analysis of normal and pathological behavior patterns. *The Journal of Nervous and Mental Disease* 143(4). 338–347.

Condon, William C. & Richard Ogston. 1967. A segmentation of behavior. *Journal of Psychiatric Research* 5. 221–235.

Conlin, Frances, Paul Hagstrom & Carol Neidle. 2003. A particle of indefiniteness in American Sign Language. *Linguistic Discovery* 2(1). 1–21.

Croft, William. 2001. *Radical Construction Grammar: Syntactic Theory in Typological Perspective*. Oxford: Oxford University Press.

Daddesio, Thomas C. 1995. *On minds and symbols: The relevance of cognitive science for semiotics*. Walter de Gruyter.

Jorio, Andrea de. 1832/2000. *Gesture in Naples and gesture in classical antiquity. A translation of La mimica degli antichi investigata nel gestire napoletano (Fibreno, Naples 1832) and with an introduction and notes by Adam Kendon*. Bloomington & Indianapolis: Indiana University Press.

Saussure, Ferdinand de. 1916. *Grundfragen der allgemeinen Sprachwissenschaft*. Berlin: Mouton de Gruyter.

Donegan, Patricia J. & David Stampe. 1979. The study of natural phonology. *Current approaches to phonological theory*. 126–173.

Duncan, Susan D. 2002. Gesture, verb aspect, and the nature of iconic imagery in natural discourse. *Gesture* 2(2). 183–206.

Duncan, Susan D. n.y. Coding "Manual" http://mcneilllab.uchicago.edu/pdfs/Coding_Manual.pdf (accessed 27.06.2010).

Eco, Umberto. 1984. *Semiotics and the philosophy of language*. Bloomington: Indiana University Press.

Efron, David. [1941] 1972. Gesture and Environment]. *Gesture, race and culture*. Paris & The Hague: Mouton.

Ehlich, Konrad. 1987. so – Überlegungen zum Verhältnis sprachlicher Formen und sprachlichen Handelns, allgemein und an einem widerspenstigen Beispiel. In Rosengren,

Inger (ed.), *Sprache und Pragmatik. Lunder Symposium 1986*, 279–298. Stockholm: Almqvist & Wiksell.

Ekman, Paul & Wallace V. Friesen. 1969. The repertoire of nonverbal behavior: Categories, origins, usage, and coding. *Semiotica* 1 (1). 49–98.

Enfield, Nick J. 2009. *The anatomy of meaning: speech, gesture, and composite utterances*. Cambridge, UK & New York: Cambridge University Press.

Engberg-Pedersen, Elisabeth. 2002. Gestures in signing: The presentation gesture in Danish Sign Language. In Schulmeister, Rolf & Heimo Reinitzer (eds.), *Progress in sign language research: In honor of Siegmund Prillwitz / Festschrift für Siegmund Prillwitz*, 143–162. Hamburg: Signum.

Engle, Randi A. 1998. Not channels but composite signals: Speech, gesture, diagrams and object demonstrations are integrated in multimodal explanations. In Gernsbacher, In M.A. & S.J. Derry (eds.), *Proceedings of the Twentieth Annual Conference of the Cognitive Science Society*, 321–326. Mahwah: NJ: Erlbaum.

Engle, Randi A. 2000. *Toward a theory of multimodal communication combining speech, gestures, diagrams, and demonstrations in instructional explanations*. Standford: Stanford University: Dissertation thesis.

Evans, Vyvyan. 2007. *A glossary of cognitive linguistics*. Edinburgh: Edinburgh University Press.

Evans, Vyvyan & Melanie Green. 2006. *Cognitive Linguistics: An Introduction*. Edinburgh: Edinburgh University Press.

Feyaerts, Kurt, Geert Brône & Bert Oben. 2017. Multimodality in interaction. In Dancygier, Barbar (ed.), *The Cambridge Handbook of Cognitive Linguistics*, 135–156. Cambridge: CUP.

Feyereisen, Pierre. 1987. Gestures and speech, interactions and separations: A reply to McNeill (1985). *Psychological review* 94(4). 493–498.

Feyereisen, Pierre & Jacques-Dominique de Lannoy. 1991. *Gestures and speech: Psychological investigations*. Cambridge: Cambridge University Press.

Fillmore, Charles. 1985. Frames and the semantics of understanding. *Quaderni di Semantica* 6 (2). 222–254.

Fiumara, Corradi Gemma. 1995. *The metaphoric process: connections between language and life*. London: Routledge.

Frege, Gottlob. 1892. Über Sinn und Bedeutung. *Zeitschrift für Philosophie und philosophische Kritik* 100(1). 25–50.

Fricke, Ellen. 2007. *Origo, Geste und Raum: Lokaldeixis im Deutschen*. Berlin: De Gruyter Mouton.

Fricke, Ellen. 2012. *Grammatik multimodal. Wie Gesten und Wörter zusammenwirken*. Berlin: Mouton de Gruyter.

Fricke, Ellen. 2013. Towards a unified grammar of gesture and speech: A multimodal approach. In Müller, Cornelia, Alan Cienki, Ellen Fricke, Silva H. Ladewig, David McNeill & Sedinha Teßendorf (eds.), *Body – Language – Communication: An International Handbook on Multimodality in Human Interaction* (Handbooks of Linguistics and Communication Science 38.1.), 733–754. Berlin & Boston: De Gruyter Mouton.

Fricke, Ellen, Jana Bressem & Cornelia Müller. 2014. Gesture families and gesture fields. In Müller, Cornelia, Alan Cienki, Ellen Fricke, Silva H. Ladewig, David McNeill & Jana Bressem (eds.), *Body – Language – Communication. An International Handbook on Multimodality in Human Interaction* (Handbooks of Linguistics and Communication Science 38.2.), 1630–1640. Berlin & Boston: De Gruyter Mouton.

Frishberg, Nancy. 1975. Arbitrariness and Iconicity: Historical Change in American Sign Language. *Language* 51(3). 696–719.
Garfinkel, Harold. 1967. *Studies in ethnomethodology*. Englewood Cliffs, N.J.: Prentice-Hall.
Geeraerts, Dirk & Hubert Cuyckens. 2007. Introducing cognitive linguistics. In Geeraerts, Dirk & Hubert Cuyckens (eds.), *The Oxford handbook of cognitive linguistics*, 3–23. Oxford: Oxford University Press.
Geeraerts, Dirk, Stefan Grondelaers & Peter Bakema. 1994. *The structure of lexical variation: meaning, naming, and context*. Berlin & New York: Mouton de Gruyter.
Gibbs, Raymond W., Jr. 1993. Process and products in making sense of tropes. In Ortony, Andrew (ed.), *Metaphor and Thought*, 252–276. Cambridge: Cambridge University Press.
Gibbs, Raymond W., Jr. 1994. *The poetics of mind: figurative thought, language, and understanding*. Cambridge: Cambridge University Press.
Givón, Talmy. 2001. *Syntax. An introduction*. Amsterdam & Philadelphia: John Benjamins.
Goldberg, Adele E. 1995. *Constructions: A construction grammar approach to argument structure*. Chicago: University of Chicago Press.
Goldberg, Adele E. 2006. *Constructions at work: The nature of generalization in language*. Oxford University Press on Demand.
Goodwin, Charles. 1986. Gesture as a resource for the organization of mutual orientation. *Semiotica* 62. 29–49.
Greifenstein, Sarah. 2019. *Tempi der Bewegung – Modi des Gefühls. Expressivität, heitere Affekte und die Screwball Comedy*. Berlin & Boston: De Gruyter Mouton.
Grote, Klaudia. 2004. 'Mediale Relativität'? Auswirkungen der gestisch-visuellen und vokal-auditiven Sprachmodalität auf semantische Strukturen. In Jäger, Ludwig & Erika Linz (eds.), *Medialität und Mentalität. Theoretische und empirische Studien zum Verhältnis von Sprache, Subjektivität und Kognition*, 193–220. München: Wilhelm Fink Verlag.
Gullberg, Marianne & Sotaro Kita. 2009. Attention to speech-accompanying gestures: Eye movements and information uptake. *Journal of Nonverbal Behavior* 33(4). 251–277.
Hadar, Uri & Brian Butterworth. 1997. Iconic gestures, imagery, and word retrieval in speech. *Semiotica* 115(1–2). 147–172.
Haiman, John. 1985. *Natural syntax: iconicity and erosion*. Cambridge & New York: Cambridge University Press.
Hampe, Beate. 2005. *From Perception to Meaning: Image Schemas in Cognitive Linguistics*. Berlin & New York: Mouton de Gruyter.
Harrison, Simon. 2009. The expression of negation through grammar and gesture. In Zlatev, Jordan, Mats Andren, Marlene Johansson Falck & Carita Lundmark (eds.), *Studies in Language and Cognition*, 405–409. Cambridge: Cambridge Scholars Publishing.
Harrison, Simon. 2010. Evidence for node and scope of negation in coverbal gesture. *Gesture* 10(1). 29–51.
Harrison, Simon. 2014. The organisation of kinesic ensembles associated with negation. *Gesture* 14(2). 117–140.
Harrison, Simon. 2018. *The Impulse to Gesture: Where Language, Minds, and Bodies Intersect*. Cambridge: Cambridge University Press.
Harrison, Simon & Pierre Larrivée. 2016. Morphosyntactic correlates of gestures: A gesture associated with negation in French and its organisation with speech. *Negation and polarity: Experimental Perspectives*, 75–94. Springer.
Haviland, John B. 2000. Pointing, gesture spaces and mental maps. In McNeill, David (ed.), *Language and gesture*. Cambridge: Cambridge University Press.

Haviland, John B. 2013a. The emerging grammar of nouns in a first generation sign language: Specification, iconicity, and syntax. *Gesture* 13(3). 309–353.
Haviland, John B. 2013b. Introduction: Where does "Where do nouns come from?". *Gesture* 13(3). 245–252.
Hjelmslev, Louis. 1974. *Prolegomena zu einer Sprachtheorie*. M. Hueber.
Hoemann, Harry W. 1975. The Transparency of Meaning or Sign Language Gestures. *Sign Language Studies* 0(7). 151.
Hoffmann, Thomas. 2017. Multimodal constructs – multimodal constructions? The role of constructions in the working memory. *Linguistics Vanguard* 3(s1). 219–210.
Hoffmann, Thomas & Graeme Trousdale. 2013. *The Oxford handbook of construction grammar*. Oxford University Press.
Hopper, Paul J. 1988. Emergent grammar and the a priori grammar postulate. *Linguistics in context: Connecting observation and understanding* 29. 117–134.
Horst, Dorothea. 2018. *Meaning-Making and Campaign Advertising. The Dynamics of Audio-visual Figurativity in German and Polish Campaign Commercials*. Berlin & Boston: De Gruyter Mouton.
Horst, Dorothea, Franziska Boll, Christina Schmitt & Cornelia Müller. 2014. Gestures as interactive expressive movement: Inter-affectivity in face-to-face communication. In Cienki, Alan, Ellen Fricke, Silva H. Ladewig, David McNeill & Jana Bressem (eds.), *Body – Language – Communication: An International Handbook on Multimodality in Human Interaction* (Handbooks of Linguistics and Communication Science 38.2.), 2112–2125. Berlin & Boston: De Gruyter Mouton.
Ishino, Mika. 2007. *Metaphor and metonymy in gesture and discourse*. The University of Chicago, ProQuest Dissertations Publishing.
Jakobson, Roman. 1956. Two aspects of language and two types of aphasic disturbances. In Jakobson, Roman & Morris Halle (eds.), *Fundamentals of Language*, 55–82. The Hague: Mouton.
Jakobson, Roman. 1965. Quest for the Essence of Language. *Diogenes* 13(51). 21–37.
Jantunen, Tommi. 2015. How long is the sign? *Linguistics* 53(1). 93–124.
Janzen, Terry. 2012. Lexicalization and grammaticalization. In Pfau, Roland, Markus Steinbach & Bencie Woll (eds.), *Sign Language: An International Handbook* (Handbuch zur Sprach- und Kommunikationswissenschaft / Handbooks of linguistics and communication science.), 816–840. Berlin & Boston: De Gruyter Mouton.
Janzen, Terry & Barbara Shaffer. 2002. Gesture as the substrate in the process of ASL grammaticization. *Modality and structure in signed and spoken languages*. 199–223.
Johnson, Mark. 1987. *The body in mind. The bodily basis of meaning, imagination, and reason*. Chicago, IL: University of Chicago.
Johnson, Mark. 2005. The philosophical significance of image schemas. *From perception to meaning: Image schemas in cognitive linguistics*. 15–33.
Kaplan, David. 1976. How to Russell a Frege-church. *The Journal of Philosophy* 72(19). 716–729.
Kappelhoff, Hermann. 2004. *Matrix der Gefühle. Das Kino, das Melodrama und das Theater der Empfindsamkeit*. Berlin: Vorwerk 8.
Kappelhoff, Hermann, Jan-Hendrik Bakels, Hye-Jeung Chung, David Gaertner, Sarah Greifenstein, Matthias Grotkopp, Michael Lück, Christian Pischel, Cilli Pogodda & Franziska Seewald. 2015. eMAEX–Ansätze und Potentiale einer systematisierten Methode zur Untersuchung filmischer Ausdrucksqualitäten. (accessed 13.08.2017).

Kappelhoff, Hermann, Jan-Hendrik Bakels & Sarah Greifenstein. 2019. *Die Poiesis des Filme-Sehens. Methoden der Analyse audiovisueller Bilder*. Berlin & Boston, MA: Walter de Gruyter.
Kappelhoff, Hermann & Sarah Greifenstein. 2015. Audiovisual metaphors: Embodied meaning and processes of fictionalization. In Fahlenbrach, Kathrin (ed.), *Embodied Metaphors in Film, Television, and Video Games: Cognitive Approaches*, 183–201. London: Routledge.
Kappelhoff, Hermann & Cornelia Müller. 2011. Embodied meaning construction. Multimodal metaphor and expressive movement in speech, gesture, and feature film. *Metaphor in the Social World* 1(2). 121–153.
Keevallik, Leelo. 2013. The Interdependence of Bodily Demonstrations and Clausal Syntax. *Research on Language and Social Interaction* 46(1). 1–21.
Kellerman, Eric & Anne-Marie van Hoof. 2003. Manual accents. *International Review of Applied Linguistics* 41. 251–269.
Kelly, Michael H. & J. Kathryn Bock. 1988. Stress in time. *Journal of Experimental Psychology: Human Perception and Performance* 14(3). 389.
Kendon, Adam. 1972. Some relationships between body motion and speech: An analysis of an example. In Siegman, Aron Wolfe & Benjamin Pope (eds.), *Studies in Dyadic Communication*, 177–210. New York: Elsevier.
Kendon, Adam. 1980a. A description of a deaf-mute sign language from the Engaprovince of Papua New Guinea with some comparative discussion: part II. *Semiotica* 32(1–2). 81–117.
Kendon, Adam. 1980b. Gesticulation and speech: two aspects of the process of utterance. In Key, Mary R. (ed.), *Nonverbal Communication and Language*, 207–227. The Hague: Mouton.
Kendon, Adam. 1983. Gesture and speech: How they interact. In Wiemann, John M. & Randall P. Harrison (eds.), *Nonverbal Interaction*, 13–45. Beverly Hills: Sage Publications.
Kendon, Adam. 1988a. How gestures can become like words. In Poyatos, Fernando (ed.), *Crosscultural Perspectives in Nonverbal Communication*, 131–141. Toronto: C. J. Hogrefe, Publishers.
Kendon, Adam. 1988b. *Sign languages of aboriginal Australia: cultural, semiotic and communicative perspectives*. Cambridge: Cambridge University Press.
Kendon, Adam. 2004. *Gesture. Visible action as utterance*. Cambridge: Cambridge University Press.
Kendon, Adam. 2008. Language's matrix. *Gesture* 9(3). 355–372.
Kertész, András & Csilla Rákosi. 2009. Cyclic vs. circular argumentation in the Conceptual Metaphor Theory. *Cognitive Linguistics* 20(4). 703–732.
Kita, Sotaro. 2000. How representational gestures help speaking. In McNeill, David (ed.), *Language and Gesture*, 162–185. Cambridge: Cambridge University Press.
Kita, Sotaro, Ingeborg van Gijn & Harry van der Hulst. 1998. Movement phases in signs and cospeech gestures and their transcription by human encoders. In Wachsmuth, Ipke & Martin Fröhlich (eds.), *Gesture and sign language in human-computer interaction*, 23–35. Berlin: Springer.
Klima, Edward S. & Ursula Beluggi. 1979. *The signs of language*. Harvard: Harvard University Press
Koffka, Kurt. 1938 [1915]. On the foundation of the psychology of perception. A reply to Vittorio Benussi. In Ellis, W. D. (ed.), *A Source Book of Gestalt Psychology*, 371–378. London: Routledge & Kegan Paul.

Köhler, Wolfgang. 2007 [1938]. Physical Gestalten. In Ellis, W. D. (ed.), *A Source Book of Gestalt Psychology*, 17–54. London: Routledge & Kegan Paul.

Kok, Kasper. 2016. *The Status of Gesture in Cognitive-functional Models of Grammar*. Utrecht: LOT Publications.

Kok, Kasper & Alan Cienki. 2016. Cognitive Grammar and gesture: Points of convergence, advances and challenges. *Cognitive Linguistics* 27(1). 67–100.

Kolter, Astrid, Silva H. Ladewig, Michela Summa, Sabine Koch, Thomas Fuchs & Cornelia Müller. 2012. Body memory and emergence of metaphor in movement and speech. An interdisciplinary case study. In Koch, Sabine, Thomas Fuchs, Michela Summa & Cornelia Müller (eds.), *Body Memory, Metaphor, and Movement*, 201–226. Amsterdam & Philadelphia: John Benjamins.

Kopp, Stefan, Paul Tepper & Justine Cassell. 2004. Towards integrated microplanning of language and iconic gesture for multimodal output. *Proceedings of the 6th International Conference on Multimodal Interfaces, ICMI 2004*. State College, PA, USA: ACM.

Ladewig, Silva H. 2010. Beschreiben, suchen und auffordern – Varianten einer rekurrenten Geste. *Sprache und Literatur* 41(1). 89–111.

Ladewig, Silva H. 2011. Putting the cyclic gesture on a cognitive basis. *CogniTextes* 6.

Ladewig, Silva H. 2012. *Syntactic and semantic integration of gestures into speech: Structural, cognitive, and conceptual aspects*. Frankfurt (Oder), European University Viadrina: Dissertation thesis.

Ladewig, Silva H. 2014a. Creating multimodal utterances: The linear integration of gestures into speech. In Müller, Cornelia, Alan Cienki, Ellen Fricke, Silva H. Ladewig, David McNeill & Jana Bressem (eds.), *Body – Language – Communication. An International Handbook on Multimodality in Human Interaction* (Handbooks of Linguistics and Communication Science 38.2.), 1662–1677. Berlin & Boston: De Gruyter Mouton.

Ladewig, Silva H. 2014b. The cyclic gesture. In Müller, Cornelia, Alan Cienki, Ellen Fricke, Silva H. Ladewig, David McNeill & Jana Bressem (eds.), *Body – Language – Communication. An International Handbook on Multimodality in Human Interaction* (Handbooks of Linguistics and Communication Science 38.2.), 1605–1618. Berlin & Boston: De Gruyter Mouton.

Ladewig, Silva H. 2014c. Recurrent gestures. In Müller, Cornelia, Alan Cienki, Ellen Fricke, Silva H. Ladewig, David McNeill & Jana Bressem (eds.), *Body – Language – Communication. An International Handbook on Multimodality in Human Interaction* (Handbooks of Linguistics and Communication Science 38.2.), 1558–1575. Berlin & Boston: De Gruyter Mouton.

Ladewig, Silva H. 2019. Konzeptuelle Integration von Sprache und Geste am Beispiel gestisch vervollständigter Äußerungen. In: *Mitteilungen des Deutschen Germanistenverbandes* 66(4). 393–401.

Ladewig, Silva H. & Jana Bressem. 2013a. New insights into the medium 'hand': Discovering recurrent structures in gestures. *Semiotica* 197. 203–231.

Ladewig, Silva H. & Jana Bressem. 2013b. The notation of gesture phases – a linguistic perspective. In Müller, Cornelia, Alan Cienki, Ellen Fricke, Silva H. Ladewig, David McNeill & Sedinha Tessendorf (eds.), *Body – Language – Communication. An International Handbook on Multimodality in Interaction* (Handbooks of Linguistics and Communication Science 38.1.), 1060–1079. Berlin & Boston: De Gruyter Mouton.

Ladewig, Silva H. & Lena Hotze. in press/2020. Zur temporalen Entfaltung und multimodalen Orchestrierung von konzeptuellen Räumen am Beispiel einer Erzählung. In Zima, Elisabeth & Clarissa Weiß (eds.), *Multimodales Erzählen*.

Lakoff, George & Mark Johnson. 1980. *Metaphors we live by*. Chicago & London: Chicago University Press.
Langacker, Ronald W. 1986. An Introduction to Cognitive Grammar. *Cognitive Science* 10(1). 1–40.
Langacker, Ronald W. 1987a. *Foundations of cognitive grammar: Theoretical Prerequisites*. Stanford: Stanford University Press.
Langacker, Ronald W. 1987b. Nouns and verbs. *Language*. 53–94.
Langacker, Ronald W. 1991a. *Concept, image, and symbol: the cognitive basis of grammar*. Berlin & New York: Mouton de Gruyter.
Langacker, Ronald W. 1991b. *Foundations of Cognitive Grammar: Descriptive application*. Stanford: Stanford University Press.
Langacker, Ronald W. 1999. *Grammar and Conceptualization*. Berlin & New York: Walter de Gruyter.
Langacker, Ronald W. 2000. Why a mind is necessary. Conceptualization, grammar and. In Albertazzi, Liliana (ed.), *Meaning and cognition: A multidisciplinary approach*, 25–38. John Benjamins.
Langacker, Ronald W. 2001. Discourse in cognitive grammar. *Cognitive Linguistics* 12(2). 143–188.
Langacker, Ronald W. 2005. Construction Grammars: cognitive, radical, and less so. In Ibáñez, Francisco José Ruiz de Mendoza & Maria Sandra Peña Cervel (eds.), *Cognitive linguistics: Internal dynamics and interdisciplinary interaction*, 101–159. Berlin: Mouton De Gruyter.
Langacker, Ronald W. 2006. Introduction to *Concept, Image, and Symbol*. In Geerarts, Dirk (ed.), *Cognitive Linguistics: Basic Readings*, 29–66.
Langacker, Ronald W. 2007. Cognitive Grammar. In Geeraerts, Dirk & Hubert Cuyckens (eds.), *The Oxford Handbook of Cognitive Linguistics*, 421–462. Oxford: Oxford University Press.
Langacker, Ronald W. 2008a. *Cognitive grammar: a basic introduction*. Oxford: Oxford University Press, USA.
Langacker, Ronald W. 2008b. Metaphoric gesture and cognitive linguistics. In Cienki, Alan & Cornelia Müller (eds.), *Metaphor and Gesture*, 249–251. Amsterdam: John Benjamins.
Langacker, Ronald W. 2008c. Sequential and summary scanning: A reply. *Cognitive Linguistics* 19(4). 571–584.
Lanwer, Jens Philipp. 2017. Apposition: A multimodal construction? The multimodality of linguistic constructions in the light of usage-based theory. *Linguistics Vanguard* 3(s1). 143–112.
Lascarides, Alex & Matthew Stone. 2009. A Formal Semantic Analysis of Gesture. *Journal of Semantics* 26(4). 393–449.
Lausberg, Hedda, Robyn F. Cruz, Sotaro Kita, Eran Zaidel & Alain Ptito. 2003. Pantomime to visual presentation of objects: left hand dyspraxia in patients with complete callosotomy. *Brain* 126(2). 343–360.
Liddell, Scott K. 2002. Modality effects and conflicting agendas. In Stokoe, William C., David F. Armstrong, Michael A. Karchmer & John V. Van Cleve (eds.), *The Study of Signed Languages: Essays in Honour of William C. Stokoe*, 53–81. Gallaudet University Press.
Lindwall, Oskar & Anna Ekström. 2012. Instruction-in-Interaction: The Teaching and Learning of a Manual Skill. *Human Studies* 35(1). 27–49.
Liszka, James Jakób. 1996. *A general introduction to the Semeiotic of Charles Sanders Peirce*. Bloomington MA: Harvard University.
Loehr, Dan 2004. *Gesture and Intonation* Washington, D.C.: Georgetown University.

Mandell, Mark. 1977. Iconic devices in American Sign Language. In Friedman, Lynn A. (ed.), *On the other hand. New perspectives on American Sign Language*, 57–108. New York: Academic Press.
Mayerthaler, Willi. 1981. *Morphologische Natürlichkeit*. Akademische Verlagsgesellschaft Athenaion.
McCleary, Leland Emerson & Evani Viotti. 2009. Sign-Gesture Symbiosis in Brazilian Sign Language Narrative. In Parrill, Fey, Vera Tobin & Mark Turner (eds.), *Meaning form, and body*, 181–201. Chicago: University of Chicago Press.
McNeill, David. 1985. So you think gestures are nonverbal? *Psychological review* 92(3). 350–371.
McNeill, David. 1989. A straight path – to where? Reply to Butterworth and Hadar. *Psychological review* 96(1). 175–179.
McNeill, David. 1992. *Hand and mind. What gestures reveal about thought*. Chicago: University of Chicago Press.
McNeill, David. 2005. *Gesture and Thought*. Chicago: University of Chicago Press.
McNeill, David. 2007. Gesture and thought. In Esposito, Anna, Maja Bratanić, Eric Keller & Maria Marinaro (eds.), *Fundamentals of Verbal and Nonverbal Communication and the Biometric Issue*, 20–33. Amsterdam: IOS Press.
McNeill, David & Susan D. Duncan. 2000. Growth points in thinking-for speaking. In McNeill, David (ed.), *Language and Gesture*, 141–161. Cambridge: Cambridge University Press.
McNeill, David & Elena Tevy Levy. 1982. Conceptual representations in language activity and gesture. *Speech, Place, and Action*. 271–295.
McNeill, David, Francis Quek, Karl-Erik McCullough, Susan Duncan, Nobuhiro Furuyama, Robert Bryll, Xin-Feng Ma & Rashid Ansari. 2001. Catchments, prosody and discourse. *Gesture* 1(1). 9–33.
Meir, Irit. 2012. Word classes and word formation. In Pfau, Roland, Markus Steinbach & Bencie Woll (eds.), *Sign Language. An International Handbook* (Handbücher zur Sprach- und Kommunikationswissenschaft / Handbooks of Linguistics and Communication Science (HSK) 37), 77–111. Berlin & Boston: De Gryuer Mouton.
Merleau-Ponty, Maurice. [1962] 2005. *Phenomenology of perception*. London & New York: Routledge.
Merrell, Floyd. 1997. *Peirce, signs, and meaning*. Toronto: University of Toronto Press.
Michaelis, Laura A. 2004. Type shifting in construction grammar: An integrated approach to aspectual coercion. *Cognitive Linguistics* 15(1). 1–68.
Mittelberg, Irene. 2006. *Metaphor and Metonymy in Language and Gesture: Discoursive Evidence for Multimodal Models of Grammar*. Cornell University. Ann Arbor, MI: UMI (ISBN: 9780542533464).
Mittelberg, Irene. 2008. Peircean semiotics meets conceptual metaphor: Iconic modes in gestural representations of grammar. In Cienki, Alan & Cornelia Müller (eds.), *Metaphor and Gesture*, 145–184. Amsterdam: Benjamins.
Mittelberg, Irene. 2010a. Geometric and image-schematic patterns in gesture space. In Evans, Vyvyan & Paul Chilton (eds.), *Language, Cognition, and Space: The State of the Art and New Directions*, 351–385. London: Equinox.
Mittelberg, Irene. 2010b. Interne und externe Metonymie: Jakobsonsche Kontiguitätsbeziehungen in redebegleitenden Gesten. *Sprache und Literatur* 41(105). 112–143
Mittelberg, Irene. 2013. The exbodied mind: Cognitive-semiotic principles as motivating forces in gesture. In Müller, Cornelia, Alan Cienki, Ellen Fricke, Silva H. Ladewig, David McNeill & Sedinha Tessendorf (eds.), *Body – Language – Communication. An International*

Handbook on Multimodality in Interaction (Handbooks of Linguistics and Communication Science 38.1.), 755–784. Berlin & Boston: De Gruyter Mouton.

Mittelberg, Irene. 2017a. Embodied frames and scenes: Body-based metonymy and pragmatic inferencing in gesture. *Gesture* 16(2). 203–244.

Mittelberg, Irene. 2017b. Multimodal existential constructions in German: Manual actions of giving as experiential substrate for grammatical and gestural patterns. *Linguistics Vanguard* 3(s1). 1–14.

Mittelberg, Irene & Linda R. Waugh. 2009a. Metonymy first, metaphor second: A cognitive-semiotic approach to multimodal figures of thought in co-speech gesture. In Forceville, Charles J. & Eduardo Urios-Aparisi (eds.), *Multimodal Metaphor*, 329–358. Berlin & Boston: De Gruyter Mouton.

Mittelberg, Irene & Linda R. Waugh. 2009b. Multimodal figures of thought: A cognitive-semiotic approach to metaphor and metonymy in co-speech gesture. In Forceville, Charles & Eduardo Urios-Aparisi (eds.), *Multimodal Metaphor*, 329–356. Berlin & New York: Mouton de Gruyter.

Mittelberg, Irene & Linda R. Waugh. 2014. Gestures and metonymy. In Müller, Cornelia, Alan Cienki, Ellen Fricke, Silva H. Ladewig, David McNeill & Jana Bressem (eds.), *Body-language-communication. An international handbook on multimodality in human interaction* (Handbooks of Linguistics and Communication Science 38.2.), 1747–1766. Berlin & Boston: De Gruyter Mouton.

Mosher, Joseph A. 1916. *The essentials of effective gesture for students of public speaking.* The Macmillan company.

Müller, Cornelia. 1998. *Redebegleitende Gesten: Kulturgeschichte, Theorie, Sprachvergleich.* Berlin: Arno Spitz.

Müller, Cornelia. 2000. Zeit als Raum. Eine kognitiv-semantische Mikroanalyse des sprachlichen und gestischen Ausdrucks von Aktionsarten. In Hess-Lüttich, Ernest W. B. & H. Walter Schmitz (eds.), *Botschaften verstehen. Kommunikationstheorie und Zeichenpraxis. Festschrift für Helmut Richter*, 211–218. Frankfurt a.M.: Peter Lang.

Müller, Cornelia. 2004. Forms and uses of the Palm Up Open Hand. A case of a gesture family? In Müller, Cornelia & Roland Posner (eds.), *Semantics and Pragmatics of everyday gestures*, 234–256. Berlin: Weidler.

Müller, Cornelia. 2007. A dynamic view on gesture, language and thought. In Duncan, Susan D., Justine Cassell & Elena T. Levy (eds.), *Gesture and the dynamic dimension of language*, 109–116. Amsterdam & Philadelphia: John Benjamins.

Müller, Cornelia. 2008a. *Metaphors dead and alive, sleeping and waking: a dynamic view.* Chicago: Chicago University Press.

Müller, Cornelia. 2008b. What gestures reveal about the nature of metaphor. In Cienki, Alan & Cornelia Müller (eds.), *Metaphor and Gesture*, 249–275. Amsterdam: Benjamins.

Müller, Cornelia. 2009. Gesture and Language. In Malmkjaer, Kirsten (ed.), *Routledge's Linguistics Encyclopedia* (Third Edition), 214–217. Abington, New York: Routledge.

Müller, Cornelia. 2010a. Mimesis und Gestik. In Koch, Gertrud, Martin Vöhler & Christiane Voss (eds.), *Die Mimesis und ihre Künste*, 149–187. Paderborn & München: Fink.

Müller, Cornelia. 2010b. Wie Gesten bedeuten. Eine kognitiv-linguistische und sequenzanalytische Perspektive. *Sprache und Literatur* 41(105). 37–68.

Müller, Cornelia. 2013. Gestures as a medium of expression: The linguistic potential of gestures. In Müller, Cornelia, Alan Cienki, Ellen Fricke, Silva H. Ladewig, David McNeill & Sedinha Teßendorf (eds.), *Body – Language – Communication: An International Handbook*

on Multimodality in Human Interaction (Handbooks of Linguistics and Communication Science 38.1.), 202–217. Berlin & Boston: Mouton de Gruyter.
Müller, Cornelia. 2014a. Gestural modes of representation as techniques of depiction. In Müller, Cornelia, Alan Cienki, Ellen Fricke, Silva H. Ladewig, David McNeill & Jana Bressem (eds.), *Body–language–communication: An international handbook on multimodality in human interaction* (Handbooks of Linguistics and Communication Science 38.2.), 1687–1702. Berlin & Boston: Mouton de Gruyter.
Müller, Cornelia. 2014b. Gesture as "deliberate expressive movement". In Seyfeddinipur, Mandana & Marianne Gullberg (eds.), *From gesture in conversation to visible action as utterance: Essays in honor of Adam Kendon*, 127–152. Amsterdam: John Benjamins.
Müller, Cornelia. 2016. From mimesis to meaning: A systematics of gestural mimesis for concrete and abstract referential gestures. In Zlatev, Jordan, Göran Sonesson & Piotr Konderak (eds.), *Meaning, mind and communication: Explorations in cognitive semiotics*, 211–226. Frankfurt am Main: Peter Lang.
Müller, Cornelia. 2017a. How recurrent gestures mean: Conventionalized contexts-of-use and embodied motivation. *Gesture* 16(2). 278–306.
Müller, Cornelia. 2017b. Waking Metaphors. Embodied Cognition in Multimodal Discourse. In Hampe, Beate (ed.), *Metaphor. Embodied Cognition in Discourse*, 291–316. Cambridge: Cambridge University Press.
Müller, Cornelia. 2018. Gesture and Sign: Cataclysmic Break or Dynamic Relations? *Frontiers in Psychology* 9. 1651.
Müller, Cornelia, Jana Bressem & Silva H. Ladewig. 2013. Towards a grammar of gesture: A form-based view. In Müller, Cornelia, Alan Cienki, Ellen Fricke, Silva H. Ladewig, David McNeill & Sedinha Tessendorf (eds.), *Body – Language – Communication. An International Handbook on Multimodality in Interaction* (Handbooks of Linguistics and Communication Science 38.1.), 707–733. Berlin & Boston: De Gruyter Mouton.
Müller, Cornelia, Jana Bressem & Silva H. Ladewig. to appear. *Gesture and Language*. Routledge.
Müller, Cornelia & Alan Cienki. 2009. Words, gestures, and beyond: Forms of multimodal metaphor in the use of spoken language. In Forceville, Charles J. & Eduardo Urios-Aparisi (eds.), *Multimodal Metaphor* (Applications of Cognitive Linguistics), 297–328. Berlin & New York: Mouton de Gruyter.
Müller, Cornelia & Hermann Kappelhoff. 2018. *Cinematic metaphor: experience–affectivity–temporality*. Berlin & Boston: Walter de Gruyter.
Müller, Cornelia & Silva H. Ladewig. 2013. Metaphors for sensorimotor experiences. Gestures as embodied and dynamic conceptualizations of balance in dance lessons. In Dancygier, Barbara, Jennifer Hinnell & Mike Borkrent (eds.), *Language and the creative mind*, 295–324. Stanford: CSLI.
Müller, Cornelia, Silva H. Ladewig & Jana Bressem. 2013. Gestures and speech from a linguistic perspective: a new field and its history. In Müller, Cornelia, Alan Cienki, Ellen Fricke, Silva H. Ladewig, David McNeill & Sedinha Teßendorf (eds.), *Body – Language – Communication: An International Handbook on Multimodality in Human Interaction* (Handbooks of Linguistics and Communication Science 38.1.), 55–81. Berlin & Boston: De Gruyter Mouton.
Müller, Cornelia & Christina Schmitt. 2015. Audio-visual metaphors of the financial crisis: meaning making and the flow of experience. *Revista Brasileira de Linguística Aplicada* 15(2). 311–342.

Müller, Cornelia & Susanne Tag. 2010. The Dynamics of Metaphor. Foregrounding and Activating Metaphoricity in Conversational Interaction. *Cognitive Semiotics* 6. 85–120.
Murphy, Gregory L. 1996. On metaphoric representation. *Cognition* 60(2). 173–204.
Neisser, Ulric. 1976. *Cognition and reality. Principles and implication of cognitive psychology.* San Francisko: WH Freeman Company.
Nesher, Dan. 1984. Are There Grounds for Identifying "Ground" with "Interpretant" in Peirce's Pragmatic Theory of Meaning? *Transactions of the Charles S. Peirce Society* 20(3). 303–324.
Neville, Henry. 1904. Gesture. In Blackman, Robert D. (ed.), *Voice, Speech and Gesture: A Practical Handbook to the Elocutionary Art*, 103–169. Edinburgh: Grant.
Ningelgen, Jana & Peter Auer. 2017. Is there a multimodal construction based on non-deictic so in German? *Linguistics Vanguard* 3(s1). 70–15.
Nobe, Suichi. 2000. Where do most spontaneous representational gestures actually occur with speech. In McNeill, David (ed.), *Language and gesture*. Cambridge: Cambridge University Press.
Nunez, Rafael E. & Eve Sweetser. 2006. With the Future Behind Them: Convergent Evidence From Aymara Language and Gesture in the Crosslinguistic Comparison of Spatial Construals of Time. *Cognitive Science* 30(3). 401–450.
Ott, Edward Amherst. 1902. *How to gesture*. New York City: Hinds & Noble.
Padden, Carol A. 1988. Grammatical theory and signed languages. In Newmeyer, Frederick J. (ed.), *Linguistics: The Cambridge Survey: Volume 2, Linguistic Theory: Extensions and Implications*, 250–266. Cambridge: Cambridge University Press.
Padden, Carol A., Irit Meir, So-One Hwang, Ryan Lepic, Sharon Seegers & Tory Sampson. 2013. Patterned iconicity in sign language lexicons. *Gesture* 13(3). 287–308.
Panther, Klaus-Uwe. 2005. The role of conceptual metonymy in meaning construction. *Cognitive linguistics: Internal dynamics and interdisciplinary interaction*. 353–386.
Panther, Klaus-Uwe & Günter Radden. 1999. *Metonymy in language and thought*. Amsterdam: John Benjamins.
Panther, Klaus-Uwe & Linda L. Thornburg. 2003. *Metonymy and pragmatic inferencing*. John Benjamins Publishing Company.
Parrill, Fey. 2008. Form, meaning, and convention: A comparison of a metaphoric gesture with an emblem. In Cienki, Alan & Cornelia Müller (eds.), *Language*, 195–217. Amsterdam & Philadelphia: John Benjamins.
Parrill, Fey, Benjamin K. Bergen & Patricia V. Lichtenstein. 2013. Grammatical aspect, gesture, and conceptualization: Using co-speech gesture to reveal event representations. *Cognitive Linguistics* 24(1). 135–158.
Peirce, Charles Sanders. 1931. *Collected papers of Charles Sanders Peirce*. Cambridge: Harvard University Press.
Peirce, Charles Sanders. 1960. *Collected papers of Charles Sanders Peirce (1931–1958), Vol. I.: Principles of philosophy, Vol. II: Elements of logic*. Cambridge: The Belknap Press of Harvard University Press.
Peirce, Charles Sanders. 2009. *Writings of Charles S. Peirce: A Chronological Edition, Volume 8: 1890–1892*. Bloomington: Indiana University Press.
Peña Cerval, Maria Sandra. 2003. *Topology and Cognition: What Image-schemas Reveal about the Metaphorical Languages of Emotions*. München: Lincom Europa.
Perniss, Pamela, Robin L. Thompson & Gabriella Vigliocco. 2010. Iconicity as a General Property of Language: Evidence from Spoken and Signed Languages. *Frontiers in Psychology* 1. 227.

Pfau, Roland & Markus Steinbach. 2006. Modality-independent and Modality-specific Aspects of Grammaticalization in Sign Language. *Linguistics in Potsdam* 24(3). 3–98.
Pfau, Roland, Markus Steinbach & Esther van Loon. 2014. The Grammaticalization of Gestures in Sign Languages. In Müller, Cornelia, Alan Cienki, Ellen Fricke, Silva H. Ladewig, David McNeill & Jana Bressem (eds.), *Body – Language – Communication. An International Handbook on Multimodality in Human Interaction* (Handbooks of Linguistics and Communication Science 38.2.), 2133–2149. Berlin & Boston: De Gruyter Mouton.
Pike, Kenneth Lee. 1967. *Language in relation to a unified theory of the structure of human behavior*, 2nd, rev. edn. The Hague: Mouton.
Radden, Günter. 2000. How Metonymic Are Metaphors? In Barcelona, Antonio (ed.), *Metaphor and Metonymy at the Crossroads. A Cognitive Perspective*, 93–108. Berlin & New York: Mouton de Gruyter.
Ramscar, Michael & Robert Port. 2015. Categorization (without categories). In Dabrowska, Ewa & Dagmar Divjak (eds.), *Handbook of Cognitive Linguistics* (Handbooks of Linguistics and Communication Science / Handbücher zur Sprach- und Kommunikationswissenschaft), 75–99. Berlin & New York: Mouton de Gruyter.
Richards, Ivor Armstrong. 1936. *The Philosophy of Rhetoric*. New York: Oxford University Press.
Rose, Miranda L. 2013. Releasing the constraints on aphasia therapy: the positive impact of gesture and multimodality treatments. *American Journal of Speech-Language Pathology* 22(2). 227–239.
Ruesch, Jürgen & Gregory Bateson. 1951. *Communication, the social matrix of psychiatry*. New York: Norton.
Ruesch, Jurgen & Weldon Kees. 1969. *Nonverbal communication*. University of California Press.
Ruth-Hirrel, Laura. 2018. *A construction-based approach to cyclic gesture functions in English and Farsi*. University of New Mexico Dissertation Thesis.
Ruth-Hirrel, Laura & Silva H. Ladewig. in preparation. *The embodied nature of aspect – a cross-linguistic comparison of the cyclic gesture in English, Farsi, and German*.
Ruth-Hirrel, Laura & Sherman Wilcox. 2018. Speech-gesture constructions in cognitive grammar: The case of beats and points. *Cognitive linguistics* 29(3). 453–493.
Savan, David. 1987. *An Introduction to CS Peirce's Full System of Semeiotic*. Toronto Semiotic Circle, Victoria College in the University of Toronto.
Schegloff, Emanuel A. 1984. On some gestures' relation to talk. In Atkinson, Maxwell J. & John Heritage (eds.), *Structures of Social Action*, 266–296. Cambridge: Cambridge University Press.
Schmid, Hans-Jörg. 2007. Entrenchment, salience, and basic levels. In Geeraerts, Dirk & Hubert Cuyckens (eds.), *The Oxford handbook of cognitive linguistics*. Oxford: Oxford University Press.
Schmid, Hans-Jörg. 2015. A blueprint of the Entrenchment-and- Conventionalization Model. *Yearbook of the German Cognitive Linguistics Association* 3(1). 3–25.
Schoonjans, Steven. 2017. Multimodal Construction Grammar issues are Construction Grammar issues. *Linguistics Vanguard* 3(s1). 143–148.
Schoonjans, Steven. 2018. *Modalpartikeln als multimodale Konstruktionen. Eine korpusbasierte Kookkurrenzanalyse von Modalpartikeln und Gestik im Deutschen*. Berlin & Boston: De Gruyter.
Schoonjans, Steven, Geert Brône & Kurt Feyaerts. 2015. Multimodalität in der Konstruktionsgrammatik: Eine kritische Betrachtung illustriert anhand einer Gestikanalyse der Partikel'einfach'. In Bücker, Jörg, Susanne Günthner & Wolfgang Imo (eds.),

Konstruktionsgrammatik V – Konstruktionen im Spannungsfeld von sequenziellen Mustern, kommunikativen Gattungen und Textsorten, 291–308. Tübingen: Stauffenburg Verlag.
Selting, Margret. 1995. Der ‚mögliche Satz' als interaktiv relevante syntaktische Kategorie. *Linguistische Berichte* 158. 298–325.
Selting, Margret. 1998. Fragments of TCUs as deviant cases of TCU-production in conversational talk. *University of Konstanz, InLiSt 9*. http://kops.ub.uni-konstanz.de/voll texte/2000/2467/pdf/2467_2001.pdf.
Selting, Margret. 2001. Fragments of units as deviant cases of unit production in conversational talk. In Selting, Margret & Elizabeth Couper-Kuhlen (eds.), *Studies in interactional linguistics*, 229–258. Amsterdam & Philadelphia: John Benjamins.
Selting, Margret, Peter Auer, Dagmar Barth-Weingarten, Jörg Bergmann, Pia Bergmann, Karin Birkner, Elizabeth Couper-Kuhlen, Arnulf Deppermann, Peter Gilles, Susanne Günthner, Martin Hartung, Friederike Kern, Christine Mertzlufft, Christian Meyer, Miriam Morek, Frank Oberzaucher, Jörg Peters, Uta Quasthoff, Wilfried Schütte, Anja Stukenbrock & Susanne Uhmann. 2011. A system for transcribing talk-in-interaction: GAT 2 translated and adapted for English by Elizabeth Couper-Kuhlen and Dagmar Barth-Weingarten. *Gesprächsforschung–Online-Zeitschrift zur verbalen Interaktion* 12. 1–51.
Sereno, Joan A. 1986. Stress pattern differentiation of form class in English. *The Journal of the Acoustical Society of America* 79. S 36.
Seyfeddinipur, Mandana. 2004. Meta-discursive gestures from Iran: Some uses of the 'Pistol Hand'. In Müller, Cornelia & Roland Posner (eds.), *The semantics and pragmatics of everyday gestures*, 205–216. Berlin: Weidler.
Seyfeddinipur, Mandana. 2006. *Disfluency: Interrupting speech and gesture*. MPI Series in Psycholinguistics, 39: U. Nijmegen.
Shaffer, Barbara & Terry Janzen. 2000. Gesture, Lexical Words, and Grammar: Grammaticalization Processes in ASL. *Annual Meeting of the Berkeley Linguistics Society* 26(1). 235–245.
Sheets-Johnstone, Maxime. 2011. *The primacy of movement*, Expanded second edn. Amsterdam: John Benjamins.
Short, Thomas L. 1996. Interpreting Peirce's interpretant: A response to Lalor, Liszka, and Meyers. *Transactions of the Charles S. Peirce Society* 32(4). 488–541.
Singleton, Jenny L., Susan Goldin-Meadow & David McNeill. 1995. The cataclysmic break between gesticulation and sign: Evidence against a unified continuum of gestural communication. In Emmorey, Karen & Judy S. Reilly (eds.), *Language, Gesture, and Space*, 287–311. Hillsdale, N.J.: Lawrence Erlbaum Associates.
Slama-Cazacu, Tatiana. 1976. Nonverbal components in message sequence: "Mixed syntax". In McCormack, William Charles & Stephen A. Wurm (eds.), *Language and Man: Anthropological issues*, 217–227. The Hague: Mouton.
Slobin, Dan. 1987. From thought and language to thinking for speaking. In Gumperz, John J. & Stephen C. Levinson (eds.), *Rethinking Linguistic Relativity*, 70–96. Cambridge: Cambridge University Press.
Sowa, Timo. 2006. *Understanding coverbal iconic gestures in object shape descriptions*. Berlin: Akademische Verlagsgesellschaft Aka GmbH.
Sparhawk, Carol. 1978. Contrastive-Identificational Features of Persian Gesture. *Semiotica* 24(1/2). 49–86.

Steinbach, Markus, Ruth Albert, Heiko Girnth, Annette Hohenberger, Bettina Kümmerling-Meibauer, Jörg Meibauer, Monika Rothweiler & Monika Schwarz-Friesel. 2007. Gebärdensprache. *Schnittstellen der germanistischen Linguistik*, 137–185. Springer.

Stickles, Elise. 2016. *The interaction of syntax and metaphor in gesture: A corpus-experimental approach.* UC Berkeley: Dissertation thesis.

Stokoe, William C. 1960. *Sign Language Structure.* Buffalo, NY: Buffalo Univ. Press.

Streeck, Jürgen. 1988. The significance of gesture: How it is established. *Papers in Pragmatics* 2(1/2). 60–83.

Streeck, Jürgen. 1993. Gesture as communication. I: Its coordination with gaze and speech. *Communication Monographs* 60(4). 275–299.

Streeck, Jürgen. 1994. Gesture as Communication II: The Audience as Co-Author. *Research on Language and Social Interaction* 27(3). 239–267.

Streeck, Jürgen. 2002. Grammars, Words, and Embodied Meanings: On the Uses and Evolution of So and Like. *The Journal of Communication* 52(3). 581–596.

Streeck, Jürgen. 2009. *Gesturecraft: Manufacturing understanding.* Amsterdam & Philadelphia: John Benjamins.

Streeck, Jürgen. 2013. Praxeology of gesture. In Müller, Cornelia, Alan Cienki, Ellen Fricke, Silva H. Ladewig, David McNeill & Sedinha Teßendorf (eds.), *Body – Language – Communication: An International Handbook on Multimodality in Human Interaction* (Handbooks of Linguistics and Communication Science 38.1.), 674–685. Berlin & Boston: De Gruyter Mouton.

Streeck, Jürgen. 2016. Gestische Praxis und sprachliche Form. In Deppermann, Arnulf, Helmuth Feilke & Angelika Linke (eds.), *Sprachliche und kommunikative Praktiken*, 57–80. Berlin & Boston: De Gruyter.

Streeck, Jürgen & Ulrike Hartge. 1992. Previews: Gestures at the transition place. In Auer, Peter & Alsdo di Luzio (eds.), *The Contextualization of Language*, 135–157. Amsterdam: John Benjamins.

Stukenbrock, Anja. 2010. Überlegungen zu einem multimodalen Verständnis der gesprochenen Sprache am Beispiel deiktischer Verwendungsweisen des Ausdrucks „so". In Dittmar, Norbert & Nils Uwe Bahlo (eds.), *Beschreibungen für gesprochenes Deutsch auf dem Prüfstand*, 165–193. Frankfurt: Peter Lang.

Stukenbrock, Anja. 2014. Take the words out of my mouth: Verbal instructions as embodied practices. *Journal of Pragmatics* 65. 80–102.

Stukenbrock, Anja. 2015. *Deixis in der face-to-face-Interaktion.* De Gruyter.

Stukenbrock, Anja. 2016. *Deiktische Praktiken: Zwischen Interaktion und Grammatik.* Berlin & Boston: De Gruyter.

Sweetser, Eve. 1990. *From Etymology to Pragmatics: Metaphorical and Cultural Aspects of Semantic Structure.* Cambridge: Cambridge University Press.

Sweetser, Eve. 1998. Regular metaphoricity in gesture: bodily-based models of speech interaction. Actes du 16e Congre`s International des Linguistes [CD-ROM]. Elsevier. edn.

Sweetser, Eve. 2007. Looking at space to study mental spaces Co-speech gesture as a crucial data source in cognitive linguistics. In Gonzalez-Marquez, Monica, Irene Mittelberg, Seana Coulson & Michael J. Spivey (eds.), *Methods in Cognitive Linguistics*, 201–224. Amsterdam: John Benjamins.

Sweetser, Eve & Marisa Sizemore. 2008. Personal and interpersonal gesture spaces: Functional contrasts in language and gesture. In Tyler, Andrea, Yiyoung Kim, Mari Takada

(eds.), *Language in the Context of Use: Cognitive and Discourse Approaches to Language and Language Learning*, 25–52. Berlin: Mouton de Gruyter.
Talmy, Leonard. 1988. Force dynamics in language and cognition. *Cognitive Science* 12(1). 49–100.
Talmy, Leonard. 1996. Fictive motion in language and "ception". In Bloom, Paul, Mary A. Peterson, Lynn Nadel & Merrill F. Garrett (eds.), *Language and Space*, 211–276. Cambridge, MA: MIT Press.
Taub, Sarah F. 2001. *Language from the body: Iconicity and metaphor in American Sign Language*. Cambridge: Cambridge University Press.
Taylor, John R. 2003. *Cognitive grammar*. Oxford: Oxford University Press.
Teßendorf, Sedinha. 2014. Pragmatic and metaphoric gestures– combining functional with cognitive approaches. In Müller, Cornelia, Alan Cienki, Ellen Fricke, Silva H. Ladewig, David McNeill & Jana Bressem (eds.), *Body – Language – Communication. An International Handbook on Multimodality in Human Interaction* (Handbooks of Linguistics and Communication Science 38.2.), 1540–1558. Berlin & Boston: De Gruyter Mouton.
Tuite, Kevin. 1993. The production of gesture. *Semiotica* 93 (1–2). 83–105.
Leeuwen, Theo van. 2005. *Introducing Social Semiotics: An Introductory Textbook*. London & New York: Routledge.
Vendler, Zeno. 1957. Verbs and times. *The philosophical review* 66(2). 143–160.
Vendler, Zeno. 1967. *Linguistics in philosophy*. Cornell University Press.
Watzlawick, Paul, Janet H. Beavin & Don D. Jackson. 1967. *Pragmatics of human communication: A study of interactional patterns, pathologies, and paradoxes*. New York, NY: Norton.
Webb, Rebecca. 1996. *Linguistic features of metaphoric gestures*. Universtiy of Rochester, New York: Dissertation thesis.
Webb, Rebecca. 1998. The lexicon and componentiality of American metaphoric gestures. In Santi, Serge, Isabelle Guaitella, Christian Cavé & Gabrielle Konopczynski (eds.), *Oralité et gestualité: communication multimodale, interaction*. 387–391. Paris: L'Harmattan.
Wilcox, Phyllis Perrin. 2000. *Metaphor in American Sign Language*. Washington, D.C.: Gallaudet University Press.
Wilcox, Phyllis Perrin. 2006. A cognitive key: Metonymic and metaphorical mappings in ASL. *Cognitive Linguistics* 15(2). 197–222.
Wilcox, Sherman. 2002. The iconic mapping of space and time in signed languages. In Albertazzi, Liliana (ed.), *Unfolding perceptual continua*, 255–281. Amsterdam: John Benjamins.
Wilcox, Sherman. 2004a. Cognitive iconicity: Conceptual spaces, meaning, and gesture in signed languages. *Cognitive Linguistics* 15(2). 119–147.
Wilcox, Sherman. 2004b. Gesture and language. *Gesture* 4(1). 43–73.
Wilcox, Sherman. 2005. Routes from gesture to language. *Revista da ABRALIN – Associação Brasileira de Lingüística* 4 (1–2). 11–45.
Wilcox, Sherman & Barbara Shaffer. 2006. Modality in American Sign Language. In Frawley, William, Erin Eschenroeder, Sarah Mills & Thao Nguyen (eds.), *The Expression of Modality*, 207. Berlin & New York: Mouton De Gruyter.
Wilcox, Sherman & Phyllis Perrin Wilcox. 1995. The gestural expression of modality in ASL. In Bybee, Joan L. & Suzanne Fleischman (eds.), *Modality in grammar and discourse*. 135–162.
Wilcox, Sherman & André Nogueira Xavier. 2013. A framework for unifying spoken language, signed language, and gesture. *Todas as Letras-Revista de Língua e Literatura* 15(1). 88–110.
Willems, Klaas & Ludovic De Cuypere. 2008. *Naturalness and iconicity in language*. Amsterdam & Philadelphia: John Benjamins Pub. Co.

Williams, Robert F. 2004. *Making Meaning from a Clock: Material Artifacts and Conceptual Blending in Time-telling Instruction*. University of California, San Diego.

Williams, Robert F. 2008. Gesture as a conceptual mapping tool. In Cienki, Alan & Cornelia Müller (eds.), *Metaphor and Gesture*, 55–92. Amsterdam: Benjamins.

Wittenburg, Peter, Hennie Brugman, Albert Russel, Alex Klassmann & Han Sloetjes. 2006. ELAN: A professional framework for multimodality research. *Proceedings of Language Resources and Evaluation Conference*.

Wundt, Wilhelm. 1916. *The Elements of Folk Psychology, translated by Edward Leroy Schaub*. Allen & Unwin.

Wundt, Wilhelm. 1921 [1901]. *Völkerpyschologie: Eine Untersuchung der Entwicklungsgesetze von Sprache, Mythus und Sitte. Erster Band. Die Sprache*. Stuttgart: Alfred Körner Verlag.

Zeshan, Ulrike. 2006. *Interrogative and negative constructions in sign languages*. Ishara Press.

Ziem, Alexander. 2017. Do we really need a Multimodal Construction Grammar. *Linguistics Vanguard* 3(s1). 35–39.

Zima, Elisabeth. 2014a. English multimodal motion constructions. A construction grammar perspective. *Linguistic Society of Belgium* 8. 14–29.

Zima, Elisabeth. 2014b. Gibt es multimodale Konstruktionen? Eine Studie zu [V(motion) in circles] und [all the way from X PREP Y]. 1–48.

Zima, Elisabeth. 2017. On the multimodality of [all the way from X PREP Y]. *Linguistics Vanguard* 3(s1). 255–212.

Zima, Elisabeth & Alexander Bergs. 2017. Multimodality and construction grammar. *Linguistics Vanguard* 3(s1). 501–509.

Zlatev, Jordan. 2012. Cognitive Semiotics: An emerging field for the transdisciplinary study of meaning. *Public Journal of Semiotics* 4(1). 2–24.

Zlatev, Jordan. 2014. Image schemas, mimetic schemas and children's gestures. *Cognitive Semiotics* 7(1). 3–29.

Index

affect 184, 185
aspectuality 34–37

conceptual archetype 23, 55, 83–93, 95–97, 99, 101, 103, 104, 181
conceptualization 4, 7, 9, 10, 14, 18, 28, 58, 82, 84, 103, 122, 123, 126, 130, 145, 147, 154, 165, 167, 170, 174, 175, 178, 184
construal 1, 3, 6–8, 15, 18, 20–23, 27, 36, 72, 79, 82, 85, 86, 89, 90, 93, 97–100, 103–105, 111, 112, 119–123, 126, 129–147, 151, 152, 156, 157, 165–167, 174, 175, 178, 183–185

emblem 75, 80, 113, 151, 172
extension 24, 50, 132, 148, 163–174, 178

foregrounding
– foregrounding techniques 94, 153, 155
– Iconicity Principle 95, 153, 155, 157, 159, 160, 162, 163
– Interactive Principle 153, 155, 160, 162
– Syntactic and Semantic Principle 153, 155, 162

gestural modes of representation
– acting mode 88, 181, 182
– acting gestures 87, 88, 90, 91, 127–130, 134, 182
– drawing, drawing gestures 87
– molding, molding gestures 90
– representing mode 88, 97, 119, 136
– representing gestures 87, 88, 90, 91, 129, 130, 182
grammar of gesture 22, 25–33
grammaticalization 30, 33–38, 49
grounding 9, 15, 18, 19, 58–60, 63, 67, 68, 70, 76, 83, 101, 142, 177, 184

iconicity 3, 117, 118, 119–126, 129, 130
– cognitive iconicity 23, 122–126, 130
inherent meaning 23, 111, 116, 126, 127, 163, 165, 168, 173

integration 1, 2, 5, 6, 10, 11–14, 16, 22, 23, 26, 33, 43, 46–51, 53, 54, 55–101, 103–146, 147–152, 155, 156, 163, 172, 173, 178–181, 187, 188
intension 24, 148, 163–174, 178
interpretant 23, 110, 120, 121, 123, 130, 132, 134, 143–146

metaphor 3, 17–21, 94, 110, 118, 121, 153–156, 166
– metaphoricity 21, 153
metonymy
– external metonymy 20, 91, 96
– internal metonymy 20, 91
modality 3, 21, 26, 32, 33, 35, 50, 51, 79, 94, 95, 117–119, 121, 125, 132, 152, 153, 159, 169, 179, 181, 183, 189
multimodal construction 22, 33, 38–46, 51, 52, 54
multimodal grammar 22, 30, 32–54
multimodal reference object 103–146, 178
multimodal salience structure 21, 94, 148, 157, 159, 162, 163
multimodality 3, 22, 24, 25–54, 152, 179, 180
– linguistic multimodality 24, 51, 179

nominal 50, 58, 59, 63, 70, 72, 75–80, 82, 88, 101, 136, 140, 142, 165, 166, 170, 172, 177, 181, 182, 187
noun position 23, 60, 61, 68, 70, 80, 82, 98, 101, 103, 105, 165, 172, 177
– slot of a noun 63, 70, 75, 77, 142, 170, 172

perception experiment
– discourse condition 57, 148, 151
– gesture-only condition 57, 75, 111, 130
– manipulated multimodal utterance condition 58
– multimodal utterance condition 57, 105, 145, 148, 151
– speech-only condition 57, 68, 105, 108, 145

https://doi.org/10.1515/9783110668568-009

profile 63, 92, 96–98, 100, 101, 121, 142, 144, 156, 159, 166, 168, 174, 178
– THING, PROCESS 63, 82, 85, 86, 91, 96, 97, 98, 101, 138, 140, 142, 145, 168, 169, 178, 181

recurrent gesture
– Brushing aside gesture 16, 32, 48
– Cyclic gesture 16, 28, 29, 35–37, 42, 80
– Palm up open hand 16, 32, 34, 80, 108
– Ring gesture 16, 32, 140
– Throwing away gesture 40, 41, 80
– Wiping Away gesture 28
reification 7, 85, 101, 177, 178

schema
– image schema 18, 19, 104, 121, 126
– mimetic schema 19
– schematization 5, 35, 37, 39, 40, 42, 121

sequentially constructed multimodal utterance 55, 57, 65, 68, 130, 156, 163, 177
sequential scanning 7, 23, 85, 99, 100, 101, 103, 178
– sequential view 98, 99
sign language 1, 15, 20, 26, 30, 32–35, 37, 38, 66, 86, 89, 91–93, 117, 118, 123, 125, 126, 130, 180–182
summary scanning 7, 23, 85, 98, 99, 101, 177
– summary view 8, 98
symbolic unit 1, 3, 5, 23, 103, 110, 119, 123, 125, 126–134, 144–146, 178

verb position 23, 58, 65, 68, 70, 82, 88, 98, 99, 101, 165, 172
– slot of a verb 67, 70, 77, 80, 170, 172, 178, 182

www.ingramcontent.com/pod-product-compliance
Lightning Source LLC
Chambersburg PA
CBHW070801230426
43665CB00017B/2445